High Stakes

Poverty, Testing, and Failure in American Schools

Second Edition

Dale D. Johnson and Bonnie Johnson

ROWMAN & LITTLEFIELD PUBLISHERS, INC.
Lanham • Boulder • New York • Toronto • Oxford

ROWMAN & LITTLEFIELD PUBLISHERS, INC.

Published in the United States of America
by Rowman & Littlefield Publishers, Inc.
A wholly owned subsidary of The Rowman & Littlefield Publishing Group, Inc.
4501 Forbes Boulevard, Suite 200, Lanham, Maryland 20706
www.rowmanlittlefield.com

PO Box 317
Oxford
OX2 9RU, UK

British Library Cataloguing in Publication Information Available

Library of Congress Cataloging-in-Publication Data

Johnson, Dale D.
   High stakes : poverty, testing, and failure in American schools / Dale D. Johnson and
Bonnie Johnson.— 2nd ed.
      p. cm.
   Includes bibliographical references and index.
   ISBN 0-7425-3531-2 (cloth : alk. paper)—ISBN 0-7425-3532-0 (pbk. : alk. paper)
1. Educational tests and measurements—Louisiana—Case studies. 2. Educational
accountability—Louisiana—Case studies. 3. Educational equalization—Louisiana—Case
studies. 4. Poor children—Education—Louisiana—Case studies. I. Johnson, Bonnie,
1948– II. Title.
   LB3052.L8J66 2005
   371.26'4'0973—dc22

                                                                              2005010745

Printed in the United States of America

♾™ The paper used in this publication meets the minimum requirements of American
National Standard for Information Sciences—Permanence of Paper for Printed Library
Materials, ANSI/NISO Z39.48-1992.

*To our former third and fourth graders at
Redbud Elementary School: You taught us well.*

CONTENTS

Foreword by Carl A. Grant   ix

Acknowledgments   xiii

Introduction   xv

1   The Realities of an Underfunded School   1

2   September: The Children We Teach   21

3   October: Regulating Teaching   47

4   November: Drugs, Poverty, and Test Scores   67

5   December: "Clamp Down"   85

6   January: Test Preparation—The Pace Quickens   93

7   February: Pep Rallies for Tests   111

8   March: Test-Day Traumas   127

9   April: Freedom to Teach and Learn   143

10 May: "I Don't Want to Spend My Time on Paperwork"   157

11   How Can We Build a Better Future? Recommendations
     for Policy Change   179

12   Today a Nation of Testing   193

Epilogue   219

References   239

Index   249

About the Authors   257

FOREWORD

In the spirit of *Washington Post* investigators Bob Woodward and Carl Bernstein, whose dedicated work helped America and the world understand the political and social abuse of the Nixon administration, Dale and Bonnie Johnson's book *High Stakes: Poverty, Testing, and Failure in American Schools* will help America, especially the education community, understand the tyranny and privilege related to high-stakes testing. *High Stakes* connects the oppression and opportunities created by high-stakes testing to the actors who are influenced or victimized by the currents driving this movement.

The character of educational thought and practice in the United States has always been determined by wider social, political, economic, and intellectual movements. The Russian launching of *Sputnik* in 1957 influenced and dramatically changed school practice in the United States. More recently in the 1980s and 1990s, the challenge to U.S. business and technology enterprises by foreign markets influenced the character of educational thought. The lightning rod this time was not a foreign country's satellite but the National Commission on Excellence in Education report *A Nation at Risk* (1983). This report placed a major part of the responsibility for the invasion of technology (e.g., Sony televisions) and automobiles (e.g., Hyundais) on the American educational system. The report stated, "If only to keep and improve on the slim competitive edge we still retain in world markets, we must rededicate ourselves to the reform of the educational system for the benefit of all" (7). The reform discourse then became the character of educational thought and practice. Federal, state, and local political leaders and officials took control of this discourse. They directed it toward a return to the basics. "Back to the basics," "excellence and accountability in education," and the "New Basics" became education slogans.

The reform effort of the 1980s is alive and well today in the form of accountability and high-stakes testing. The social, economic, and especially political discourse directed by presidents and officials at all levels are fanning the flames of the accountability movement. Being tough on schools—and on teachers and students—will bring about change and will win elections, or so it is believed. Testing companies, test preparers and scorers, instructional material and software developers, and tutoring enterprises stand to benefit financially, so they eagerly endorse the testing craze. On the other hand, teachers and administrators feel helpless and overwhelmed as test prep skilling-and-drilling consumes the school day. Teachers and principals know that poor test results will bring harsh consequences. Students know that the track to which they are assigned—and eventually promotion and graduation—will be based on test scores. Parents are caught up in the uncertainty about the intellectual and emotional costs of this accountability mania.

To understand the impact of accountability in schools, it is necessary to see it in operation day by day. Illuminations—voices of children, teachers, parents, and school administrators—are best told as an accounting that allows the reader to know the range of attitudes and behaviors of the people caught up in this testing whirlwind. *High Stakes: Poverty, Testing, and Failure in American Schools* enables us to feel, see, and experience firsthand the tyranny and oppression that the accountability movement is causing. The Johnsons demonstrate how and explain why there is a daily suppression of *real* teaching and learning. Both separately and together, students and teachers are pressured by those in positions of authority. Teachers want to help young people learn and acquire the kind of education that will allow them to escape the harsh poverty of their lives in Redbud, Louisiana. Instead, the Johnsons show us how official policies have exacerbated the problem by stripping teachers of their autonomy, depriving them of necessary resources, and intensifying the stress levels in public schools.

The tyranny of testing is spelled out vividly by the students and teachers. The increasing opposition to high-stakes testing is described, and the Johnsons question the silence of some in the education community, including professional organizations of teacher educators. The financial gains to educational consultants, instructional developers, and testing corporations, as well as the political points politicians earn through their support for this testing movement, are discussed and critiqued.

The voices of the children whom the Johnsons taught remain with you long after you close their book. The teachers who are introduced to you, who are striving to make a difference in their students' lives, become a source of inspiration. You realize you need to dedicate yourself to derailing the accountability movement that spawned high-stakes testing so destructive of equity and sensible educational practice.

After many years of researching and observing what takes place in classrooms, I must say that this book is in a class by itself. Jonathan Kozol's visits to schools across the United States vividly informed us in *Savage Inequalities* (1991) of the unequal funding of American public schools. The Johnsons did much more than visit schools. They taught, full time, for one year as regular teachers without any of the trappings of their professorships. The result of their labor is fruit that the educational community and the American public would be wise to harvest and use to make learning productive for all students.

CARL A. GRANT
Hoefs-Bascom Professor
University of Wisconsin–Madison

ACKNOWLEDGMENTS

We are grateful to Alan McClare, executive editor; Jason Proetorius, production editor; Alex Masulis, editorial assistant; and Bruce Owens, copy editor, of Rowman & Littlefield for their insightful suggestions and unwavering support in the development of this work. We also thank Carl Grant, Hoefs-Bascom Professor at the University of Wisconsin–Madison, for writing the foreword to this volume and Daniel Ness, professor of human development and learning at Dowling College on Long Island, for his late-night assistance.

INTRODUCTION

*H*igh Stakes: Poverty, Testing, and Failure in American Schools (second edition) is an account of the school year in one of the most impoverished schools in America. Redbud Elementary School in Redbud, Louisiana, has 611 students, 95 percent of whom qualify for free breakfast and free lunch. Its teachers are among the lowest paid in the nation. Built in 1948, its main structure badly needed repairs, paint, and the services of an exterminator. The local tax base ensures its status as an underfunded school. Redbud, like every public school in Louisiana, is regulated, monitored, assessed, and labeled by the state's school accountability bureaucracy. Its designation is "academically below average." Louisiana currently is one of only eight states in the nation that mandate failure and grade repetition for elementary and middle school students who fail the state's high-stakes achievement tests, although other states are heading in that direction.

Many of the children who attend Redbud are the poorest of the poor. Their homes are substandard and include trailers, shotgun houses, and housing project apartments. Some lack electricity or running water. Most of the children, 80 percent of whom are African American, live with a single parent, an aunt, or a grandmother who holds a minimum-wage job in a fast-food restaurant or discount store. Many of the children do not receive medical or dental care. Their neighborhoods teem with alcohol and drug abuse. Several have witnessed shootings and other types of violence. The children often come to school hungry and leave nothing on their school breakfast and lunch trays.

Despite these conditions, the resilient children of Redbud come to school eager to learn and filled with hope. They exhibit compassion, selflessness, and a sense of humor. The children are too young to know the score.

Redbud Elementary School serves children from preschool through grade 4. When we taught at Redbud, the school had no library, no playground equipment, no counselor, no art classes, no hot water (except for a faucet in the teachers' lounge), inadequate window heating and cooling units, and no regular school nurse. There was no place for sick children to lie down. There was one telephone available for seventy-two staff and 611 children and one other telephone available for the principal and secretary. Most of the thirty-four teachers were white, and most of the paraprofessionals and other staff were African Americans. Some lived in Redbud, and some commuted from other towns in Louisiana and Arkansas.

The push for toughening the standards and reforming the schools through accountability measures began with the publication of *A Nation at Risk* in 1983. The report spoke of the need to make American education more rigorous and demanding, and it decried education policies that permitted the social promotion of undereducated youth. Critics of schools claimed that school change would have to be guided by experts who understand the requirements of business and the economy. With *A Nation at Risk*, the accountability movement was born, and since its inception, it has pitted some parents, employers, professors, and politicians against teachers and the education community.

Proponents of standards and accountability for schools want to improve education. They believe that high standards are essential to motivate students, teachers, and school administrators to work ever harder to improve scores. Some employers support the accountability movement because of their concern that high school graduates lack academic skills requisite for success in the workplace. Proponents of accountability demand public reporting of test results to inform the public of achievement differences among schools, districts, and specific student groups.

Opponents of high-stakes testing as a means of achieving higher standards and improving the schools muster a number of arguments in support of their position:

1. The use of test scores to determine educational advancement or to affect a student's life chances must never be the sole criterion for such important decisions. Test scores should be but one indicator of a student's achievement.

2. Students should not be held to the same high standards when there is a wide disparity in the funding and public support of schools. Children with uncertified teachers, outdated schoolbooks, inadequate access to technology, and other outgrowths of school funding cannot be expected to perform at the same levels as children in schools of affluence or schools with selective admission policies.

3. Unless books and other resources that are aligned to the state standards and tests are available to all teachers and students, the standards will remain out of the reach of many learners. Teachers cannot be expected to teach what is unavailable to them.

4. The validity of both test content and score levels used to determine reporting categories such as "basic" and "proficient" must be established on psychometric—not political—foundations.

5. Appropriate attention and accommodation must be given to students in special education and to students who lack mastery of the language used in the assessment. Test scores must be interpreted in light of these factors.

Other criticisms of high-stakes testing include the neglect of those subjects not tested, loss of instructional time, and centralized decision making that is harmful to children. In many American schools, tests are driving instruction, and education has become primarily about improving test scores. Teachers spend much of their instructional time preparing their pupils, in one way or another, for tests. Test preparation books, supplements, and computer programs fill the education catalogs and teacher-convention exhibit space.

Despite its entrenchment, there is growing opposition to the accountability movement and especially to high-stakes testing. Professional organizations of teachers, specialists, researchers, and administrators are being joined by parents and citizens who are concerned about the direction public schooling has taken. Students in some states have begun to boycott state-mandated tests. Reports of testing abuse have been documented by the media. Politicians and policymakers are beginning to feel pressure in some states.

In the summer of 2000, we applied for and received unpaid leaves of absence for one year from our university. We secured teaching positions—one in third grade and one in fourth grade. As teacher education professors, we wanted to refresh ourselves with real-life teaching experience, and we wanted to see firsthand the effects of the accountability movement on life in school. We kept a journal so that we could share our experiences with our university students who are preparing to become teachers. As the year unfolded, we realized that the story of Redbud, an underfunded, struggling school working hard to educate its children in a time of accountability and high-stakes test pressures, was a story that had to be told beyond personal journal pages. Throughout this story, you will hear the voices of the children with whom we spent all day, every school day, from August 21, 2000, until June 1, 2001. You will hear the voices of our Redbud faculty colleagues, and you will hear the voices of elected and appointed politicians, policymakers, and pundits.

We treasure Louisiana with its rich cultural and ethnic diversity; its friendly, bright, caring people; its varieties of music, cuisine, and visual arts; its histories and religions. Nonetheless, all is not well in Louisiana. Despite its great wealth from oil, gas, lumber, tourism, cotton, and rice, Louisiana has one of the highest percentages of children and adults living in poverty in America, and Louisiana is choking on bureaucratic red tape—especially in matters pertaining to public education.

Three major themes are addressed throughout this book: the grinding effects of acute poverty on all aspects of life, the negative consequences of the continuing drive for accountability in the schools, and the unreasonable demands placed on teachers that stifle their creativity and enthusiasm and hasten their exodus from the profession.

Other issues surface in the book: the rising growth of for-profit ventures feeding off the accountability movement, the developing alliances between policymakers and such profiteers, and the increasing need for standard setters and politicians to be held accountable for the conditions of schools and schooling—after all, the standard setters and politicians are the ones who make the rules and control the purse strings.

This work is an honest report of what we did, how we felt, and what we saw and heard as full-time classroom teachers during one academic year. The feelings conveyed are those we had. If we seem disgusted or angry at times, it is because we were. We didn't write this book after we completed the year but rather as we lived it, while events were fresh and while we dealt with the daily demands of teaching. We wrote about things that mattered to us on a particular day. Perhaps other teachers, other participant observers, would have seen things differently. This is the story of Redbud Elementary as viewed through our eyes in 2000–2001 as we brought with us our prior knowledge and our many years of experience in public education.

Redbud Elementary existed exactly as described. We have changed the names of students and school personnel to ensure anonymity. We have also changed the town and school names. We have not changed any names of elected or appointed officials, journalists, or others whose public comments we cite. Our account is intended to serve as a voice for children too little to be heard.

For this edition, we have added two chapters. Chapters 1 through 11 constitute a critical ethnography of our year at Redbud Elementary School, as we lived it, and they remain largely intact from the first edition. Chapter 12, "Today a Nation of Testing," describes how accountability mandates and high-stakes testing have become the dominant influence in public education from preschool through graduate school. The final chapter is an epilogue. It describes the situation in Redbud and the state of Louisiana in the time since our departure from Redbud Elementary. Readers will see that, if anything, the accountability system has intensified and become fully entrenched. Readers also may note similarities to conditions in the public schools in their own states. The story of Louisiana's Redbud portrays what is happening nationwide.

ONE

THE REALITIES OF AN
UNDERFUNDED SCHOOL

The swamps and woods of Louisiana hold tales as spicy and enticing as a simmering pot of gumbo. For starters, the state was home to Jean Lafitte, the Gentleman Pirate. Prior to the War of 1812, Louisiana Governor William Claiborne posted a $500 reward for Lafitte's capture. On hearing this, Lafitte, never one to be outdone, posted a $5,000 reward for nabbing Claiborne. In 1815, during the Battle of New Orleans, Lafitte and his fellow pirates fought under General (and future president) Andrew Jackson to help secure a victory over the British. To this day, people talk of booty that was hidden by Lafitte in Louisiana's moss-draped waterways.

Marie Laveau, the Voodoo Queen, came from Santo Domingo to New Orleans in the early 1800s. Although her official occupation was "hairdresser," she acquired fame and wealth through fortune-telling, spell casting, and selling potions allegedly concocted from alligator innards and other delights. Laveau had a daughter who was nearly identical to her, so she could give the impression that she was in two places at the same time. She became known as the "boss woman of New Orleans" because she established an intricate network of eavesdroppers who would relay information about the people of New Orleans to her. This information came in handy when she had to make predictions.

Huey Pierce Long, "the Kingfish," was elected governor of Louisiana in 1928. One observer likened his campaign style to "a circus hitched to a tornado" (Williams 1969, 591). Long, in addition to building bridges over the Mississippi and increasing paved roads from three hundred miles to over fifteen hundred, still is held in esteem by many Louisiana educators because he supplied all schoolchildren with free textbooks. Long said of himself, "There may be smarter men in the United States, but they ain't in Louisiana" (Eakin and Culbertson 1992, 404).

Louisiana is also the home of musicians Louis Armstrong, Van Cliburn, Fats Domino, and Winton Marsalis; writers Lillian Hellman and Truman Capote; singer Mahalia Jackson; chef Paul Prudhomme; and a long list of other well-known Americans. Jazz, Cajun, Gospel, Zydeco, and Swamp Pop were born and nurtured in the state. Its kitchens serve up jambalaya, crawfish etoufée, blackened redfish, red beans and rice, hot water cornbread, and smothered steak.

THE TOWN OF REDBUD

The roads that we drove daily on our way to Redbud Elementary have names and histories as colorful as Louisiana's personalities and cultures. We began in Ruston, where, in 1933, Bonnie Parker and Clyde Barrow stole a Chevy, took an undertaker and county agent as hostages, and eventually released them some miles away with a gift of $5 so they could get back home. From Ruston we traveled along Goodgoin Road, where recycling is not yet the fashion or the law. Large green Dumpsters accept all sorts of nasty discards. A sign attached to one of the Dumpsters warns "No Dead Animals." Just beyond Stone's Throw Road, Goodgoin changes its name to Louisiana 146—better known as White Lightning Road. The meandering two-laner gets its name from Prohibition days. There was moonshining in the dense forests in the area, and several locals were caught and thrown in jail. When it came time to build the state highway through the woods, the bootleggers were released during the day to work on the project—hence the name White Lightning Road. Past the town of Hilly and St. Rest cemetery, White Lightning Road continues northwest to Redbud.

It was a rainy day in early June when we made our first visit to Redbud Elementary. As we turned off the highway, we saw laundry hanging on lines in the steady drizzle. Doorless shotgun houses, with their rooms one behind the other, explained that clothes were hung outside out of necessity—not for the fresh-air scent.

The town of Redbud, population 3,788 (2000 census), lies in northwest Louisiana, about twenty miles south of the Arkansas state line. About 25 percent of the population of Redbud receives federal or state aid. Redbud is the parish seat of 766-square-mile Deerborne Parish. The average household income in Deerborne Parish is $20,000. The percentage of residents below the poverty level is 29.5 (nearly three times the national percentage). There are 16,851 residents of the parish. Louisiana is the only state that uses the term "parish" instead of "county." The word comes from earlier divisions of the territory by the Catholic Church. Under the Spanish, the church parishes were treated as sections of local government. Redbud is situated between sections of the Kisatchie National Forest, where Teddy Roosevelt and Joseph Pulitzer hunted. It often comes as a surprise to out-of-staters that about half of Louisiana is forestland and that lumber is one of Louisiana's most valuable crops. Belying the sprawl of poverty on top of the soil in Deerborne Parish are the underground Redbud and Hines oil fields.

The town square, like many other commercial areas of contemporary small-town America, has vacant stores interspersed with those still open for business. In the middle of the square is the Deerborne Parish Courthouse, completed in 1861. The Greek Revival–style building is still fully functional, and with its massive columns and graceful staircases, it is not hard to imagine groups of Confederate soldiers departing from its grounds—which is just what happened. A statue of a young soldier stands on the courthouse lawn with a CSA (Confederate States of America) inscription on its base.

Across from the courthouse is the stately old Hotel Deerborne, built in 1890. It now houses the Dodge Museum, established in 1918 and begun with a World War I German helmet that a Dodge family member picked up at the local dump.

We drove up North Main Street, off the square, and took a right turn on Pine Street to the school. A plaque near the main entrance noted that the building was erected in 1948. We introduced ourselves to Pam Porter, the principal. Ms. Porter is a kindly, effervescent woman who grew up in the area and taught in Redbud for many years. We soon learned that her gentle manner belies her tenacious stance in what she knows to be best for the children she leads—even when it is at odds with some legislative prattlers or fadmeisters. The woman is no creampuff.

Ms. Porter told us that the children in the school now wear school uniforms. We asked her thoughts on this mode of dress and lack of individual clothing choice. She replied, "There is a child here who wore the same long T-shirt every day to school. It was all she had. The girl told me she was happier now because she looked like the rest of the kids and she wasn't teased."

Ms. Porter forewarned us of day-to-day frustrations. "You will have parents who intentionally give you the wrong phone number. That way you can't reach them," she said.

Unknown to us, the editor of the local paper was in the principal's office waiting to interview us. In response to her questions about our motivations for returning to the classroom, we told the editor that it had been too long since we handled all the responsibilities of a classroom teacher. Our graduate students reported that teaching had changed since they started in the classroom, and one had to "be there" to understand the extent and ramifications of the changes. In addition, we told her that we felt somewhat ill at ease instructing teacher education majors about classroom realities when we had not dealt with the realities on a daily basis for several years.

The editor, we learned, is a friend of education. She commented on low teacher salaries. "When it didn't rain, the governor said to pray for rain, and it hasn't stopped raining. Maybe he should tell the people to pray for higher teacher salaries. There are eighteen thousand people in this parish," the editor continued, "of those two thousand are inmates. The schools don't come any worse than here. It's poverty—we can't break the cycle. We don't attract industry because the workforce is unskilled so there are no jobs. Without jobs, how can people improve their lot? They don't even have money to move." We were getting a glimpse of our upcoming year. Ms. Porter must have read our disconcerted faces. With a wink she reassured us, "You eat an elephant one bite at a time."

Redbud Elementary School is home to 611 prekindergarten through fourth-grade children. Approximately 95 percent of the pupils are categorized as economically deprived and qualify for free breakfast and free lunch. About 80 percent are African American children. During the previous school year, one of the four fourth-grade classes had fourteen different teachers who stayed from a few days to a few months. A second class had five more teachers after the regular teacher resigned midyear.

The school, with a performance score of 44.1, was one of the 497 schools that were labeled academically below average in the fall of 1999. During the spring semester of 2000, the Iowa Test of Basic Skills and the LEAP tests were again administered across the state. The spring of 2000, the second year of LEAP testing, was when "high stakes" took on serious meaning. Children who failed the LEAP test, given to all public school children in grades 4 and 8, would have to repeat the grade unless they could pass a retake of the test following a remedial summer session. Schools and churches in most communities held spirit and pep rallies to encourage students to do well. Some schools and semiprivate or private organizations offered expensive LEAP prep tutorials for parents and children. Many teachers, especially in grades 4 and 8, reported doing little except preparing their pupils for the test during the months preceding the test dates. Some teachers in our graduate courses had reported that their students suffered insomnia, nausea, and other symptoms of test anxiety and that some teachers did as well.

Performance on the LEAP test earns test takers a performance label similar to those on the school report card. In each of the principal school subjects tested (English language arts, mathematics, science, and social studies), students score at advanced, proficient, basic, approaching basic, or unsatisfactory levels. Fourth-grade children who perform at the unsatisfactory level in English language arts or mathematics must repeat the grade.

We devoted the first week of August to preparing our rooms for the school year. One of us had been assigned a third-grade classroom, Room B, and the other a fourth-grade classroom down the hall, Room H. The custodians had just completed their yearly floor waxing (they also mop the floors during winter break), so our rooms were "ready for occupancy." They were anything but ready. The floors showed over a half century of filth waxed over annually. Apparently, no attempt had been made, at least in recent decades, to remove the buildup of grime from the perimeter and especially the corners of the floors. The windows, tops of the fluorescent lights, and rickety ceiling fans looked as if they had never been cleaned. Apparently, the walls had not been painted since the construction of the school. Scuff marks, holes, cracks, tape, falling plaster, and other signs of neglect were everywhere. Parts of the overhead light fixtures were missing. The ceilings were water stained. In Room B, a large glass section above a wall was broken off, and in another part of the room, a hole offered a view into the next classroom. In both rooms, the poor fit of the wheezing window air conditioners allowed daylight to come in around the units. A major job was to rid the rooms of spider webs, as dense as well-preserved medieval tapestries, in areas of the windows. The rooms were no place for arachnophobics. We sprayed, swatted, and stepped on spiders, some with bodies as large as silver dollars—only thicker and with impressive legs. They were fast, too. The rooms and hallways had the smell of age—mildew and decades of accumulated dirt.

A custodian thought for a moment when we asked where we could get some hot water for scrubbing the walls, our few gouged and scraped bookshelves, and tippy, timeworn student desks. "No place I can think of. There's no hot water in the building. There might be some over there in the high school." We began to wonder how we would teach hand-washing hygiene to children without hot water.

We emptied our bookshelves so we could clean them. In the cupboard in Room B, silverfish skittered as we pulled out old student papers, worksheets, and catalogs from some bygone time. A few beetles lumbered out of their well-established homes. Also in Room B sat a sizable unidentifiable piece. Our guess was that it served as a bookcase. It resembled a humongous fungus that one might find in a primordial forest. We tried to move the rotting hulk, but it wouldn't budge. We were relieved. Whatever was living under it and behind it would have to wait for another day to be discovered.

We found basal reading series from 1989 and spelling books from 1986. The language arts, math, science, and social studies materials were of a more recent vintage, having been published in the 1990s. Room B's science equipment consisted of a dusty beaker and a cardboard box of rocks, labeled *Rocks*. Some of the rocks and most of the labels were missing. There were no wall maps in either room, although both of us were to teach social studies. There was only one globe between us. There were no decorations to make the room cheerful. We saw a chunk of our $34,904-a-year salary (top of the pay scale, Ph.D. with twenty-five or more years of experience) going toward making the rooms somewhat more habitable.

In 1952, British Prime Minister Winston Churchill visited America, Dwight D. Eisenhower was the president-elect, and Ernest Hemingway's *The Old Man and the Sea* was published. It also was the year that the dictionaries we were to use in our classrooms were updated. The copyright date was 1952. In the books, *Alaska* was defined as a U.S. territory, and *Hawaii* wasn't listed (both became states in 1959). A perusal of the dictionaries uncovered obsolete words such as *hayrick*, *hight*, and *hitherward*. Some of the entry words were insulting to ethnic groups: *mammy* was defined as "a colored woman in charge of white children; an old Negro woman," and *redskin* was included as the word for "a North American Indian." We compared our 1952 dictionaries with a 1997 children's dictionary that we had at home. The latter included *airbag*, *air conditioner*, *astronaut*, *condo*, *contact lens*, *fast-food*, *high-rise*, *microwave*, *mouse* (related to computers), *software*, and hundreds of words that have entered our language in the past fifty years. Of course, our Redbud dictionaries contained none of these words. In Room H, we also found an even older dictionary, copyright 1941 but not "updated." It had a new words section with such entries as *baby sitter*, *bobby pin*, *bobby soxer*, *bulldozer*, *freezer*, *juke box*, *helicopter*, *iron lung*, *nylon*, *penicillin*, *soap opera*, and *walkie-talkie*.

During our cleaning bee, several teachers stopped by to greet us and welcome us to the school. Ruth, starting her third year and earning a salary of $24,221, told us about the many things she bought for her classroom out of her own pocket. "Last year the school provided $200 to each teacher for supplies. But it doesn't go very far. I just paid $8.50 for this poster for my wall. Maybe we'll get the $200 again this year, but maybe not. We don't know yet."

Another teacher, Monique, said, "We each get ten reams of paper a year. I run out in the fall, and from then on I buy my own at a discount store. This year, because of the budget, we may get less paper. There is a list of supplies that each student is supposed to bring from home, such as pencils, markers, notebook paper, and glue. Of course, many students bring nothing. They are too poor. Their unemployed mother may have six or eight other children to worry about. So I go to Wal-Mart and buy the things they need. What else can I do?"

"You have to be careful in Room H," Ruth warned. "Last year I bought some shrimp eggs for the kids to watch for science class. One morning most of the eggs were missing. I discovered a long line of ants carrying them outside through the hole in the wall. Did you see the hole?" We had seen the hole.

Belinda, a third-grade teacher, added, "There have been rats going between Rooms B and C in the past."

"I don't deal well with rodents," said Nikki with a wry grin. She was a first-year teacher and was assigned Room C. We commented that we weren't exactly the Pied Pipers of Hamelin either.

Ruth told us that last year there was a sample LEAP test question on the use of a thesaurus. There are no thesauri for the children. The teachers had to create worksheet lessons on the thesaurus to accommodate the presumed upcoming questions on the test.

We asked Ruth about classes such as art, music, and physical education. She told us there were no art classes. There is a "gifted art program." Children take a test to see if they are artistically inclined. Those children go to the high school occasionally for art. We asked what percentage of the children pass the test. "There was just one child last year in my class who passed," Ruth said. "He was really talented. There were fifteen in the whole school." Ruth also mentioned that the music teacher probably would not be coming back and that they still needed to hire a physical education teacher.

Jane, a new first-grade teacher, just out of college, was part of the conversation. She looked at us, at the condition of the room, and at the outdated materials; heard the latest news about "special classes," the ant brigade, and the darting rats; and said in a tiny voice, "I'm scared."

The children come from almost indescribable poverty. Ruth said that in her two years on the faculty, only two students, one per year, had to pay a reduced lunch fee. All other children had qualified for free breakfast and free lunch.

She said, "I live near the apartments where a number of our students live. It's rough. Many times I'll see third and fourth graders out on the streets at 10:30 or 11:00 at night. They are unsupervised. They come to school hungry and dirty. Some fall asleep in class."

Ruth explained that the tired air conditioners in our rooms are also the heating units, which are needed especially in December, January, and February. "Last year the units often broke down, leaving the room without heat for several weeks. One little girl had no coat, so I gave her one that my cousin had outgrown. She wore it every day for over a month and then started wearing it inside out. She refused to take it off until it got very warm. One day when she was at recess, I peeked inside the coat. There was some paint on it. Apparently the child didn't want to hurt my feelings, so she wore the coat inside out. Many of the children who have coats don't want to take them off in school. Maybe it's because the coats are security blankets for them or maybe it's because they have something they can call their own and don't want to lose them."

Martha, a second-grade teacher with over twenty years of experience, told us that she kept blankets in her room. "Some children come to school with high fevers and chills. No one will pick them up or there is no one at home. I try to keep them warm with blankets. I just ache for them. They have to sit at their desks, heads down and very sick, because there is no place for them to lie down." The school has no nurse's room or cots.

We learned that Redbud Elementary School has no library. There is one girls' and one boys' bathroom for all students in grades K, 1, 3, and 4. There are separate restrooms for the second graders, who are in portable buildings. There is one toilet and a small sink—cold water only—for the seventy-two teachers and staff in the building. Redbud Elementary has no playground equipment except for a few plastic pieces that the prekindergarten children use. There are no swings, climbing structures, slides, merry-go-rounds, or see-saws. When we asked teachers what the children do during recess, we were told, "They wrestle."

A TOUR OF REDBUD

Carla Peterson and her sister Tina invited us on a tour of Redbud and Deer-borne Parish. We had met Carla as a doctoral student the previous year. She works as director of education at Warton Correctional Institution, a maximum-security prison with about fifteen hundred inmates. Tina had taught at Redbud Elementary School for seventeen years and currently was working as a teacher at Warton. They showed us the main sections of Redbud from which most of the elementary school students came. The sections included the projects, the apartments, the Dr. Martin Luther King Jr. Street area, and River Bottom. In all our years and in all the places we ever lived in or visited, we had never encountered such dire poverty. Past experiences included teaching stints in Africa, living in pregentrified downtown Boston, visits to communist Czechoslovakia and East Berlin before the Wall came down, and assignments from Trinidad to the Native American reservations in Wisconsin. None of it prepared us for the "living accommodations" that were home to our Redbud pupils.

Housing consisted of project buildings and apartments built in recent decades by HUD (Housing and Urban Development), decaying mobile homes, unpainted or peeling shotgun houses, and shacks without doors. Carla and Tina informed us that many of the homes had no water or electricity because bills had gone unpaid. Some dwellings had dirt floors, and some had no indoor plumbing. Perhaps as a testimony to the hopelessness felt by the occupants, some of the small yards were covered with trash of every description. Outside several of the homes, people were sitting on their little porches where it probably was cooler, despite the ninety-eight-degree August temperature, than inside. Some of the homes appeared to be abandoned, but Carla informed us that there were people living in these places. She often knew the families by name.

Tina said, "One of my kindergarten kids went out to the playground during recess, pulled down her pants, and pooped. She didn't know any better. That's what she had to do at home. There was no bathroom inside or out."

We asked how many people typically lived in the squalid dwellings and were told there were sometimes many children and more often than not only one parent, usually a young mother.

Tina said, "I have several students, inmates at Warton, whom I taught years ago in second grade. Now they are good students and they are learning. The difference is this: They have to go to bed at night, they have to get up in the morning, they have three meals a day, they have clean clothes, I have plenty of teaching supplies and books to teach with. Even though they are incarcerated, they are in some ways better off than when they were students at Redbud Elementary."

Carla and Tina warned us that if we had to take a child home, we should do so before 5:00 P.M. They said that the areas were not safe later than that because of the crack cocaine trade and the concomitant drive-by shootings and robberies.

Carla said, "Do you see some of the tidy houses and clean yards? These families are African Americans who don't let their children play outside in the evening." We stopped at a neat frame dwelling and were introduced to Ms. Eleanor, an aide at Redbud Elementary School. Tina said, "If you have any trouble with any of the children, you talk to Ms. Eleanor. She knows all of the children and their families."

The tour included a trip down Turtle Drive, an all-white neighborhood with large homes, golf-green lawns, and other signs of prosperity. The children from these homes do not attend Redbud Elementary School. They are sent to the private Deerborne Academy on the road from Redbud to Hines. The annual tuition rivals that of a small university, $3,000 to $4,000 per child per year. Shady Lake Christian School is another private school that attracts white children and a few African Americans whose parents can afford tuition. A benefit of attending Deerborne Academy or any of the numerous private schools in Louisiana is that the children do not have to take the LEAP test and subject themselves to anxiety over the test and possible repetition of a grade. We have learned that some families are willing to pay the tuition just to avoid the consequences of high-stakes testing mandated by the state for the public schools.

Our tour of Redbud and Deerborne Parish ended with a surprise. We were taken to the home of Carla and Tina's mother, Ann, and her husband, Bill, for a lunch that only southern cooks can prepare. At the lunch we were welcomed to the community by Mayor David Duncan; Sheriff Bill Waters; Judge Toni Blake; Warden Howard Smythe; Deputy Phil Demster; Hilda Smith, the Redbud public librarian; Kathy Dulin, a local reporter; Barbara Manzer, curriculum supervisor for Deerborne Parish schools; and Tina's husband, Joel, a quality controller at the local factory. Conversation was spirited and free-flowing. It was clear that the guests cared a great deal about the conditions in which most of the Redbud children lived.

The warden said over lunch, "I wish we would be put out of business. If some of the money shoveled into our end of the pipeline could be rerouted to children for food, decent housing, and well-equipped schools with current textbooks, maybe we could begin to be put out of business." Judge Toni relayed a tale about a mother who wanted to give up her newborn child because she could not afford to care for the baby. "The barely habitable house had a dirt floor, the water had been turned off, and cardboard covered some of the broken windows. Three hungry-looking siblings played on the floor. When we asked if she wanted us to take them too, the mother said, 'No, they're old enough to steal food.'"

The judge said, "Something has to be done, and I think it's time the churches stood up. The rest of us all have restrictions on what we say. I have restrictions as a judge, you have restrictions as a teacher, even you, warden, have restrictions. But the churches don't have any restrictions. They are the ones that need to take the lead."

Mayor Duncan spoke of moral dilemmas. "If someone doesn't pay the water bill, and the water gets turned off, there will be no water for the children. But if we don't turn the water off, everyone else will want free water. It's a predicament. I don't want to see anybody without water, but I was elected to uphold the laws."

"Yes," added Judge Toni. "Justice and doing what's right aren't always the same. If people come before a judge arrested for their third DWI, the law says they go to jail. If they go to jail, they can't work, and there's no money for the family. Sending the offender to jail may be justice, but it might not be the right thing to do."

The African American and white guests at the luncheon were knowledgeable, insightful, wise, and compassionate. We saw firsthand the lack of a tax base in Deerborne Parish. There was little industry and few people of even the upper middle class to pay taxes. The leaders of Redbud were desperately trying to find a better way for the many children in need.

RULES TEACHERS MUST FOLLOW

Back at the school that afternoon, we began to wade through the Redbud Elementary teacher handbook. The handbook has more than one hundred pages packed with information, including emergency telephone numbers, faculty addresses, philosophies of the school district, the school calendar, and an assortment of rules and regulations. Among the school rules are the following:

- Breakfast duty begins at 7:15 and ends at 7:55. There should be an empty row of tables dividing high school students and elementary students.
- Restroom breaks for fourth grade will be from 10:05–10:15, 1:00–1:15, and 2:40–2:50 P.M. [Actually, there are only two restroom breaks.]
- Boys and girls are assigned to different areas on the playground. Teacher in charge is to have students follow playground rules and keep students in designated areas. [Recall that there is no playground equipment at Redbud Elementary.]
- At lunch teachers, unless otherwise assigned, will go to the cafeteria with their class daily. Noise should be kept to a minimum in the cafeteria.
- Teachers' first priority is to get the students to work. An effective teacher begins class immediately with an assignment, not roll taking.
- You should paddle as a *last form of discipline* after other forms have been unsuccessful. No child should be paddled more than once a day and no more than 3 "licks" should be given. When you paddle, take students to the hall and have another *teacher* as a witness. . . . Do not carry paddles to the lunchroom, playgrounds, or while walking in halls. Do not spank a child that is not in your homeroom.

- Students should move to the right when meeting another line of students and keep their hands/arms down and to themselves.
- Playing in the halls is unnecessary.
- Throwing rocks, dirt, pinecones, or sticks on the playground is not permitted due to the possibility of student injury.

Also in the handbook are rules governing general conduct, classroom conduct, and the detention room. There are rules for homework, homework charts, and sending papers home. There is an array of school policies directed to teachers. For example, every teacher must teach *Character Counts*, bus safety, and sixteen hours of drug awareness. Each teacher must keep a personal folder containing a professional growth plan, self-evaluation, teaching certificate, and several observations and evaluations. All phone calls to parents must be recorded in a log. No personal calls are allowed. (There is only one phone for 611 students and seventy-two faculty and staff members.) Another regulation states, "Checks are not accepted at Redbud Elementary from parents or school personnel." Other rules for teachers include these:

- Employees are to sign in by 7:40 A.M. in the main entrance (if they don't have early duty).
- A form will be filled out and signed by the teacher for all absences or leaving early (name, reason, date, etc.). These will be kept in your file.
- When you are absent send your grade book and plan book to school.
- *It is your responsibility to call another teacher to do your duty when you are out.*
- *Take their duty when you get back.* This includes recess, early duty, concession duty, and late duty.
- Teachers will run their own papers. Each grade will have access to a ditto machine in the grade representative's classroom.
- The Xerox machine is to be used to make "master copies" only, *not to run student copies.* Teachers will be allowed to use this machine as long as it is not abused. [It is permissible to paddle students but not to abuse a machine.]
- *All classes* should be incorporating some form of Iowa/LEAP preparation on a weekly basis. Do not wait until spring to prepare.

There are more than two pages of rules governing lesson planning that require, among other things, objectives, specific skills, activities and materials, modifications, assessment, and correlating the appropriate Louisiana content standards and benchmarks. Some of the previously mentioned are to be underlined in green, yellow, or red. Report cards are given every six weeks, and grades for each subject are reported as percentages: an A is 94 to 100, a B is 87 to 93, a C is 77 to 86, a D is 70 to 76, and an F is 0 to 69.

There are also rules governing teacher use of the resource room (e.g., "do not check out materials from the resource room until the second week of school") and machines (e.g., "keep them clean") as well as rules concerning teacher professionalism (e.g., "make an effort to reduce friction, anger, tension, and negativity in self and those with whom you work"). A "chain of command" specifies that "teachers should go first to the principal with any school-related problem, and only then to the superintendent if the problem cannot be resolved. This is to be strictly adhered to." There are also miscellaneous rules for teachers: "When help from custodians is needed, contact the office. Do not go directly to the custodians with jobs, projects, etc. Talk to students about flushing the toilets and not playing in the restroom. They are not to write on or scratch the walls." The rules even specify the precise number of minutes per week that are to be devoted to each subject area. For example, in grade 3, language arts is to be taught for 165 minutes, five days a week, and music, arts, and crafts are to be taught for thirty minutes, five days a week. (Recall that Redbud Elementary has no art teacher.) There are many other rules in the handbook that regulate the daily lives of the teachers.

At a district meeting for new teachers in mid-August, the superintendent shared several pieces of information. We learned that the average family income in Deerborne Parish is under $20,000 a year and that, by the end of first grade, 90 percent of the children already are reading below grade level. Forty-five new teachers—20 percent of the total district faculty—were present. Superintendent Miller also let us know that he was not a fan of high-stakes testing and state policies requiring that children be retained in grades 4 and 8.

Mr. Barnes, principal of the alternative school, described the "boot camp" atmosphere of his school. "We have an eight-foot fence with razor wire on top. Our job is to change attitudes." He described some of the problems we new teachers would face. "In some families, incest is a problem. I've had students who were pregnant in the seventh grade. Last year there were seven. A mother who is a crackhead needs the money her daughter brings in as a prostitute. The FBI says we have one of the highest rates of unsolved murders. We have a serious gang problem. The Crips are in Redbud, and the Bloods are in Hines. Don't back down to these hoods. If you see graffiti, report it so that we can paint over it. If it remains, it means that gang has won that territory. Some teachers," he continued, "don't even call parents anymore because they're sick of being cussed out. I'm an advocate of spanking. But I didn't spank more than ten kids my first year."

Mr. Barnes gave us a handout that included eleven tips for our first day of teaching. Number 8, for example, was "Slowly get to know your children one

on one." Some worried that we might get to know the children rather quickly
if Mr. Barnes's stories were accurate. His handout included a list of fourteen
classroom procedures, such as "*Pencil Sharpener:* Go only with teacher permission—only one at a time—no talking to and from." We hoped we wouldn't
have to say this twice to any Crips.

Among the forty-five new teachers, some were retired teachers who were
coaxed into helping to fill the needs of the parish. Many newcomers, however,
were raw recruits with no classroom experience. A number of them were uncertified teachers who held a bachelor's degree in a field other than education.
The state permits them to teach on the condition that they take course work
each year and pass the dreaded Praxis examinations if they want to continue
teaching in Louisiana. Mr. Barnes's handout was the first of many we were to
receive. The forty-five of us were bombarded with rules, regulations, and requirements presented to us by the various district central office administrators.

We first learned about the teacher observation/evaluation instrument that
administrators would use when they came into our classrooms. The instrument
contained the forty-four Louisiana components of effective teaching grouped
into four categories. Included under the category Professional/Personal Traits,
for example, were "exhibits a neat, attractive appearance; demonstrates loyalty
to school and administration." That handout contained a set of fifteen market-
ing tips for teachers. Number 6 stated, "Ethics: be fair with everyone." The
closed campus policy handout included nine regulations, among them, number 2: "Cars that are driven on campus should be parked and locked and not
entered until school is dismissed, except as authorized by the principal's office."

The "Revised Personnel Evaluation Plan, 2000–2001" contained a
whopping 103 pages with all sorts of rules, regulations, forms, tips, mission
statements, philosophies, and even a glossary. Under the heading "Focus on Educational Improvement," goal 2, number 3, stipulates, "All certified and professional personnel will be encouraged to participate in professional organizations
as measured by dues paid." The beginning teacher's salary in Deerborne Parish
is among the lowest in the state; some professional organizations for educators
and unions can cost $100 to $200 per year or more.

CODED LESSON PLANS

A forty-one-page "Job Description/Plan/Personnel Eval. In-service Packet"
was distributed. It contained such teaching tips as "Consider the use of Bloom's
taxonomy." Most of the time spent on this in-service packet dealt with com-

pleting the weekly lesson plans. For each subject, teachers needed to include a description of the lesson objectives, a list of the materials needed, and, using codes, a citation of the activities to be undertaken, the modifications to be made for individual students, and assessment. There was a separate sheet that defined the forty-four codes we had to use for each lesson taught. There were fifteen activity codes (e.g., "LC—Lecture, BW—Boardwork"), nineteen modification codes (e.g., "MS—Multisensory Instruction, ITA—Individual Teacher Assistance"), and nine assessment codes (e.g., "TMT—Teacher Made Test, DM—Duplicating Masters"). Presumably, the principal, supervisors, someone from the state, or all three monitored these plans. We wondered how we would ever have time to prepare engaging, sound instruction while spending inordinate amounts of time working with all the codes. In addition, each lesson had to contain the appropriate state standards and benchmarks.

The standards and benchmarks have an abbreviated form similar to a code. For example, the grade 3 benchmark "write legibly in manuscript/cursive form" should be written on the lesson plan as follows: "3/ELA-3-E1/pg 24." No foolin'. Defined, 3 is the standard number, ELA-3-E1 is the benchmark number, and 24 is the curriculum guide page number. There are fourteen pages of these abbreviations for English language arts, eight pages for math, and seven pages for social studies (broken down into the disciplines of economics, geography, civics, and history); science has seven pages. The task of completing a single lesson plan with all the codes and abbreviations seemed senseless and mind-boggling—and we hold Ph.D.s in the field. We began to fear for the beginners in the group. Their faces registered disbelief and rightly so. The supervisor, though, told us that relief was in sight. Within weeks, a computer program would enable us to do all of this much faster and even code in "Bloom's taxonomy" as well.

There seemed to be an assumption that listing codes and benchmarks in a lesson-plan book ensured that they would be well taught and understood by the students. What it amounts to is busywork for the teacher. Designers and authors of instructional materials provide scope and sequence skills listings. Sound materials are based on the best of what is known from research and seasoned practice. It would save everyone time and make much more sense if teachers could simply refer to a page or two in the materials they are using. Competent teachers know what they are going to teach, and they take their work seriously. They are not helped by listing codes and symbols in their plan books. The incompetent teachers don't know what to do, they don't care, and they never will, no matter how much listing and coding they are required to do.

Louisiana teachers work hard to develop mechanisms to ease the paperwork burden imposed on them by the forces of accountability. One elementary

education supervisor told us that she had spent three years developing a simplified correlation of skills and benchmarks. Teams of teachers worked for months
to develop computer-generated lists keyed to this and that. Think of what could
happen for the children of Louisiana if all this time and energy were devoted to
convincing state legislators, the Department of Education, and the accountability committee that what they have mandated is driving some of the best teachers out of the state or out of the classroom.

During the meeting, we were warned never to let our grade books out of
sight. "People steal them," cautioned Mr. Green. In the grade books, we had to
record the number of the textbook assigned to each student, numbers correct
on all assignments, and then percentages and letter grades for each grading period. There are six reporting periods, and we learned that we must send home
progress reports every three weeks.

The leave policy packet was next. We were told that we could take two
personal days per year; however, these days would be deducted from our ten
days of sick leave per year. Children are not the only ones who need a doctor's
excuse when they are absent for a period of time. The handout stated, "When
a teacher is absent for six or more consecutive days because of personal illness,
he shall be required to present a certificate from a physician certifying such illness." We were told that this was a more generous period of time before a physician's certificate was needed. In prior years, it was two days. It was explained that
every teacher's attendance had to be reported to the Louisiana Department of
Education, which planned to look at correlations between teacher absentee
rates and LEAP scores. "You will be reprimanded by the state if you have too
many absences," cautioned Mr. Green. We also were told that all faculty must
sign in every morning, and some schools have a time clock to check tardiness.

A final handout that morning was the forty-six-page student handbook,
which covered such areas as metal detector policy, corporal punishment,
weapons policy, dress code, communicable disease control policy, and fifteen
other categories. We all knew we had some homework to do before school
started. We'd certainly be pulling all-nighters on those lesson plans.

More than three decades ago, historian Michael B. Katz (1971), in *Class,
Bureaucracy, and Schools*, wrote,

> Even people who have been willing to accept a poor salary and who can
> remain indifferent to status have been repelled by the lack of autonomy, the
> rigid and petty authoritarian ethos of the schools. Bright, creative, and well-
> educated people want to function as professionals, to make the decisions
> about how they will do their job. Education has not suffered from any free-
> dom granted teachers to run schools as they see fit; it has suffered from the
> suffocating atmosphere in which teachers have had to work. (131)

Now the bureaucracy has added standards, accountability, and high-stakes testing to further diminish teachers' range of choices. They are told what to teach, how to teach it, and how many minutes to spend on it. Every societal ill or politician's whim signals an addition to the elementary school's already bloated curriculum. Educator Garrett Keizer (2000) pointed out,

> Whenever our society changes, wants to change, or pretends that it wants to change, schools and teachers are enlisted in the cause. If we as a society decide that cyberspace is the place to go, we'll start by sending the third grade. If we as a society come to fear that we're going to hell in a handbasket, we'll start talking about "values-based education." No teacher or school administrator can hear the phrase "launching a new initiative" without suspecting that the launching pad is going to look a lot like a blackboard. (83)

Teachers, however, are not given more time to teach all the new material, nor is any of the old material deleted from the curriculum.

Critics of teachers say, "If they don't like the job, why don't they get out?" That's exactly what many have done and what many more will do. Real estate agents are taking out ads in local newspapers inviting teachers and former teachers to join their teams. Some insurance companies have tried similar appeals.

After the LEAP results were released in May 2000, the Louisiana Department of Education issued a revised testing policy that softened the "all or nothing" existing policy (Louisiana Department of Education 2000). The revision permitted exceptions to "fail the test—repeat the grade" by establishing mechanisms of appeal for a promotion to three categories of students: students with disabilities, students who had already repeated grade 4, and students who had scored at the proficient level on either math or English but scored unsatisfactory on the other or had achieved high report card grades in the subject(s) of the failed test. Students, their teachers, and principals were held captive until August 14, when the second LEAP scores were finally announced. Before the announcement, fourth- and eighth-grade students who had retaken the LEAP did not know to which grade they would be assigned. Teachers could not plan properly, and the principal could not assign any of the students who had failed in May to a classroom until just before the start of the school year. Such planning by the state caused needless anxiety for students, parents, teachers, and principals.

WORKSHOPS AND MEETINGS

We began to get to know our colleagues at Redbud Elementary during a three-day workshop a week and a half before school started. The workshop was designed to give teachers information about the new balanced literacy program that had been adopted for the school. In a nutshell, balanced literacy involves integrating reading, writing, spelling, literature, and oral language through the use of small-group instruction and small-group learning centers. We learned about the methods and materials that were scheduled to arrive the following week, but mainly we learned how creative and selfless the teachers are. Kim Bridges, the workshop leader, is a captivating storyteller. We howled with laughter as she told her version of "The Gingerbread Boy." Kim's characters included Lily, the southern belle who did little but always was "about to DAH [die] from exhaustion," and Bubba, king of the grease pit, who lived on fried food. We heard Virginia Hanks read poetry, and Kay Barker led us in guided reading. Other teachers shared some of their specialties. We had forgotten how much fun it is to be among elementary school teachers. They love what they do. They have a sense of humor. They deserve medals of honor and a lot of money.

One feature of the balanced literacy program is called "daily news" or "daily oral language." Each morning, the teacher invites students to write sentences that describe something of interest to them. A teacher, pretending to be a child, wrote, "Last night my mamma and daddy had a fight and the cops came." Teachers often hear a lot of family stuff. It reminded us of an incident that happened in one of our classrooms several years ago. A boy named Henry asked if he could show the class some pictures his uncle had taken of his Christmas tree. He was given permission. Henry proudly passed around two pictures of the tree. On one photo, mom lay sleeping under the tree with an empty beer bottle near her head. In the other pic, Dad, mouth open, slept beside the tree with a beer bottle between his legs. All the children admired the beautifully decorated tree.

During the three-day workshop, we also learned about the items teachers are expected to buy out of their own pockets in order to do a good job of teaching. The handbook says, "Teachers must purchase paper clips, glue, tape, staples, pens, and highlighters for classroom use." At the workshop, many other items were mentioned that are not provided by the school but are necessary for the success of the program: clipboards, cassettes, spray bottles, dowels, folders (one for each child for each center), small pocket charts, large pocket charts, metal chart holders, chart racks, easels, timers, paint, crayons, colored paper, little magnets, metal trays, magnetic letters, magnetic words, felt, batteries, plastic tubs, plastic carts on rollers, cookie sheets, and more. Glenda, a second-year teacher, told a group of us that she was worried about buying the necessary supplies and even the basic materials, such as cursive letter cards, for her classroom. She explained that she had not had a paycheck since May. We wouldn't get our first paychecks until the end of September. Her salary, when she does get paid, will be $23,868 for the year. One of the veteran teachers said she should talk to the district about an advance. All of us chuckled weakly.

Critics have been heard saying, "Teachers chose to work with kids. They should buy things for them to use." No one, however, expects pediatricians to buy medicine to keep their patients healthy, nor do they expect orthodontists to buy the braces to straighten their patients' teeth. Yet these professionals make more money than teachers. It is only in education that practitioners are expected to pay for the things children need that should be provided by the school district or state.

Similarly, many people believe teachers deserve poor salaries because they work only nine months. Summer courses, workshops, seminars to improve teaching, cleaning and readying rooms during the weeks before school begins, shopping for supplies, working every night and every weekend planning lessons, finding materials, and preparing needlessly complex lesson plans coded to state standards and benchmarks all belie the nine-month myth.

Toward the end of the workshop, we were shown a videotape of a California school that uses balanced literacy. It made clear to all of us the difference between "have" and "have-not" schools. The school was carpeted; in the classrooms were children reading on plush sofas, rockers, and beanbag chairs or seated at new tables. Little lamps with dainty lampshades adorned the tables. There were art supplies and books everywhere. Groups of cheery, well-dressed, well-fed children played games on the floor. We watched longingly.

Most teachers went home for lunch or ate at Ming Shui's Bakery and Mexican Cafeteria, where a chicken enchilada and salad go for $4.50 and a full buffet is $6.00. After the second day, Belinda told us that she wasn't going back the next day for lunch. "I just can't afford to go there three days in a row. It adds up, you know, and I have a lot of supplies to buy for this new program."

Two days before the start of the school year, there were two more days of in-service meetings. The first meeting was for the two hundred teachers in the school district and was held at Redbud High School. We entered the auditorium to the rhythm of a "yakkety-sax," drum, and bass guitar. The small combo, led by the Redbud High School band director, easily fulfilled its task of rallying the returning teachers. Some even danced a little at 7:45 A.M. Coffee, soda, and doughnuts were provided by a regional bank. One faculty member noted, "This is Louisiana. We don't do anything without music and food."

"That's why we're here," we responded.

The Mardi Gras mood was sobered by Ms. Randall from the Louisiana attorney general's office, who spoke about the need for crisis plans and drills. She relayed statistics on guns and gangs and described some Internet hate sites.

"In the last six months, kidnapping in the state has risen 6 percent," she stated. The speaker urged us to have a teacher buddy across the hall or in the room next door so we could help each other manage stress. Ms. Randall said that last year a teacher had snapped on receiving a bad evaluation from her principal. The teacher had intended to kill the principal and then turn the gun on herself. Apparently, the teacher buddy prevented the tragedy.

After Ms. Randall was finished speaking, we were reminded to sign the attendance sheet in the hall. "We have to report our hours and numbers to the state," announced Mr. Green. Before the day was over, we had to sign our names three times to three different sheets to verify our presence at all sessions. Various announcements were made. The technology director reported that the state had cut funds this year but that she was working on refurbishing some computers for the high school.

During the mid-morning break, returning teachers greeted old friends and welcomed newcomers. They were a vivacious bunch. We learned more about the rat situation. A kindergarten teacher said, "Last year I was sitting in the teachers' room and I saw a tail on a cushion. The tail was attached to a rat. Some had babies behind the Coke machine."

As is typical of teachers, they continued to chat as they returned to the auditorium and were seated. Mr. Green attempted to get everyone's attention. He tried a couple of times, and then, to our astonishment, he screamed at the teachers to be quiet. The room became silent, and the Mardi Gras mood was over. Mr. Green spoke to us as if we were naughty children. "In my thirty years in education, I've never had to do *that*," he bellowed. "I demand respect. I'm disappointed in you."

The remaining presentation on yet more rules and regulations was made to a defeated audience. "Pick up your empty cans and cups and put them in the trash cans before you leave," Mr. Green barked.

Our final day of in-service was presented by a consultant from the company who supplied the materials for the reading program the school was using. The consultant began the session by reading a dry storybook to us. She told us endless tales about her teenage son. She remarked that she knew nothing about technology. She whined that she wanted bigger closets at home. She confided that her husband, who was an engineer, was too exacting. We were read to, line by line, from her countless transparencies. They contained "valuable" information, such as "Teach kids how to handle books. Plan the first week of school. Skimming and scanning are important for middle school kids." This nonsense went on all day. We never got to the meat of the matter—how to teach reading with the company's materials. It was an endurance test unlike any we had had so far.

TWO

SEPTEMBER

THE CHILDREN WE TEACH

WEEK 1, AUGUST 21–25: THE DAILY ROUTINE

The children arrived today. Twenty-one bright-eyed boys and girls in school uniforms found their desks in Room B, grade 3. Twenty-two others made their way to fourth grade, Room H. The school uniforms are varied. Choices include red, white, blue, or plaid tops and navy or khaki bottoms. Some wear pants, others shorts or skirts. Everyone is neat and clean. Many children carry their required school supplies (scissors, glue, notebook paper, pencils, crayons, and so on), but several children are empty-handed. Third and fourth graders come in all sizes and shapes. We learn quickly that their levels of reading and writing abilities are as dissimilar as their heights and weights. Rosters reveal that six of the twenty-one third graders are in special education, as are four of the fourth graders. These children are nonreaders. Of the twenty-one third graders, only four are approaching reading on a third-grade level. In the fourth grade, about half the children are reading at the fourth-grade level, according to a quick pretest.

Among the twenty-two fourth graders is Dwayne, a slender boy with large eyes, a ready smile, and a timid demeanor. Joshua, one of the five white children in the class, is the opposite of Dwayne. He is quick with the hand in the air and filled with questions and suggestions. De'Lewis appears nervous as he stacks and restacks his crayons on his desk. His mother, a prison guard up the road, accompanies him that first morning and urges, "Stay on top of him. But you can't reach me at the prison. I'm in the field all day. Last year school tried to call me too much." Other boys—Dario, Malcolm, Derek, Victavius, and Damien—find their seats. Letrinette, Tashanee, LaDelle, Emerald, and Jaylene chatter near the doorway, exuding nervous energy.

Among the third graders, there are five white children. The African American pupils and the white children mix freely. Third graders, at least in this classroom, seem to be unconcerned about skin color. A few personalities stand out from the others. Kanzah is alone and sulking near the back of the room. Manuel and Jaron talk loudly and nonstop. Jelani is swatting his neighbor. Delicate Shantel whispers to her friend Cherise. Keaziah is running around the room. Leon is playing with a metal pull cord from a lamp. The rest of the children are seated and staring toward the front of the room in anticipation.

Teachers work the entire day with practically no break from their children. When it is their weekly duty day, they are with children from 7:15 A.M. until 3:35 P.M., when the last bus leaves. On other days, start-up time is 7:55 A.M. The teachers accompany the children to and from their ten-minute recess and to the two toilet breaks (following recess and lunch), and they walk with their children one block to the cafeteria building and eat with them there. Just thirty minutes are allotted to march to the cafeteria, wash all hands in a trough, stay in line to get food, gobble down the meal, return the trays, and walk as a group to the toilets. Classes that have music or physical education after lunch have only twenty minutes for the entire procedure. Each teacher's only break from class comes during the twenty-five minutes daily when the class has music or physical education. The teacher must, however, walk the children to the music room, which is in a portable classroom at the far end of the building, and then return to the portable building to walk them back. On alternate days, students are walked to the gym. Net "free time" per day is ten minutes. This is when the teacher must use the restroom (one adult toilet and sink with cold water only for the faculty and staff of seventy-two), as there is no other time during the day. It is also during this "planning time" when teachers are expected to return or make phone calls to parents. There is only one telephone available for teacher use in the school.

Louisiana is in the thick of a scorching heat wave. Records are broken daily as temperatures soar well above one hundred degrees. The intense Louisiana sun beats down on the dry, cracked playground as the two hundred third and fourth graders run out for their ten-minute morning recess. The playground is divided by imaginary lines into quadrangles. Boys and girls are kept separate, as are third and fourth graders. There is no playground equipment, so most pupils run around under the relentless sun, playing tag or throwing the one or two rubber balls a child has brought from home. Forbidden are tackling, doing flips, or using hardballs and bats. Teacher voices can be heard above the din, reminding the fourth-grade boys not to go near the softball diamond because "That's not ours." As a security measure, girls are warned to stay away from the far fences. Children who fall on the hard ground have scrapes and cuts. Here and there a child cries because of an injury or, more often, because of an insult from another child. We are told that the insults usually refer to a child's mother (e.g., "Your mama is a crackhead") or a deceased relative. All too quickly they must line up again by class for the march to the bathrooms or, for third graders, to their classrooms.

We are somewhat in awe of the assembly-line restroom process. When it is necessary for two hundred boys and girls to use their small bathrooms at the same time, the organization rivals that of a Disneyland waiting line. In the boys' restroom, there are four stalls and a trough that can accommodate four standing urinators. In the girls' room, there are eight stalls. A few children have specific duties. One holds the door open. Another assigns incoming students to a spot. A third oversees a quick hand wash (in cold water), and a fourth presses the drinking fountain button for a count of three. Hence, one hundred children of each gender are relieved, washed, and watered—all within ten minutes. You have to see it to believe it.

"My farter food is hot dogs. My farter state is California," writes Nikeya, a fourth-grade girl in response to the prompt "Write about some of your favorite things." A day at Redbud is not without its smiles and laughs. When asked to describe Mr. Johnson, one child observes, "He talk funny." Another notes, "Mr. Johnson smell good." A third child pens, "He is very old but still smart." Haden, a third-grade child, writes, "Dear Ms. Johnson. if it weren't for you I'd be dom you tolt me everything I know."

Not all instruction has to do with academic work. We find that a few of our third and fourth graders need to be taught rudimentary table manners. They do not know how to use a fork. Some children scoop food off the cafeteria trays with their hands—a handful of green beans, another handful of taco salad. When told to use forks, not their hands, Milo says, "This is the way we eat when we're hungry." Some of the children are scrawny and don't leave a scrap of food behind. With the short time allotted for lunch, students may have discovered that they must scoop their food to get it all in. Veteran teachers tell us that for many children, the school breakfast and lunch are the only food they get all day.

Even though it is just the first week of school, we know that if we could work one on one with some of the children, they could learn to read and write. Chalese is an African American fourth grader whose appearance resembles that of a starving child seen in photographs of Sudan. She has big brown eyes and a sweet smile. Chalese is a nonreader and a nonwriter. She knows two sight words, "go" and "look," and can write a few letters, some of them backward. Chalese, like many of the children, yearns for attention. She often comes to the teacher's desk to proudly show her scribbles. If Chalese received the attention and time she craves, she could succeed. A few children, however, seem to have given up as early as the third grade. Most of the nonreaders simply do not attempt to do anything. They sit and snip paper, play with glue, and doodle. Any type of written material is ignored. We suspect that some can do better. Fourth graders De'Lewis, Antron, and Tony do nothing until prodded and hounded by the teacher; however, each of the three has shown that he can read and write a little. Third graders Leon, Kanzah, and Chikae cannot read even one word. Their writing consists of random letters that make no sense. By age eight, they have stopped trying. They spend their class time drawing and pestering others or just staring into space.

While lining up to enter the building one morning, third grader Cherise asks if she will get a warning if she falls asleep in class. She is told that she will not.

"Our neighbor in the next apartment played music loud until one o'clock last night," she reports.

Wendice and Leon fall asleep in their third-grade classroom every day this week. Wendice is lethargic and has a deep cough. He complains of chest pains. Leon, who constantly is in motion, wears himself out by noon. Fourth grader Yolande has to be awakened every day. Most of the pupils report bedtimes of eleven o'clock, midnight, or later.

There are three computers in each classroom. In the third-grade room, two are broken, and the one with an Internet connection has lost the connection. The overhead projector has a three-prong plug, but the electrical outlet accommodates only two prongs.

A group of fourth graders reads a story about a boy whose mother dies and whose father later remarries. The child in the story isn't sure about this stepmother, but eventually the two agree they can be friends. When asked if any of them have stepmothers or stepfathers, two pupils reply that they had stepmothers. Dwayne grimaces, "I hate her. She don't like me." Derek, a white child, joins in, "Mine was so bad my dad dumped her. She had tattoos all over and metal in the skin. She was awful." Letrinette says, "My stepdad is very nice, but I love my daddy."

The pupils come up with all kinds of observations and questions. Third grader Jaheesa, in the middle of a science lesson, asks, "Do teachers cuss at home?" Demetrius confides to his fourth-grade teacher, "I live with my mama and daddy, but mostly I live with my aunt. My mama have five babies and they was too much for her. I like living at my aunt's house."

We quickly learn that the principal, Ms. Porter, and her staff are extraordinary. They often arrive at school by 6:45 A.M. and sometimes stay until 11:00 P.M. We also learn of another extraordinary person during our first week. We had asked a friend, Bob Zuvanich of Continental Press, if he possibly could help us out by "adopting" Redbud Elementary School and sending us badly needed instructional materials. In August, UPS drivers deliver more than seventy large, heavy boxes to our house. The boxes contain ten copies each of thirty-five different children's books as well as instructional materials for math, problem solving, reading comprehension, phonics, and language development. The materials span all the grades, and there are enough copies for the entire school. Continental Press bills us nothing—not even shipping charges. The children are so thrilled that they write thank-you notes to Mr. Zuvanich. The following are a few examples of their messages.

Demetrius's note reflects what he considers valuable: "I will buy you shoe one day. I belive you have a wive. I love your wive to."

Carlonna writes, "I thank you for what you have done for us. And I hop we all past the Leap 21 test this year."

Dawnyetta comments, "How wonderful you is."

From Shonora comes, "We all love you and your family. You are so nice and kin so keep up the good work Mr. Zuvanich."

Antinesha observes, "You are a nice men."

The first week closes with 109-degree temperatures and two broken water fountains. Redbud children return from recess, lunch, and the un-air-conditioned gym with no water to drink. Driving back to Ruston after school, we hear the radio broadcaster warning listeners to make sure their pets have plenty of drinking water. It irks us when we think of our morning drive past the magnificent Temple Baptist Church, which sits on lush, green acreage. In the middle of a record-setting heat wave and drought, Temple's underground water sprinklers work overtime lavishing precious water on its golf course–like grass carpets. On the weekend we stock up on paper cups so our pupils can at least drink some tepid water from a faucet in the building.

According to educator Ruby Payne (1998), children of poverty often talk incessantly. We find this to be true during our first week of teaching. A great deal of our time is spent trying to convince the children that unless they listen and are attentive, we cannot help them learn.

We know that we will have to spend a large part of the upcoming weekend poring over the mountain of forms and memoranda that come our way daily. These are handed to us during an after-school teachers' meeting. We wish that we could spend time preparing useful instructional activities for our pupils—especially for our nonreaders who have given up. Instead, our time will be spent looking up the codes for standards, benchmarks, activities, modifications, and assessments and attaching these codes to instructional plans. We had been warned by Mr. Green that he could come at any time to check our plan books for these codes. There will be little time left for actual meaningful planning. In just one week, we have come to understand that a major culprit hampering the education of children and souring the professional lives of teachers is useless state-mandated busywork.

WEEK 2, AUGUST 28–SEPTEMBER 1: HEAT WAVE

Third Grade

Jimmy is coughing and complaining of chest pains. I ask him if he has told his mother. He says that he has. "Have you seen a doctor?" I inquire. "No," he mumbles. Many children complain of tooth pain. Cherise has tears running from her eyes. She isn't crying, she is in pain. I ask how many children ever have been to a dentist. Only five of the twenty-one raise their hands. Every day some of the pupils report stomachaches. We attribute this to hunger.

Each day I read to the class, usually just before lunch. Four or five children fall into a deep sleep during this time. Some sleep so soundly that it is difficult to wake them for lunch.

In previous years, Pam Porter has been in charge of her six-hundred-plus pupil school with no administrative assistance. Now there is a new face. Greta Dawson has been hired as an assistant principal in charge of discipline. At an after-school meeting, Ms. Dawson introduces the faculty to her three-strikes method of discipline. Strike 1 is a warning, strike 2 requires that the child be isolated from the rest of the class for the day, and strike 3 means being sent to Ms. Dawson's office for a lecture, a paddling, or suspension. Within days, pupils learn that they do not want to be sent to Ms. Dawson. She has her own three-strikes procedure. The first time children are sent to her, they are lectured or paddled and made to apologize to the teacher. The second visit nets them in-school suspension. This means being sent to a separate room, supervised by Ms. Eleanor, where they do schoolwork but are allowed no contact with anyone. Bathroom and lunch breaks are taken when no other children are present. They are required to perform duties such as picking up litter around the school, inside and out. Strike 3 means removal from Redbud Elementary for several days.

Ms. Dawson is a statuesque woman with ebony skin and a gold front tooth. She is capable of a warm, inviting smile and a hug for a kindergartner or a scary scowl. Three signs rotate on her office door: a smiley face, a frowning face, and a weeping face. We aren't sure if they indicate her mood that day or if they suggest what's happening behind her closed door. Ms. Dawson is not shy about telling teachers how to discipline their classes. On the playground, she tells us firmly and up close, "Don't let children lie on the ground!" Veteran teachers say that the hallways and cafeteria are much quieter this year because of Ms. Dawson. One can always tell when Ms. Dawson is in the vicinity; small heads turn in unison, and little eyes grow big. Usually accompanying Ms. Dawson is a string of students, some silent and chagrined, others weeping. Misbehavior in the cafeteria means standing at attention on a square tile in the front of all the students. The effect is similar to the stocks or dunking stool in days of yore. Third grader Jelani says, "She mean. She everywhere."

I tell Leon that I will help him learn to read and write, but for now he should just draw in his journal when the others are writing. He completes his picture and calls out to me. It is a picture, he says, of a mother rat and a baby rat. Leon clearly is familiar with rats. The pictures are unmistakable. I help him spell the word "rat." Sometimes the children's dialect and my midwestern accent make it difficult for us to understand each other. Chikae tells the class, "I saw a baa last night." I cannot interpret what the child is saying. Helpful Manuel sticks out his front teeth and flaps tiny imaginary wings. "You know, one of these," he says. "Oh, a *bat*," I say.

Despite the harshness of their environment, many of the children are touchingly innocent. Shantel writes in her journal, "I love you to deth. I want you and Mr. Johnson to come to my house tonit. My adres is. . . ."

There are three after-school curriculum-related meetings this week. Tuesday's meeting is an attempt by local teachers to wade through the math standards and benchmarks and to key and sequence objectives to six-week periods for each grade level. All teachers, however, must find and note the resources they use to meet these objectives. The math objectives do not sequentially correlate to any math books available in the school. There is no money for additional resources other than the rumored $200 per year per teacher. The meeting ends at 5:15 P.M.

On Wednesday after school, we are shown how to do "running records," a method for evaluating the oral reading of an individual child using an elaborate system of coding. This technique was intended to be an informal, quick measure for the teacher's use. Now mandated, it has become cumbersome. The district wants each teacher to test each child individually using a running record analysis several times during the year. One teacher whispers, "When will we find time to teach? All we do is test." Most of us already know the children's reading levels through several days of observation and oral and written work. The meeting drags on until 5:30 P.M.

The DRA (developmental reading assessment) is the topic of Thursday's after-school session. This assessment requirement is state mandated. It is to be given individually twice a year to every child in the classroom. In theory, the DRA would give a teacher about the same information as the running record procedure; however, the coding system is entirely different, time consuming, and elaborate. Any elementary school teacher could diagnose children's reading difficulties through informal observation. We teach our undergraduate students how to do just that. None of these complicated evaluation systems is necessary. The meeting ends at 5:40 P.M. In Louisiana, elementary students must take the Iowa Test of Basic Skills annually, the high-stakes LEAP test in fourth and eighth grades, the individually administered DRA assessment twice annually, and the individually administered running records assessments several times annually. We wondered which high-powered sales reps or product promoters had such success convincing the people in Baton Rouge to burden teachers and frustrate and frighten children with so much unnecessary formal testing.

We learned that in addition to the balanced literacy training we had before school started and the previously mentioned after-school training this week, week 4 would include three days of after-school training in a particular phonics methodology. On the drive home, the two of us agreed that if we were new teachers, not experienced educators, we would reconsider our career choice. No wonder the scores in Louisiana are so low. There is no time to teach. The new Redbud teachers are overwhelmed and are walking around glassy-eyed. We worry about how many of them will stick it out until the end of the school year.

Fourth Grade

Victavius arrives at 7:15 A.M. with tears running down his cheeks. I ask what's wrong. "My ear hurts." I ask Mrs. Larson, another fourth-grade teacher, if we can give him a children's aspirin for the pain. I learn that is not permissible even if the child has no adverse reactions to aspirin. I also learn that the district school nurse comes once a week and has already been there this week. Just before the morning bell, I have Victavius call his mother. "She'll come at 10:30," he reports. His face is contorted in pain. By noon, no mother. Ruth had Victavius last year in class. She knows a cousin of the boy and contacts her. "I can't find his mother, and his grandmother is drunk," says the cousin. At 2:30, the cousin finds the mother—inebriated. The mother rides to school with a friend to pick up Victavius. Ruth explains to me that Victavius's older brother was shot and killed earlier in the summer and that the mother has been drinking since that time. She has four other children.

The second week of school begins with a temperature of 107 degrees and ends with a record-setting 111 degrees. North Louisiana had no rain in August and a half inch in July. The grass is brown, and the deciduous trees are losing their leaves. Burn bans are in effect in this heavily forested part of the country. One benefit of all the heat is that we have fewer huge cockroaches to squash before the children arrive.

The class is discussing the Pecos Bill tall tale and shows an interest in rodeos. Two or three students have been to a rodeo in the nearby communities of Arcadia or Monroe. I mention that the major Louisiana men's penitentiary, Angola, holds a rodeo each year with the inmates as participants. Streetwise and ever smiling Tony raises and waves his hand. "I know about Angola. My daddy there." The child says that he'll ask his father about the rodeo during the next phone call to him in prison.

WEEK 3: SEPTEMBER 5–8: MORE CODES

Like most teachers, we find that our pupils are never far from our minds. On Saturday we went to a megabookstore in Shreveport to look for a rhyming dictionary and an idiom dictionary. We noticed that the children's book section was filled with healthy, vibrant, mostly white children, many of whom were being read to by adults. Several of them chose books for purchase. We thought of our students, most of whom own no books and probably have never seen the inside of a bookstore.

The heat wave broils on. The gym is 120 degrees—a teacher brings a thermometer. Our loud classroom window air conditioners pant out some cool air. We learn from a friend in a Chicago suburb that her children's school closed at noon in the ninety-degree heat because the children were "getting light-headed." We hear no talk of light-headedness among our children of poverty taking physical education in a 120-degree gym. The drivers report that it is also 120 degrees or higher on their un-air-conditioned buses.

Third and Fourth Grades

On Tuesday there is another after-school meeting. This one is held to describe a new coding system for the Louisiana English/language arts standards and benchmarks. Each elementary teacher in the district is given a packet the size of a ream of paper. The document lists 326 different English language objectives, each one keyed to the LEAP test, the Iowa Test of Basic Skills, the Bloom taxonomy, and a "Strand." Also listed are the hours it should take to teach the objectives and a blank space for the teachers to write the resources they use to achieve the objective. Here is an example:

1. Word attack: blends   Initial sound   Fourth Content Standard
   use blends   (ELA-1-E1/pg 1
                                                        #1)/LEAP/IOWA

This objective is listed at the "comprehension level" on the Bloom taxonomy and is estimated to take 1.0 hour of instruction.

5. Syllabication   Inference   Fourth Content Standard
   distinguish syllables   (ELA-1-E1/pg 2
    in words   #4)/LEAP/IOWA

This objective is categorized as being at the analysis level on Bloom's taxonomy and is allotted 2.0 hours for instruction.

Not only is this list dizzying to the teachers expected to teach it (especially with most of the children well below grade level), but it is riddled with ambiguities. We can't discern how the "syllabication" objective is related to the Strand "inference" or to the "analysis" level on Bloom's taxonomy because syllabication is simply a pronouncing task.

The packet also contains a forty-two-page curriculum grade book spreadsheet that lists each of the 326 objectives followed by "days 1–30." It is to be used by the teachers to track what they teach and when they teach it. This is how Louisiana interprets the concept "teacher accountability." All the previously mentioned material is to be fed by us into our weekly lesson plan book, and it is to direct our classroom instruction. There are no materials available, however, that are keyed—sequentially or topically—to the objectives document. The presenter urges us to list the resources we use when we teach each objective. "At the end of the year, these resources will be shared with a compiling committee so that other teachers may get your great ideas," she woos. The previous week we received one of these behemoths for math too, and more are promised for social studies and science.

The person who presents the English language standards is a middle-grade teacher from another parish. She admonishes, "You must teach to mastery all the objectives that will be tested on the LEAP and Iowa tests. Skip the others until after the tests next March. We have no time to teach fluff." Once again, many teachers leave the meeting stunned. It has become clear even to the most optimistic that school is no longer for education. Schools are now test prep centers, and woe be to those who don't do enough prepping. Nikki, a beginner, says, "I don't know how much longer I can last. I just can't get anything accomplished, and it just keeps piling on."

As we leave our meeting after 5:00 P.M., we notice, as we have on many late days, how the neighborhood atmosphere changes and takes on the feel of "mean streets." Clusters of thin men congregate outside seemingly vacant houses—crack houses, we are told. We are reminded of what Tina, the teacher who gave us a tour of Redbud, told us: "Don't drive into these neighborhoods after 5:00. They just become too dangerous."

Fourth Grade

Victavius returns to school after the Labor Day weekend complaining that his ear still hurts. I inform the school nurse who visits Redbud Elementary each Tuesday morning. She telephones Victavius's mother, who says, "He didn't complain all weekend. So he can just stay at school. I ain't coming to get him." Does he have an earache? I don't know.

During a restless night with little sleep, I am feeling the frustrations and inadequacies that a beginning teacher feels. I can't seem to get on top of it all. There has been no time to get the children on the three classroom computers to see what programs they can handle. I haven't been able to look at the cumulative folders of my pupils. They cannot be taken out of the office. There is no time during the day, and after-school time is consumed by mandatory meetings. I want to put the children into reading centers, but I worry about the lack of self-discipline. I ponder ways to orchestrate teaching those who can't read or write one word with those who can read and write on grade level. My frustration stems from a desire to help them catch up and develop some listening habits combined with the relentless pressure of the continual mention of the LEAP test at every after-school meeting. I have been an educator for years, and I can't imagine the anguish felt by the first-year teachers.

The September 7 issue of the *Guardian Journal*, the local Redbud newspaper, has a front-page editorial by Susan T. Herring (2000b), "Failure of LEAP Test Prompts Suicide Attempt by Fifteen Year Old Student." Teachers in our building express deep concern:

> One fifteen-year-old student felt life was not worth living anymore after she failed the LEAP test in July for the second time. She had been a good student with no behavior or discipline problems, had had problems grasping math problems, but had managed to make a passing grade, then she failed the math portion of the LEAP test.

Although she was faithful attending summer remediation courses and said the teachers did a good job, her score in math was lower than her first test score in March. This is the worst case scenario of the pressure exerted upon fourth and eighth graders across the State of Louisiana due to the new high stakes testing. In an effort to raise test scores, the State enacted a new accountability program which not only punishes a child for failing one test, but also punishes schools and school districts for not making their growth target within a set amount of time. (1)

In the same newspaper, Walter Lee, a member of the Board of Elementary and Secondary Education in Louisiana said, "Louisiana simply does not put enough money into education in relation to other states. . . . We don't pay teachers enough. . . . We've got to redistribute the money. We've got to put it in poor parishes" (1, 5).

Ringing in my ears this morning as I drive to school are the words of yesterday's presenter, "What is not going to be tested on the LEAP test is not worth teaching—it is just fluff." I am an educator. I know how wrong this is. Being able to pronounce words in syllables will not help my students get through life. Earlier, over my morning cup of coffee, I glanced through the September issue of the *Council Chronicle*, a publication of the National Council of Teachers of English. My eyes fell on an excerpt from the book *Standardized Minds* by Peter Sacks (2000):

> Focused on test scores and the means to effect higher scores, the accountability movement has been curiously oblivious to the unintended damage to the learning environment. The movement has ignored the distortion to teaching and learning resulting from teachers, students, and others in the system acting in their own perceived best interests. Schools and teachers, under intense pressure to boost achievement scores, had discovered the educationally dubious practice of teaching to tests. (National Council of Teachers of English 2000, 24)

Third Grade

While on 7:15 A.M. playground duty, I speak with Belinda, who has taught for more than thirty years. She tells me that she feels helpless when teaching higher-order thinking skills. "They have so little background knowledge. They have so little to build on. It is sad." The farthest most of our students have been from Redbud is Minden, a trip of about twenty miles. My pupils urge me to go there. "You and Mr. Johnson has got to go to the Super Wal-Mart in Minden. They got everything." Their eyes light up as they say this. Many want to work at Wal-Mart when they grow up.

A form to be completed by parents or guardians requests information such as current work and home telephone numbers. The sheets continue to trickle back to school. Many parents are working poor. They work at fast-food restaurants or as chicken deboners at a local plant. One sheet reads, "umploy."

Third and Fourth Grades

We need to help our pupils develop listening skills. Speaking and listening development are not tested on the paper-and-pencil LEAP test, and thus the state of Louisiana will probably ignore them. This is a critical mistake because speaking and listening are two crucial building blocks of learning. Listening comprehension parallels and precedes reading comprehension. Speaking parallels and precedes writing development. These integral components of language now are presumably considered "fluff" and will be skipped in many classrooms by well-intentioned but pressured teachers.

Both of our classes complete a student survey in which they are asked to respond to a number of questions. One item asks them to describe "the number one problem today." Replies include "drugs," "drinking," "guns," "knives," "killing," and "the LEAP test." Others write "violence in school" and "school shootings." Another question asks what they would make disappear if they could. Answers include "sticks and rats," "barking dogs," "old shoes," "my brother's disease," and "the water bill."

Third Grade

Jaron reports to me that he saw a second-grade boy stick out his tongue at an adult when her back was turned. I ask the class what they think about someone doing this. Jaheesa says, "If you do that to somebody when you grow up, you could get shot." Violence is never too far away from the minds of my eight-year-olds.

After school, I work with a beginning third-grade teacher, Glenda, on her lesson plans. Her undergraduate teacher education program hasn't prepared her for this onerous chore. I tell her that my weekly plans, even after fourteen years of teaching this age-group, take me an entire Sunday to complete because of the accountability requirements.

Fourth Grade

On Wednesday the heat wave breaks, and the temperature hits only ninety degrees. On Thursday, the high is eighty degrees, and more people wear smiles. Ms. Porter, the principal, reports that Mrs. Larson of the fourth grade has been named Teacher of the Year for Deerborne Parish. After just three weeks of teaching across the hall from Mrs. Larson, I have come to realize that she is truly an expert teacher. She should be making more than twice her current salary. The award is well deserved and long overdue.

Third Grade

Something is terribly wrong with Wendice. His coughing has subsided somewhat, but he complains of a painful jaw. He continues to sleep in class. There is a pus-filled sore on his left arm. I ask him about it. He tells me that he has a lot of these sores on his feet. I take him into the hall and have him remove his shoes and socks. Several sores cover his tiny feet. I send for Ms. Dawson. The child must have medical attention. She takes Wendice away.

Third and Fourth Grades

Today's lunch includes orange halves. We have reminded our classes several times to use forks, not fingers, when they eat. Four rows of third and fourth graders stab oranges with forks and gnaw on the pulp as they rotate the orange. We walk among them saying that it is not bad manners to eat oranges with hands.

On Friday we decide to join the teachers union—the Louisiana Federation of Teachers and the American Federation of Teachers. Redbud educators belong to three different unions, but most join the latter because its dues are less expensive, $75 a year. One big reason they join a union is to get the $1 million liability insurance coverage, a necessity in this litigious age.

WEEK 4: SEPTEMBER 11–16: GETTING STUDENTS' ATTENTION

Third Grade

I have a banana for lunch today. Manuel, a rail-thin child, tries to give me one of his fried chicken wings to supplement my fruit. I am touched. Many students continue to wolf their food down in the tray line and right up to the tray window. There is no time for a leisurely meal.

Most of my students cannot read the science text. I bring in a fall planting catalog and show the class the colored pictures of tulips, daffodils, and hyacinths. They seem enthralled with the variety of colors and names. We talk about what is needed for a plant to grow and how some plants grow from bulbs and others from seeds or roots. I have their attention, and I know I can build on their interests. We discuss climate zones on the catalog map, and we talk about planting depths. A child asks what a picture of a deer with a slash through it means. Another child correctly infers that it means deer won't eat these plants.

The children design seed packets for flowers that grow from seeds. They create original names for sunflowers, snapdragons, and so on. Jaheesa calls her sunflower "Yellow Angel." Jesse, a nonreader, wants to call his sunflower "Son of Sun." I help him spell the two homophones. The pupils ask me if I know what kind of tall flower is growing next to the fast-food Chick-a-Dilly in town.

I tell the children I will have to sit sometimes today because I hurt my left foot. While I read them a story, they are seated around me. Leon sticks a smiley-face sticker on my left foot.

Fourth Grade

Joshua asks if he can read a book to the class that was similar to a book I read to them earlier. He reads the book so well that I ask if he wants to read it to the third graders. Joshua, I am told, receives Carnegie Hall applause from the third-grade class.

While on late bus duty, I tell a kindergartner to sit down. We do this for safety reasons. With bus and carpool traffic coming and going in front of the building, there is the constant fear of a child's darting out in front of a vehicle. The kindergartner tells me, "I can't sit down. I got new pants on." The legs of the pants have been rolled up several times to allow for growth. I show him how to squat so he won't get his pants dirty or torn. The little guy squats for fifteen minutes until his bus arrives.

One of the uncertified teachers who is taking courses to get certified tells me with great worry that she is going to drop the two night classes she is taking this term. She says, "I hate to be a failure, but there is no way I can teach all day, do my planning, attend after-school meetings, drive an hour to the university, and do all the assignments that Dr. Nolan has required." I tell her not to feel bad and recount that when I was about her age, I reached college burnout and joined the army for a two-year tour. Another teacher tells her that she left college for a year to work because she had to earn more tuition money.

Third Grade

Wendice is absent today, and Kanzah is crying from tooth pain. I request that the school nurse come to the school and look at his tooth. It is broken and black.

New teachers have three after-school meetings this week from 3:30 to 5:00 P.M. We are to learn about Project Read, the phonics program used at Redbud Elementary. Then from 5:00 to 6:30 P.M., there is a meeting of the Parent–Teacher Organization (PTO). Monday will be a long day, especially for the Redbud teachers who commute from small towns in Arkansas.

Third and Fourth Grades

The PTO meeting begins with Pam Porter's introducing the faculty and staff. She states, "I sent a letter to every parent in the district asking for volunteers to serve as PTO officers this year. Not one person responded." It is easy to see that there are more teachers and staff in attendance than parents. We count about thirty unfamiliar faces whom we presume are parents. There are over six hundred pupils in the school. Ms. Porter continues, "I hope you will think about serving and let me know before our next meeting." The new reading program is described, and several teachers tell about class reading projects. Only one parent asks a question, and it pertains to the LEAP test. Teachers and parents alike seem thankful when the meeting ends at 6:00 and they can leave the sweltering gym.

On our drive home, we discuss the previous evening's *60 Minutes* segment on the high-stakes TAAS test required in the state of Texas. The program emphasized the frenzy surrounding the test. It showed pep rallies, marching bands, special hats worn by children, and flags all designed to rev kids up—not for a football game but for the TAAS test. Texas teachers were interviewed. They expressed their outrage over what has happened to schooling in Texas because of the tests. One teacher reported that her school has no library but spent $20,000 on test preparation materials. The program highlighted the pressures placed on children. A small child who was interviewed was crying because the next day he had to take the test. CBS reporter Leslie Stahl commented that school administrators can receive a $25,000 annual bonus for improving TAAS scores. Educators lamented that real teaching and learning can no longer occur in Texas. All efforts must be directed toward passing the multiple-choice TAAS test. We believe that this practice will come back to haunt the businesspeople promoting it when there are no divergent, creative thinkers to move their enterprises forward. Will the schools and teachers then be blamed for these serious shortfalls?

What strikes us is the realization that the situation in Louisiana is even more harsh. Texas attaches rewards and punishments to the TAAS test, but currently failure does not impact promotion until high school. In Louisiana, fourth and eighth graders who fail the LEAP test must repeat the grade. The LEAP test does not rely solely on multiple-choice items, but the open-ended response items are read and evaluated by out-of-staters unfamiliar with Louisiana cultures and the vocabulary and syntactic structures used in the children's everyday lives. Test-grading enterprises are among the many new entrepreneurial ventures that have sprung up around the country to feed off the accountability movement.

Third Grade

I learn from the school nurse that Wendice has impetigo. His mother says that she cannot afford to take him to a doctor. He stays out of school the rest of the week.

Fourth Grade

The students change classes once a day. I teach reading/language arts and social studies to my homeroom from 8:00 to 10:40 A.M. Then Mrs. Henderson and I change classes, and she teaches math and science to my class while I teach my subjects to her class. She is a retired educator with a doctoral degree who used to teach at the local prison. She was coaxed into coming out of retirement because of the elementary teacher shortage in Louisiana. Each day we compare notes and wonder what we could be doing to better capture our students' attention and interests. Are we expecting too much? Our hearts understand the horrible living conditions they come from, but our heads tell us that if they only would listen and follow directions, we could help them learn and maybe escape the entrenched poverty in Redbud. Neither of us has found the magic formula yet.

A staff member tells us at recess that the children come from environments with constant noise. "All they are used to is people shouting at them," she says. She adds, however, "They have to learn school behavior or they won't learn at all and the cycle will continue." I have decided to have an individual conference with each of my students from both classes over the next couple of weeks to try to mutually work out some solutions.

WEEK 5, SEPTEMBER 18–22: WASTING INSTRUCTIONAL TIME

We have begun to develop our routines. The major lesson planning, with all the coding, is completed on the weekend. Weeknight evenings are taken up with fine-tuning our class sessions and grading student work. The drive to and from Redbud has become our best planning time. Today we discussed some new learning centers we could develop (e.g., a vocabulary center filled with activities for vocabulary expansion and an advertisement center to help pupils discern bias in writing and to identify persuasion strategies).

On Saturday we invested in a reading rug for each classroom: Wal-Mart, five by eight, $28.88 per rug. The children are ecstatic. Initially they won't walk on the rugs but take circuitous routes around them. We say it's okay to walk on them, but they do so tentatively. During their reading times on the rugs, some children pick grass and other debris from the rugs and fluff them up with their hands.

Third Grade

At recess one of my boys says, "Yesterday my mama whupped my ass so hard she broke the paddle." "Wow," I reply.

This morning before school starts, a tearful grandmother is waiting for me by my room. She tells me that Gerard's mother has taken him away and that she is here to gather up his things. I don't know where he has gone. He is a nervous little boy who often mentions his younger sister. She died "because something was wrong with her heart." I will miss Gerard.

Kanzah is crying again with a terrible toothache. On Tuesday morning, the school nurse checks his rotting, black molar. She tries to call his home, but the phone has been disconnected. She gives Kanzah a letter to take home. It states that the child needs immediate care. Despite Kanzah's unimaginable pain, he manages to do well on his spelling test, missing only three words.

The following day Kanzah hands me a note that says, "This is Kanzah grandmother. I am going to make him apnement for his teeth today. Thank you."

Fourth Grade

I receive a letter from a parent telling me about practices "to which I take religious exception to. . . . The practices we feel are contrary to our religious beliefs include any stories and activities that include fairies, trolls, and such to include all Harry Potter materials."

Third Grade

Some toys are missing from a child's desk. I tell the class that if the person who took them tells me confidentially, I will return the toys to the rightful owner. No one comes forward. I have seen no child take toys from another's desk. They have been in their seats all morning working. The following morning, I receive a note from the mother of the child who says his toys were stolen. "You did not spend enough time looking for those toys. You didn't go through every student's desk and book bag." We have begun to see another problem confronting teachers—parents who place unreasonable demands on them.

I am still working on the developmental reading assessments. I am also completing computerized forms for the state of Louisiana. For each child, I must write the full name (including middle initial), Social Security number, special education codes, race, and reading levels. This information I must track down in the children's cumulative folders (which do not leave the office). If the child is below grade level, the level must be indicated and an oval filled in with a number 2 pencil. Each numeral of the Social Security number must be blackened on the form. The numerals in the ovals are so tiny and faint that I need a magnifying glass to do this job. This requirement is burdensome to the thousands of first-, second-, and third-grade teachers in the state of Louisiana who must do this at least twice a year. Sometimes a child can take an entire day to find a small DRA booklet with which he or she feels comfortable. Teachers are trained to know where to place children in reading materials. There is so much testing going on that the amount of time for teaching is shamefully reduced. I feel guilty taking precious instructional time away from the pupils to fulfill these testing requirements. I know better.

The exasperating truth is that the individually administered DRA given in grades 1, 2, and 3; the high-stakes LEAP test given in grades 4 and 8; and the Iowa test given in nearly all grades are required by the state for accountability purposes—not as evaluative tools to help teachers. We wonder if Cecil Picard, state superintendent, and his staff have any idea of the amount of instructional time that is being squandered by these test-monitoring mandates. Until this overuse of testing changes, we are convinced that the state of Louisiana will remain near the bottom of the education heap. If the money the state spends on testing, test scoring, and bureaucratic fiefdoms involved in the related monitoring were rerouted to reducing class size and putting a full-time paraprofessional in each classroom, what a rosy future Louisiana could have.

Third and Fourth Grades

One of the most competent teachers we have ever seen tells us, "We are observed every three years by a person from the district office. The last time I was observed, I was using an overhead projector that I had not listed in the materials section of my lesson plan book. I needed the overhead projector to get my point across to the students. I was graded down by this evaluator for not stating 'overhead projector' in my plan book." This dedicated teacher was made to feel bad because a rigid, nitpicking administrator did not realize or care that masterful teachers must adjust their lessons frequently to accommodate learning. This obsession with monitoring the correctness of forms has caused another teacher to begin thinking of early retirement—another loss for the children of Redbud, Louisiana.

One year can impact the culinary distinctions our children make. Long, melted-cheese-covered things are served for lunch one day. We ask the third graders what they are. They shrug their shoulders. "How do they taste?" we ask. "They're really good!" they respond. We ask the fourth graders what the entrée is. They, too, shrug their shoulders. One child adds, "They're nasty," but he eats it all.

Connie Hemerly, an associate of Mr. Zuvanich who gave us the many materials for the school, sends our classes her grown son's encyclopedias, paperbacks, and other reading materials. The children cannot believe the largesse they are receiving. We have them write thank-you notes. Graham, a fourth grader, writes, "We are learning a lot of things. if you never gave us books we wouldnt have learn hardly nothing." Shantel, a third grader, notes, "I like the books. Shoot, I love them."

Third Grade

The third-grade teachers have an after-school meeting at which "greenbacks" are discussed. The term "greenbacks" refers to ledger sheets, not dollar bills. On each sheet, the classroom teacher is to record each child's name, address, telephone number, date of birth, place of birth, birth certificate number, father's name, and mother's maiden name. This information must be dug out of the cumulative folders. Then the ledger is used to record each student's daily attendance, even though this information is submitted to the office every morning. The ledger sheets are visually complex, and the print is faint. At the end of the meeting, Ms. LeGrande is writing in a notebook. I ask her what she is doing. She says, "I have to document that we are having this meeting." The message is clear: Someone doesn't trust teachers to do their job. They must document everything. This is our second year in the state of Louisiana; we spent the first as professors. We continue to be disturbed by the oppressive amounts of monitoring that occur at every level of education. The implicit message is that people in authority mistrust educators and must be shown paper-and-pencil "proof" of their compliance with every rule and regulation.

Fourth Grade

I read stories to my class nearly every day to help stimulate interest, develop listening skills, and expand background knowledge. Demetrius's desk is part of a cluster near the front of the class. As I read, I notice his chair getting closer to my desk; before long, he is directly in front of it. His arms are on my desk as he looks at me while I read. It is as though I am reading just to him. I often find Demetrius and Dwayne close beside me, and sometimes their heads find their way to my shoulders. Both boys were given to aunts to raise when they were younger because their mothers had too many children.

Third Grade

In a group of four, we are reading a short book about the human body. We discuss bones and muscles. Shantel asks about black eyes. "They're bruises," I tell her.

"My mama got a black eye because some man hit her. Then some other man came and held on to the guy who hit her. My mama, she got a pan, and hit the guy who hit her. She hit him hard on the head. Then somebody called the police."

"Is she okay?" I ask. Shantel nods yes.

"I know the guy who helped Shantel's mama," adds Cherise. "He works at the projects. I think he's mean 'cause he puts people out when they don't pay the rent." When I ask where he puts them, she replies, "Outside."

We return to reading the book.

Third and Fourth Grades

Pam Porter gives us the second- and third-grade Iowa test scores from last spring. She asks us to analyze the scores and make recommendations for ways to improve them. The scores confirm what we already know after five weeks with the children. Vocabulary, comprehension, English language, and math scores are extremely low for at least two-thirds of the children tested. We prepare a one-page analysis for her, pointing out the areas of greatest need. We also state that in our opinion, the answer is not to be found in yet another program or workshop. We recommend that teachers get more than their current ten-minute break per day and that they be relieved of some of the needless paperwork. We know that the district is poor, but finding a way to fund a full-time paraprofessional for each classroom would be a wise use of limited resources.

Thick books of objectives, accountability documentation, greenbacks, external computer consultants on objectives and codes, and expensive test-related software should not be put before additional help for the children. We point out that the children in the school are not easy to teach. They haven't developed the listening skills or self-management skills appropriate to their age-group. They have little relevant real-world knowledge. The children need human attention and interaction both as individuals and in small groups.

The rumor mill has it that beginning in October, administrators from the central office will appear unannounced in classrooms to check teachers for fidelity to their weekly plan book. Every teacher continually adapts and adjusts lessons to the needs of the children and to make the most of "teachable moments." Weekly planning is, at best, an estimate of what the teacher hopes to accomplish. It should not be viewed by anyone as a minute-by-minute blueprint of what will actually occur in the classroom.

WEEK 6, SEPTEMBER 25–29: GRADES AND MOTIVATION

Third Grade

I again spend an entire Sunday on lesson plans—not innovative lessons but long strings of codes and letters for each subject that must be entered in my red lesson plan book. I hear from a former colleague who is teaching sixth grade in a Wisconsin school. She tells me that she hasn't written a detailed lesson plan in years.

Fourth Grade

The week begins with the promise of another evening meeting. Last week, fourth-grade students had been given a note to take home inviting their parents or guardians to attend a meeting from 5:00 to 6:00 P.M. on Monday. The purpose of the meeting is to explain the LEAP test and to give suggestions for helping their children prepare for the test. The LEAP test will not be given until next March, but the pressures are already building in some students, teachers, and parents.

Third and Fourth Grades

On the drive to Redbud this morning, we lament the low grades of many of our students. It is the sixth week of school, and report cards are sent home every six weeks. Letter grades must be given as well as percentage scores based on class work and homework. We spent part of the weekend adding up each student's points in each subject and calculating the percentage scores. To our disappointment, close to half of our students were destined to receive Ds or Fs on their first report card of the year. Some students do not comply with the assignments, while others cannot do the work—even when it is greatly simplified for them. We worry that the low grades will squelch motivation; however, we are compelled by state and district mandates to teach to the standards and benchmarks and adhere to the grading policies. We decide that we must convince our students to rally, do their schoolwork with our help, and successfully complete the grade level.

Third Grade

In social studies we are talking about ancestors. "My grandma's ancestor was a slave in Shreveport," reports Jaron. Several of the children chime in to say that they, too, have slaves as ancestors.

"When did slaves get free?" asks Manuel.

"During the Civil War, a war between the northern and southern states," I reply.

"Were you around then?" inquires Manuel.

"No, I'm not that old," I respond.

"Were you sort of around then?" he continues. I tell him that I would have to be at least 140 years old to have witnessed the Civil War. Antinesha asks if Dr. Martin Luther King Jr. helped free the slaves. I briefly explain the civil rights movement and tell them that the movement came long after the Civil War and that I do remember Dr. King.

Fourth Grade

Twenty parents show up for the 5:00 P.M. meeting to discuss the upcoming LEAP test. They represent about one out of six of the fourth graders. Handouts prepared by the fourth-grade teachers are passed around, as is a list of websites with relevant instructional activities. Even though most of the parents do not have computers at home, the Redbud Public Library has several. The parents of the children who are the farthest behind academically are not in attendance.

Third Grade

Tuesday after school, the third-grade teachers meet with Pam Porter and Kim Bridges, the reading specialist. Ms. Porter reminds us that members of the central office will begin visiting our rooms, unannounced, in October to review our coded lesson plans. They will make certain that we are teaching Project Read, the phonics program, to which we new teachers have just been introduced. Kim gives us forms to review that someone designed to expedite our planning for each reading group within our classroom. Although her efforts are well intentioned, they only add to our lesson-plan format woes because the central office insists that we use the myriad codes and write for each objective, "The learner will . . ." Another precious hour is consumed. I think of my friend who teaches in Wisconsin, where poverty certainly exists but high-stakes testing and monitoring mania do not yet exist.

Third and Fourth Grades

Today it was announced that all third- and fourth-grade teachers will be required to attend a four-hour session next week Thursday after school from 3:30 to 7:30 P.M. Its purpose will be to train us in a new, complex computer program designed to help us "pinpoint" our students' needs and to offer computerized instruction addressing those needs. The teachers wonder where this add-on will fit into our fragmented schedules. We learn that the district will spend $85,500 for this software. Teachers have been with their children for six weeks, and we know what they need. What they need most is more personal interaction. The quality of this latest gimmick remains to be seen. We continue to be surprised by the number of computer and publishing ventures, consultants, "implementation teams," and similar groups that have come to feed at the standards-and-accountability trough.

Education commentator Alfie Kohn (2000b) made this observation in *Education Week*:

> When the stakes rise, people seek help anywhere they can find it, and companies eager to profit from this desperation by selling test-prep materials and services have begun to appear on the scene, most recently tailoring their products to state exams. Naturally, affluent families, schools, and districts are better able to afford such products, and the most effective versions of such products, thereby exacerbating the inequity of such testing. Moreover, when poorer schools do manage to scrape together the money to buy these materials, it's often at the expense of books and other educational resources that they really need. (46)

As we read this, we think of the 1952 dictionaries and the absence of thesauri in our classrooms. And our school has no library.

Fourth Grade

The children like to take their shoes off when they read on the reading rug. Dario comes up to me and whispers, "Verlin say bad things about my socks." I look at his socks. They are filthy and holey. I tell him not to let the comment bother him. "There will be no talking about socks if you want to be on the reading rug," I announce.

Every morning Chalese, De'Lewis, Jamal, and Antron leave my first class to spend an hour with Mrs. Buford, a special education teacher. In my second class, Tony, Nikos, and Travis do the same. All seven are African American children who read at a first-grade level or not at all. During the rest of the school day, these seven children are in their regular classrooms. This is called "inclusion."

Third Grade

We are discussing habitats in a science lesson. A forest habitat is shown in a book that I am reading to the children. It happens to be a forest located in Wisconsin. Out of the clear blue, Sam asks, "Do they have the LEAP test in Wisconsin?"

"No," I reply.

"I want to move to Wisconsin till next year is over," says Sam seriously. The other children agree.

Fourth Grade

Ms. Dawson has sent four of my students to the in-school suspension room this week. Victavius, whose brother was shot and killed during the summer, is there for fighting. Perry is there because he refused to go to a work station at the request of Mrs. Henderson. "I ain't gonna do it," he announced. Joshua is there for slamming down books and papers and throwing a temper tantrum when told he could not work on a computer until he finished writing an assignment. Jaylene is sent there for refusing to apologize for disruptive behavior during the day. Tempers are raw, and tears come easily to a number of the children at Redbud Elementary. Certain infractions (e.g., fighting and "willful and repeated disobedience") result in three days in the in-school suspension classroom. The philosophy of the school is that punishment is more effective when it excludes children from normal classroom activities. The message is, "School is a reward that can be withheld. School is not a punishment."

Third Grade

Ms. Porter comes to my room to speak with me. She says that Jaheesa's mother has phoned. Jaheesa is absent today, but she is not ill. Haden, a child in my classroom, has been taking Jaheesa's snack money from her daily. Haden has told Jaheesa that unless she hands over her money, he "will beat her up." Jaheesa stands a head taller than Haden; nonetheless, she is terrified. Haden admits taking her money, and he receives in-school suspension.

We receive a note from the school office that we should not allow the pupils to sleep in class. This catches my eye because earlier in the week, my social studies review session had put ten of my pupils to sleep. I teach social studies methods classes at the university. The memo also tells us that the school board has approved a $500 raise for the school year (less than a ten-dollar bill per week). It states, "This is recognition of a job well done."

THREE

OCTOBER

REGULATING TEACHING

WEEK 7, OCTOBER 2–6: NO MONEY FOR SCHOOL PICTURES

Third Grade

This morning before the children arrive, I am swinging my broom at one of the jumbo cockroaches that greet me every day. I stop. "Just look at what you're doing," I say to myself. My morning extermination routine has become commonplace to me. Tonight is the evening of the four-hour, after-school workshop on how to use the software package that is intended to help children pass the LEAP test. I think of the moldy, insect-infested room I am working in and the lack of hot water for hand washing. I think of having to beg and borrow any type of appropriate print material for the children. I think of no playground equipment or art classes. What computer program could be so powerful that it should come before the children's basic needs are met?

Third and Fourth Grades

An article in the *Times* of Shreveport, Louisiana, catches our eye. It describes information just released from the U.S. Census Bureau. Although the nation's poverty rate had dropped in the previous year, it grew in Louisiana to 19.1 percent, making Louisiana the number two state in overall poverty. Only New Mexico has worse poverty. The most recent data available for Deerborne Parish reveal a 29.5 percent poverty rate.

School pictures are taken. Students who wish to purchase pictures bring their money in a special envelope provided by the photography studio. Only one of the twenty-two students in the fourth-grade homeroom brings picture money and only one child of the twenty students in the third-grade classroom. The remainder will have no photographic record of this year at Redbud Elementary. Our pupils sit and smile for the photographer as he takes the pictures that never will belong to them.

A consultant for the new balanced literacy reading program spends a day at Redbud Elementary giving demonstration lessons for each grade level. She is reminiscent of the consultants who preceded her this year. The consultant sits with three to five of the best readers and asks them questions about a storybook. Meanwhile, the rest of the class exhibits sterling behavior as they work in centers. No doubt the presence of the principal and five or six teachers who are there to see the consultant "orchestrate balanced literacy" contribute to their model deportment.

The building-wide consensus among teachers was that the day was a flop. The consultant had demonstrated an aspect of the program that we all knew how to do. There isn't a teacher in the land who can't work with a small group of good readers. All the hard stuff was avoided by the consultant. Questions such as what to do with nonreaders in centers were dismissed with "Even kindergartners can do centers." Her rehearsed responses were viewed as putdowns by the teachers. Some of her comments included "You've made the centers too difficult" or "That's a management problem you have to solve" and "Don't you have any consequences for that kind of behavior?" Her answers unmasked her lack of experience with children who are not easy to teach.

Third Grade

I read a book about Thurgood Marshall to the children. There is not an African American child in the class who has not heard of him. We discuss segregation and discrimination. Antinesha tells us that her aunt and uncle were thrown in jail during the civil rights movement. "For what?" I inquire.

"For doing this," she replies. She stands up and carries an imaginary picket sign. "Oh, they were marching for civil rights," I say. Antinesha nods.

"I'm afraid of the Ku Klux Klan," reports Leon.

"Why?" I ask.

"Because they burned down a house of an old lady," he responds. "They kill people." The other children agree.

In the book about Thurgood Marshall, the children notice a sign that says "Colored" with an arrow pointing to the left. They ask me what that means. I say, "'Colored' is what people used to call blacks or African Americans."

"Why 'Colored'?" asks Chikae.

Manuel points to his face and replies, "Because we got color."

"Oh, yeah," said Chikae.

The children were on the rug as I was reading the book to them. They began to compare the colors of the skin on their arms.

"Each color is different," said Manuel.

The children seemed intrigued and pleased with these differences.

Fourth Grade

The pupils' assignment is to write a biographical sketch of a family member. Only five of my forty-four students write about their father. Most write about their mother. Graham writes, "My mama is nice woman. She sweet when you are good but when you are not nice she will get you." Jatoyia writes, "My brother is pretty, famous, and nice he is the tallest brother I ever had. He is in tenth grade he never got put out of school Mr. Johnson is that good he never got put out of school." Carlonna states, "She feed me and my brother well." De'Lewis reports, "Mama ride a horse and tote a gun." As a field guard at the nearby prison, that is exactly what De'Lewis's mother does.

Third Grade

There was an armed robbery at the local Piggly Wiggly grocery store. The suspect wore a camouflage ski mask and carried a semiautomatic handgun. He forced employees into the cooler and removed money from the safe. The children are all atwitter about this robbery because so many of them go to the Piggly Wiggly. Jaron says, "I saw a robbery before. The police shot two guys in the legs when they tried to run away."

When his class is at physical education, Mr. Johnson visits my third-grade class. The pupils are excited to see him and point out how the class bean is growing and other wonders of their day. He has taught them to sing the "from the M-i-crooked letter-crooked letter-i" song about the Mississippi River. Some days he leads them in the song, and together they do a little dance routine as they sing. There are few inhibitions in third grade.

Fourth Grade

Each student has chosen a state to study and become an "expert" on through research. We wrote to all fifty states, asking for free tourist information and maps, and more than twenty states sent materials. The tourist brochures, together with the social studies textbook, the classroom set of 1962 World Books (three volumes missing), the encyclopedias sent by Mrs. Hemerly, and the Internet are the students' information sources. They especially like the website www.50states.com. Mrs. Redd, the competent paraprofessional who runs the computer lab, has bookmarked the site. Over 75 percent of my students have no computer at home, and they are fascinated by the Internet. Some go to the public library in the evening to use the computers. Every day it strikes us that these Redbud children could soar academically if they had access to what children of the middle class—and certainly of the wealthy—take for granted. A young acquaintance of mine from Wheaton, Illinois, writes my class a pen pal letter and mentions her gymnastics class and her private violin lessons. The children seem somewhat interested in this remote bit of news. "What are gymnastics?" asks Jaylene.

"It's like when you do flips on the playground," I reply. Eyes light up and heads nod. Now they understand.

Third and Fourth Grades

At the start of the four-hour after-school workshop on the newly purchased computer program, we ask how much it cost. The technology person for the district responds, "Well, it was expensive."

"How expensive?" we prod.

"Well, we got a matching grant, and then we finagled some, so we got it for $85,500, but it should have cost us almost half a million dollars." We ask her who the authors of the program are and what their credentials are.

She says, "I don't know, but a lot of parishes are using this software, and it was correlated to a lot of tests."

"Is this another test prep program?" we ask. We explain how fragmented our curriculum is. "We already can pinpoint the needs of our students; this is the seventh week of school," we state.

"Maybe you can, but most teachers can't."

"Yes, they can," we say. "We know they can because we work with them."

She responds, in whispered tones, "Well, the word is, you should really only teach reading and math because of the LEAP test." When we ask who said so, she replies, "The superintendent."

"Isn't anyone worried about effects of depriving children of science, social studies, and the arts?" we inquire.

"Well, just integrate everything through the reading," the technologist advises.

As we sit through the presentation by the consultant who sold this program (who arrived at the school driving a new Lincoln), we quickly become aware that the software is little more than high-tech skill-and-drill. Each aspect of reading, math, and other disciplines has been fractionated into its tiniest subcomponents on which the students take practice tests, complete drill lessons, and then take posttests. Occasionally there is a paragraph to read and a short essay to write.

The amount of time it will take teachers to master the complexities of the program design is staggering. There are elaborate mechanisms for assigning students to various levels of pretests on numerous subskills to "pinpoint their needs" and then other mechanisms to assign them to various categories of instruction. When the consultant is asked if there is something in the program for our nonreaders at all grade levels, she replies, "No, this program doesn't teach them to read. Your district didn't buy that program. If you're interested, we have another program—a computerized phonics program for sale that will teach them to read."

At exactly 7:30 P.M., the consultant ends her presentation by apologizing for having talked too fast. "This actually should be a nine-hour workshop that I have crammed into four hours. On page three of the handout is my e-mail address. I don't give out my phone number. If you have problems, call Peggy [the district technologist]. Sometimes the best thing you can do is to just turn the computer off and start over again." As the meeting ends, the teachers, heads reeling, dash in a downpour to their cars. Some will drive nearly an hour through a violent thunderstorm before getting home to eat dinner, grade papers, and review lessons for the next day. Several will be on early playground duty by 7:15 A.M.

WEEK 8, OCTOBER 9–13: PARENT CONFERENCES AND PROFESSIONAL GROWTH PLANS

Third and Fourth Grades

We spent the weekend assembling materials and preparing for parent–teacher conferences, which will be held on Monday afternoon and evening. We spotted a paid advertisement in the October 5 issue of the local

Redbud newspaper announcing "job vacancies" for a third-grade teacher and a fourth-grade teacher in the parish. We don't know of anyone at Redbud Elementary who has resigned yet, but we have been told by two of the beginners at Redbud that they will not be returning next year. What a loss. Both are exceptional teachers.

Fourth Grade

I intercept a note from Letrinette to Nikeya with a heart drawn on it. "I hate him and you too, And dont say nothin else to me I going to beet your ass."

Third and Fourth Grades

Yesterday, parent/guardian/teacher conferences were held from 1:00 to 6:00 P.M. Eleven out of twenty third graders had someone attend, and thirty of forty-four fourth graders had a parent, aunt, or grandparent in attendance. With a few exceptions, those who came spoke of their support for the teachers and the school. At the other end of the building, the father of a kindergartner became loud and abusive toward a teacher. Ms. Dawson called the police. The man was arrested.

Fourth Grade

Dwayne's mother is disappointed in the grades he has earned. "I know he can do much better, but he's used to getting away with things because everybody just loves cute little Dwayne. Now he's girl crazy. You don't spank, do you Mr. Johnson?" When I told her that I didn't choose to spank, she continued, "I want you to spank Dwayne if he don't do his work. You have my support."

I tell De'Lewis's mother that De'Lewis can do the schoolwork but often does not because he seems distracted. She nods and says, "Just like his father was. He would stand and stare off into space." She demonstrates the father's look and stance.

"That's it!" I respond. "That's De'Lewis."

"His daddy got in trouble because of it, too. He lost jobs for just standing there staring off into space." We agree to keep urging De'Lewis to do his schoolwork. The boy is no discipline problem, and he has a good sense of humor. Having failed the LEAP test last spring, De'Lewis is in fourth grade for the second year. Perhaps his staring off into space is a medical problem.

Dawnyetta's mother is just as bubbly as Dawnyetta. Sometimes the apple doesn't fall far from the tree. I tell her that I am surprised that Dawnyetta failed the LEAP test last March and the retake in July. She is bright, sporadically hard-working, and a good reader. "Well," Dawnyetta's mother reflects, "in the spring, her daddy and I had some troubles. And then in the summer we got divorced. I think that was weighing on Dawnyetta's mind."

Today the fourth-grade classes each received a classroom set of dictionaries and thesauri. We had been asking for these reference books since before the school year began. The superintendent was able to use some money from a tobacco settlement in Louisiana. Only the fourth grade is given the new books, and that is because of the LEAP test. Third graders must be content with their 1952 dictionaries and no thesauri.

Third Grade

Most adults at the conferences express concern about the LEAP test that fourth graders take. They ask if it is true that children who do well in their daily work and earn good grades can fail fourth grade if they fail the LEAP test. I tell them that this information is accurate. Sam's mother says, "Parents should get together and protest this test." I tell her that's probably the only way any change will occur.

Several mothers come to the conference wearing their fast-food uniforms. They have taken time off from work to discuss their children's progress.

One mother's breath smells strongly of an alcoholic beverage. She partially covers her mouth as she speaks. Another mother laments the absence of prayer at Redbud Elementary. A couple complains that I don't send enough worksheets home. I give them a few suggestions about listening to and reading with their child every evening and perhaps taking him to the public library regularly. I explain that scads of worksheets will not enrich his reading ability or interests. I am disappointed that no parent or relative came for the seven poorest-performing children in my class.

Third and Fourth Grades

The day after conferences was called a "teacher workshop." It was a day off for the children. This eagerly anticipated teacher workday turns out to be just that; however, it is filled with completing new forms, not working in our classrooms. We looked forward to an entire day of catching up on our filing, designing instructional activities, and making the classrooms more inviting. As the day begins, the intercom summons all teachers to the tiny office to pick up some "important" forms. On entering the office, teachers go through a large computer printout of every teacher in Deerborne Parish to locate their names and write "no" if they do not want their names given to telemarketers. No one writes "yes." Then names have to be located and addresses and phone numbers verified on a teacher roster. Next we are given our "professional growth folders."

In the folder is a four-page handout titled "A Guide to the Process of Meaningful Professional Growth Plans," written by a professor in Connecticut. It appears to have been taken from a textbook because of the page numbers (e.g., 119, 120) at the bottom of the handout pages. There is no reference identifying the source of this handout. All questions are of the open-ended variety—not just checkoffs—for example, "List below two or three developments in your field that you need to become familiar with to be more current in your teaching. Identify an area where you are relatively weak and want to become more proficient. Identify an area that you could strengthen by working closely with a colleague." The professor offers such advice as "These professional growth plans are meaningful to the extent that they are based on worthwhile objectives. Sometimes teachers ask how do I get started on my objectives." (In all our years of teaching, we never have heard a teacher ask, "How do I get started on my objectives?") Another guideline stipulates, "First, a good objective is one that has an observable impact on the quality of the educational program in your school. Second, priority objectives should be important to you. They should give direction to your professional growth, excite your imagination, and provide a sense of satisfaction when achieved." Can you believe this stuff? We couldn't either if we hadn't been required to complete the handout and weren't holding a copy of it in our hands as we write this.

Next, teachers are to complete a Deerborne Parish school board professional growth plan. This form requires the "evaluatee" and an "evaluator" to review performance objectives and professional plan activities four times during the year. A note at the bottom of the form states, "One objective per page; use additional sheet(s) if necessary." When we ask Pam Porter the purpose of completing these forms, she says, "The state auditor is coming in October and will audit these forms." Ever since we arrived in Louisiana, we have heard intelligent educators speak of the "state auditors" in somewhat hushed tones. University and public school colleagues inform us that the amount of paperwork has increased enormously since the onset of the accountability movement. Every piece of paper, every form that someone completes, presumably is subject to an audit. We have been assured that these audits occur and that the consequences of failure to complete forms can be dire. Recent newspaper stories speak of the possibility that a nearby university may lose its regional accreditation because a recent state audit had turned up irregularities and incompleteness in the paperwork.

Later in the morning, grade-level teacher meetings are held. Each meeting is required to have a "recorder" whose job it is to complete a form that documents the meeting. The form contains the following elements: grade, date, presider, recorder, faculty/staff present, faculty/staff absent, topic of meeting, and report of meeting. The veteran teachers say that every meeting has to be documented for the state.

Meeting topics include a discussion of state standards and benchmarks and difficulty in finding materials to meet them, upcoming events such as the required sixteen hours of drug awareness instruction, and rules for field trips that are scheduled within the next few weeks. The grade-level representative announces that we also must copy each grade for each child for each subject into our greenbacks. This information amounts to 240 entries for each third-grade teacher. Grades already are recorded in the office computer and in the grade book, and teachers retain a copy of each report card to place in the cumulative folders.

The third-grade meeting closes with Ms. Thibeaux's announcement that she has decided not to return to Redbud Elementary for a second year. She shakes her head and says, "This whole thing is crazy." An announcement comes over the loudspeaker. Pam Porter says that all of us should go to lunch at 11:30 to beat the crowds so "we can get back in time."

The afternoon begins with the discovery of a memo in our mailboxes informing teachers that each of us will get $225 for supplies from the state. Attached to it is a form titled "Guidelines for Purchasing Instructional Materials." Teachers' initial enthusiasm over the news that they will get some reimbursement is dampened when they read the guidelines, which include the following:

> The law requires that a minimum of 75 percent of these monies shall be used for teaching materials and supplies which are not consumed within a one-year period of time (examples include instructional software, software manuals, globes, instruments, skeletal models, math manipulatives).
>
> The law also states that 25 percent of each allocation (i.e., $56.25) may be used for consumable-type instructional materials and supplies (e.g., paper, pencils, glue, chalk, markers, blank tapes, earth materials such as seeds).

Please list what you buy on the attached form and keep all receipts. [Actually, all receipts had to be attached to the form.] Put nonconsumable materials first and then consumable, if any are bought.

This is the eighth week of school. Teachers have been buying items and saving receipts since the school year began. Few, if any, have bought such costly items as globes and skeletal models. Teachers did not know that they would receive only twenty-five cents on the dollar for items such as paper, chalk, and glue. In other words, a teacher who bought stickers for sixty-seven cents would compute the following: $.67 \times .25 = .1675$. This calculation would entitle the teacher, if the original receipt had been saved and attached to the form, to seventeen cents (rounded up). What kind of mini-minded bureaucrat came up with this petty policy? And for such pathetic amounts! Most teachers have spent and will continue to spend many hundreds of dollars more for which they will receive nothing. The remainder of the workday is spent computing the figures and completing the form.

Third Grade

Jesse left our class for good. He has been living with his father, but he is going to live with his mother and attend school in another district. She is upset about his low grades and expresses her anger to the school secretary via a phone call. I had a long conference with Jesse's father—over an hour. Apparently, the lengthy discussion we had about Jesse was not relayed to the mother. She wants a private conference but does not specify a time to the secretary. I wait over an hour for her after school, but she does not appear. I do not have her new phone number.

We talk about various shapes in our environment. A picture in a book of shapes shows a saucer under the heading "circle." I ask the children what the object is. "Rich people use those so they don't spill on their clothes," points out Chikae.

Jimmy raises his hand. "We drive by a rich woman's house. She's so rich she's got her name on her house. She wears a lot of clothes." He extends his arms out from his sides. "She looks like a big puffball."

I feel like a naughty child today. First, Ms. Dawson tells a few of us on cafeteria duty that we are letting the children talk too loudly. "Teachers, keep these children quiet," she admonishes. The children can hear her, and I feel embarrassed at being scolded in front of them. After school, the evening custodian hollers at me because three of my students did not put their chairs on top of their desks. It was the first day they had not. I walk to my car with the self-esteem of a bottom feeder.

WEEK 9, OCTOBER 16–20: RELENTLESS INTERRUPTIONS

Fourth Grade

Letrinette, Joshua, Dwayne, and Emerald separately and quietly confide in me that they will work harder now in school. Joshua asks me to check his assignment book. No doubt the parent/guardian/teacher conferences and report cards initiated these comments.

Third and Fourth Grades

We learn while on playground duty that a child has run away from her grandfather because he beats her with his fists. A meeting has been held in Pam Porter's office. We also learn that a child in a third-grade class is being shuttled from relative to relative. He has no permanent home.

Both grade levels are discussing persuasive writing. The children write letters to the New Orleans Saints football team. Here are some of their letters.

Dear Saints,
   Our school has no playground equipment. Cold you send us some Narf footballs we wold like that. Maybe you can help redbud school out a littil.
Your frind,
Milo

Dear New Orleans Saints,
   May you bring us some footballs, jump rops, soccer balls. When we go on the playground we don't have nothing to play with. We would be happy if we had something to play with.
Your friend,
LaDelle

Dear Saints,
   Our school has no playground. We would like to have a football field on the boys playground and be tough guys like you boys be.
Yours truly,
Verlin

Dear New Orleans Saints,

Our school has no playground equipment. Can you help us out we need so much. I'm in the fourth grade and I hope I pass the LEAP test. Will you guys pray for us? If you do, "thanks."

Your friend,
Carlonna

Third and Fourth Grades

We arrive at 6:50 A.M. A thin woman with a black eye is waiting by the school office. The woman is dressed in a sleeveless white blouse and a straight skirt on this chilly morning. Her legs are bare, and she is wearing sandals. The woman wants to enroll her daughter in preschool. The secretary arrives as we sign in for the day. The woman is told that there is no room at Redbud Elementary for the child. The preschool classes have reached their enrollment limit.

While we're on playground duty, Shenita points to a fourth-grade boy and says, "Look at him. He's acting like a fool."

We tell her that maybe the boy has a crush on her and say, "He's twirling to show off for you."

Shenita replies with disgust, "He can twirl right on out of here." We always enjoy talking with Shenita. She is a child who is wise beyond her years and has a quick wit. Her admirer is about half her size but persistent.

Four faculty members were selected to attend ten days of technology training spread over several weeks. They are worried because their absences require substitute teachers. After they complete their training, they must train the Redbud Elementary faculty on Monday evenings. On the days when they are back at school, they report that the content of the course is predicated on the assumption that every classroom has a digital camera (Redbud Elementary has none), an Internet projection system (Redbud Elementary has one), a variety of software that requires a lot of memory (Redbud Elementary has neither the software nor the requisite memory), and other hardware and software requirements that are just dreams to the Redbud teachers. The pacing of the course is so fast that even the computer-literate teachers cannot keep up. Materials were clearly designed by people who had little classroom experience or sense of the time it takes to absorb new material. Lengthy homework assignments are given after each all-day session. The uncompensated add-ons continue to drain energy from the teachers. They worry about how they will be able to reduce their ten days of training into after-school sessions for an overburdened faculty. These experienced teachers tell us that if they had had an idea of what the training was all about, they would not have agreed to participate. Meanwhile, the students lose ten days of instruction with their regular classroom teachers.

Fourth Grade

Each week, the students prepare for and look forward to their regular Friday event, reading to the third graders in Ms. Johnson's class. In pairs, they select a book, read it to me, practice it at home, and then read the book to two or three third graders on Friday. When I ask if this practice is worth continuing, they assure me that it is. "It helps us learn to read better," points out Jatoyia, "and it helps them learn to like books."

Graham adds, "We're helping them learn to read, too. They way behind."

After school, Pam Porter gives me two thick binders, one containing LEAP test materials for social studies and science, the other English language and math. Each binder holds more than three hundred pages of information about the test's nature and type of questions, scoring procedures, and released test items from the spring 1999 and spring 2000 LEAP tests. A lot of the material prods teachers to teach to the test. What's missing is the most essential element: the materials to use with the children. For example, the social studies items contain a number of questions about federal and Louisiana governmental structures. The fourth-grade social studies text, however, focuses on the geographic regions of the United States.

Third Grade

Many of the children are still learning standard English because a southern African American dialect is spoken at home. Each morning, I put four or five sentences on the blackboard that contain errors in spelling, capitalization, punctuation, or usage. Pupils are to detect and correct these mistakes. On the board today is the sentence "'I be trying to finish my math,' said Danitha." Keaziah raises his hand and says, "It should be 'I *do* be trying to finish my math.'" This is not standard English, but it is perfect dialect, helping verb and all. Mainstream children have an advantage on standardized tests that many of our pupils do not have—standard English is spoken in their homes.

We are reading about a boy named Billy who rides his bike through a yellow light. A police officer is on the corner. Jimmy shouts out, "That is some dumb kid!" He shakes his head incredulously. Jimmy holds up his index finger and says, "First, Billy goes through the yellow light." Then Jimmy holds up a second finger and adds, "Second, he does this with a cop on the corner!" The entire class agrees that Billy isn't too bright.

Before teaching begins each day, teachers have numerous demands on their attention. For example, today Ms. Dawson tells me, at 7:55 A.M., that the children weren't lining up fast enough to enter the building. Between 7:55 and 8:10 A.M., the following incidents take place:

- I take roll call and must record the absent children on a yellow slip of paper for the office and then record the absent children in my green-back.
- Various moneys must be collected. Today, money is brought in by two children for a play. I must record the name of the child, the amount paid, and the date on a brown reservation form and write the same information on another sheet of paper.
- This sheet of paper goes into my tan money pouch, which must be sent to the office with my attendance slip.
- Three children have questions about the sentences on the blackboard. (Remember that the district wants the children to be working immediately in the morning.)
- Two children have lost their spelling lists and ask me for replacements. I make a note to myself to copy two more lists.
- One child reports that he has lost his math paper.
- A child finds another student's reading paper in his desk and reports this to me.
- A pupil tells me that she cannot see the board. I tell her to move her chair closer.
- Two children say they cannot find their pencils. I give a pencil to each child with instructions to sharpen them.
- Jelani is tardy, not absent. I must make this change in the greenback.
- A sheet comes to me from the grade-level representative. It reminds me that progress reports are due next week. I must get the report forms from the teachers' room and count out the correct number for my class.
- The children go to the restrooms. The physical education teacher and I must supervise them.
- The secretary is on the loudspeaker paging an adult.

It is 8:10, and we say the Pledge of Allegiance.

Third and Fourth Grades

A team of experts from the Governor's Office of Rural Development visited the town of Redbud to gather data. In their report, the team pointed out some contradictions. "The people are wonderful. It is a beautiful town. . . . Redbud has a jewel of a museum, a hidden treasure. . . . It is a great place, full of wonderful potential . . . but it was being undermined by poverty and drugs. . . . Drugs in Redbud are widespread and use is extremely high." The report noted that drugs are used by some children as young as eight. The drugs most commonly used are alcohol, marijuana, crack cocaine, prescription drugs, and methamphetamine (Herring 2000c, 1, 5).

Fourth Grade

The week of October 23 has been designated Drug Awareness Week. Each fourth grader prepares an essay on the topic "How Drug Abuse Affects My Family" and draws a poster about drug awareness. LaDelle proudly displays her poster. On it are detailed illustrations and captions for each of the following: "bag of weed, 1/2 oz.; a joint (weed); lighter; crack cocaine (rock form); Premoe joint (half weed, half crack); crack cocaine pipe; elastic tie-off; cocaine cooking; drug needle and spoon; rolled-up dollar bill; powder cocaine; razor blade table." I wonder how many fourth graders in America possess this knowledge.

Third Grade

Today I want to explain types of maps to the children. I have several transparencies to show them. When I want to use my overhead projector, I must first tighten a screw on the side of the mirror with a tiny Phillips screwdriver. Then I tape paper to the blackboard because the classrooms have no screens and the images cannot be seen easily on the black surface of the board. I become frustrated as the paper falls off the board. "I wish we had a screen," I say. "In my last classroom, I had a screen that I could pull down." I ask a rhetorical question: "Why do some schools have things and others don't?"

Manuel raises his hand. "Because the kids in other schools might work harder than we do," he offers.

"We work very hard," I reply.

Shantel reports, "Some schools probably have rich principals, and they might give things to the teachers and the kids."

"We could write letters to rich schools and find out how they got all that stuff," suggests Haden.

Randall says, "Maybe we could trade some of our stuff with a rich school so we could get one of their screens."

"We could trade one of our air conditioners," Sam proposes. (The classroom has two tired, sputtering window air conditioners that spit out parts of their worn filters as they run.)

"Or we could trade Jesse's desk because he moved away," says Cherise. "Some schools might be too stingy, though, and want to keep all their screens."

"We could wash dogs to get money for a screen," suggests Randall.

"We'd have to wash a lot of dogs to buy a screen," I reply. "We probably won't get a screen this year."

"That's okay," Kelvin adds consolingly. "All we need is each other."

Antinesha reports, "My cousin lives near Washington. His school has a stage and a lot of bathrooms. So the President probably decides who gets the money."

Randall nods and says, "I think that if you live close to the President, you get more money for your school. He can't send you a lot of money if you live far away like us because it might get lost in the mail." The other children nod in agreement.

WEEK 10, OCTOBER 23–27: ANOTHER "NEW" PROGRAM

Third and Fourth Grades

The weekend was spent on three tasks: lesson plans, correcting papers, and completing a progress report for each child. The progress reports, sent home every three weeks, are actually full-blown report cards. All points received in each subject must be added and percentages of the possible number of points must be determined. The percentages are then converted to letter grades. There is a section on each report for teacher comments.

The Monday faculty meeting begins at 3:00 P.M. sharp. Some of the teachers are speaking with the children who remain after the first buses leave. Ms. Dawson comes to find us. "Let the aides take care of the children. You're late for the meeting," she says firmly. We write our names on the faculty sign-in sheet. Ms. Dawson is on a tear. At the meeting she tells the teachers that they are being too lax. "The children are not to sleep in class. If they do, stand them up! Don't let them wear coats in school. The children are using more time than is necessary getting in and out of the restrooms. We need to get test scores up, and you're using too much instructional time on this. Teachers, don't stand around talking in the cafeteria. Stay on the children. There's too much talking. Teachers who can't do their job will be called in and talked to one on one."

After Ms. Dawson reprimands us, we listen to a guest speaker who talks about identifying homeless children. Then the featured attraction speaks—a consultant with the regional education agency. By now it is 3:45 P.M., and any hopes of getting away for a restroom break before the 5:00 PTO meeting begins are fading rapidly.

The consultant tells us that we will be involved in a new endeavor: "whole-faculty study groups." We are handed an article to read and then divided into three groups. The consultant has marked where the ones, twos, and threes begin reading. Of course, the twos and threes have no notion of what precedes their sections without reading that material. What they are asked to read is out of context. She says, "This is the jigsaw method. You will each be an expert on your section."

We begin reading the article. A snappy tune from the computer signals "time up" just as the twos and threes proceed to their portions of the article. "Now get together in groups. Make sure there are ones, twos, and threes in each group to talk about the article."

The author of the article, we think, seems to be writing in support of whole-faculty study groups. When we ask the consultant what research base supports using faculty time in this way, she replies, "They've been using it in St. Charles Parish for two years, and their test scores are soaring." It doesn't seem to dawn on the consultant that these soaring scores could be attributed to dozens of things other than whole-faculty study groups, such as a library in the school, parents who can afford books, or different populations of children being tested during those two years. Whole-faculty study groups choose something to study that will improve individual teaching and improve the school as a whole. Most teachers value the opportunity to share ideas with other teachers and have always done this. This "new" program formalizes a time-tested practice and destroys spontaneity. It requires each group member to serve a role and each group to keep a log (more paperwork and monitoring).

Math and technology apparently have been chosen by someone for Redbud Elementary. The consultant says that our students don't know math because we "don't teach in-depth math like the Japanese and Germans do." She lectured, "They take about eight objectives and teach them deeply." We would like to teach in depth, but the consultant seems to forget that the state math standards require that third-grade instructors, for example, teach 227 objectives. The state even tells us which objectives must be covered in each six-week period (e.g., fifty-three objectives must be covered in the first six weeks of school).

We ask where teachers, who have only ten minutes a day free, will find time to participate in a whole-faculty study group. The consultant says with an unctuous smile, "Be creative! Don't worry—I'll be here to help you. I can come every Monday for an after-school meeting." Uh-oh.

Dave Longaberger (2001), creator of one of the largest and most successful private companies in America, understood who the real experts are in any organization:

> I truly believe that the world's best source of information about any business is the people who spend eight hours a day working there. Big companies spend huge fees to bring in consultants, when all the answers (and the right answers at that) are available for free. All they have to do is listen to their employees. (49)

The teachers at Redbud Elementary School are the experts. They know their pupils, they know the community, and they know the needs. They do not need consultants to tell them what to do. But no one in the state or the district ever seems to ask the teachers how to make things better.

After the meeting with the regional consultant, teachers must again sign in—this time for the PTO meeting. As we take our seats before Pam Porter begins, a competent first-grade teacher tells us she will not be returning to Redbud Elementary next year. "I just want to teach. I can't do that here with all these add-ons," she says. A third-grade teacher who is new to Redbud Elementary chimes in, "This whole-faculty study group thing may be the add-on that pushes me over the edge."

The PTO meeting again has more teachers than parents in attendance. About fifty teachers and staff are in the gym. We count twenty parents. Pam Porter announces that she received one anonymous letter nominating PTO officers. The nominees are elected by acclamation. The new president, an African American male, says a few words and gives his phone number. A white mother, the new vice president, speaks at length. She asks that the PTO meetings be scheduled later in the evening. The teachers, especially those who commute an hour each way to and from school, wince.

Fourth Grade

Mrs. Redd is helping the fourth-grade students learn to use the $85,500 assessment program. She has completed the time-consuming task of entering all the children into both the assessment and the instructional programs. The program is slow, and the students often have to wait for a screen to change.

Sometimes they impatiently click the "enter" key more than once. When they do, nothing moves. Mrs. Redd cautions, "The pretest has two parts. Part 1 has fifty-seven questions, and part 2 has seventy-one questions. You must be careful. Say you're on question 56 and you tap 'enter' twice. It will freeze and you'll have to log out, log on, and start over." I wonder how much of a time-wasting boondoggle this large investment will be.

Third and Fourth Grades

A traveling children's theater group will present *Aladdin and the Magic Lamp* at Redbud High School, which is a block from Redbud Elementary. Wednesday morning from 10:30 to 11:30 is reserved for the performance. Each pupil must pay $2.50 to attend. The day before the performance, more than half the children have been unable to come up with the amount. Most teachers pull out their wallets so that their students do not have to stay behind and work while the children who had $2.50 walk excitedly to the high school. Something is terribly wrong when a school district spends $85,500 on a computer program to prepare children for a high-stakes test but won't spend a comparatively measly sum to send economically disadvantaged children to a play.

Redbud teachers are stunned about the news in this morning's Shreveport newspaper: "State Education Superintendent Cecil J. Picard gave 18 of his top state Education Department administrators raises of up to 12 percent" ("Education Officials Get Raises" 2000, 5B). The article points out that the eighteen officials were handpicked by Picard to oversee the state's accountability program to raise academic achievement. This news comes at a time when the governor has reneged on a promise to give teachers a raise because of budget shortfalls. Picard said that the salary increase money "was saved from months of department frugality on travel and supplies" (5B). Teachers in Louisiana could never accumulate money in this way because they have no travel or supplies budget. The worry now is that publicity about these big pay raises for state administrators might cause voters to reject a proposed tax hike that would give a small raise to teachers. Teachers are struck by the irony of giving large rewards to the people who heap busywork on them when they are among the lowest-paid educators in America.

Third Grade

I find a rotten little tooth on my classroom floor. "Who lost a tooth?" I ask. The children search their mouths with their tongues. Kanzah comes up to me and retrieves the tooth. There are no tooth fairies in Redbud.

FOUR

NOVEMBER

DRUGS, POVERTY, AND TEST SCORES

WEEK 11, OCTOBER 30–NOVEMBER 3

Fourth Grade

Two essays from the Drug Awareness Week contest were not selected as winners last week, but they are poignant testimonials to the impact of drugs on the pupils.

Malcolm wrote,

> Drugs are everywhere. I see people walking down the street acting like something wrong. They need on clean clothes a bath, hair need washing and combing. They come over fence in the backyard when we are not home and steal things from our backyard. They steal our hanging plants late at night. They come to our house trying to sell us things that they might have taken from someone else. They seem like they do not eat any food from looking at their size, sometime they ask if we have something for them to do to get money, and seem like they never go home at all.

Emerald wrote,

Drug affect my family by dad do all kinds of drug. He do dope and wed. My uncle do wed. It just hurt my hart. I feel like one day they gong to get the wrong thing. When my dad had smoke wed he try to burn my grandmother house. I was crying when my dad tried to burn up my grandmother house and he live there.

Third Grade

A new word is taught to me by my third graders: blackmoll. They, too, ask to make drug awareness posters as the fourth graders have. One poster has a bottle drawn and labeled "gine" (gin) on it. Jelani asks me how to spell "blackmoll."

"What's that?" I ask.

I hear many voices. I call on Haden. "It's like a cigar, but the stuff inside has been scraped out and weed is put in. It's got a white plastic tip on the end." I spell the word the best I can.

Kanzah is absent this morning. "Where is Kanzah?" I inquire.

Antinesha says, "He probably won't come because his mother got put in jail last night."

"Why?" I ask.

"She was fighting and the policemens came and the ambulance came."

"I saw it," adds Wendice. "They was cut and bleeding and one had a knot on her head." He points to his forehead.

Fourth Grade

The intercom announces that fourth-grade teachers are to bring their classes to the gym immediately after lunch for a meeting with Ms. Dawson. Students look from one to another murmuring, "What did we do now?"

In the lunchroom I learn from another teacher that inappropriate websites (e.g., a wrestling site) have been visited because the sites have frozen on the screen. Ms. Dawson checks all fourth-grade computers. She discovers that such visits have occurred in two classrooms. At 12:30, the children are lined up to sit in rows on the gym floor. By 12:45, teachers are mumbling about valuable time being wasted. At 12:55, Ms. Dawson and Pam Porter enter the gym. One teacher is dispatched to get a student conduct handbook from Ms. Dawson's office.

Ms. Dawson announces, "If you visit inappropriate websites, you will not use a computer for a year. You will be suspended. We will find out who you are. Teachers, monitor who is on the computers in your classrooms."

This continues until 1:10 P.M., when teachers and their classes trudge back to their classrooms to pick up the threads of instruction.

Third Grade

Yesterday was Halloween. The school had no parties or costume parades because some parents objected on religious grounds. Many of the same parents do not seem to object to their children watching violent, gory movies on television. The children report the plots and details of these movies to me regularly.

Most teachers brought small gifts, such as bookmarks and candy, to their pupils and read autumn stories to them. Some children brought candy for their classmates.

Today the children are tired and wired. Some claim that they were up until midnight or 1:00 A.M. eating trick-or-treat candy and watching television. "We're fired up from last night," says Manuel.

Kelvin tells the class, "I couldn't get to sleep because a branch was scratching my window in the wind and I kept thinking somebody was trying to get in."

Fourth Grade

I continue to be struck by the generosity of the children who live in poverty. When Dario or Victavius can't find their pencils, several students offer to let the boys borrow one. The same is true with notebook paper. Today Joshua, Jamal, and Dwayne bring their bulging bags of trick-or-treat candy to share with the class during snack time. I dimly recall hoarding my Halloween candy for weeks when I was a child. Perhaps, for these children, it is the only way of ever treating the class because they have so little.

Third and Fourth Grades

This is the week of the all-school book fair. On the first day, children are allowed, by classes, to go into the gym and browse among the books and toys for sale. On the remaining days, only children who have money to buy books are allowed into the gym at their scheduled time.

Each class can remain in the gym for fifteen minutes the first day. The children see many books they would like to own but cannot. Several children spot stuffed toy monkeys hanging from a post in the gym. They ask the aide selling the books how the monkeys keep their hands and feet together around the post. "Are there suction cups on them?" inquires a third grader.

"No, they have Velcro on them," the aide replies.

"How much do they cost?" several children ask.

"They are $8.99," responds the aide. This is an impossible amount for most of the children.

At mid-morning, the intercom summons Ashley, a white fourth-grade girl, to the office. Ashley's mother has arrived to take her to the book fair. Later Ashley returns to the classroom, smiling and carrying seven books. The other children stare in wonder.

The computer lab is closed all week. Mrs. Redd, the paraprofessional who runs the lab, has been assigned to work at the book fair this week—even though most of the children cannot afford to purchase books.

Fourth Grade

I am concerned about Rachael, who just transferred to Redbud Elementary. In her first week, she has already been in one playground fight. Today she was sent to in-school suspension by Ms. Dawson for saying unkind things to Chalese, a shy child who has learning disabilities. Rachael is the fifth child who has enrolled in my classroom since the school year began. I have learned that with each new face, the chemistry of the class changes.

Third Grade

In science class, we are talking about animal shelters. I call attention to a picture of a squirrel curled up in a hollow tree trunk. Wendice raises his hand. "Squirrel is good."

Antinesha comments, "You can have it fried or baked." I ask how many have eaten squirrel meat. Most raise their hands.

"I like possum with cream," Jaron adds.

"You're making me hungry," I fib.

During the reading block, the third-grade teachers meet with the consultant from the new reading program that the school has purchased. This is the same woman who "worked" with us in week 7. In attendance at the meeting are Pam Porter; Kim Bridges, the reading specialist; all the third-grade teachers; and an uncertified fourth-grade teacher. To be fair, the consultant does model a couple of worthwhile writing techniques with six perfectly behaved children. Her comments, however, are fatuous. Examples: "If you don't make them share, you'll have a group that goofs off. You need to know where your kids are. You need to know what your kids did. You may need to pull from lower levels."

Before school starts, we pick up the Redbud weekly paper. The third graders accurately reported the incident involving Kanzah's mother. I see her name in the arrest section of the newspaper. Bond is set at $1,500.

WEEK 12, NOVEMBER 6–10: BURGEONING NEEDS AND STAGNANT FUNDS

Third and Fourth Grades

There are two teachers who, in our opinion, should not be working with children. Ms. Pringle, a first-grade teacher, constantly screams at the top of her lungs. She carries a paddle with her even to the children's restrooms and uses it frequently for the mildest infractions of her rules. Her face has a perpetual look of anger. Another teacher, a male, gives off worrisome clues of taking enjoyment in paddling the children. Both teachers pride themselves in "keeping order."

An after-school tutoring program is scheduled for an hour every Tuesday and Thursday until March. The program is provided to help students get ready for the LEAP test and the Iowa Test of Basic Skills. There are 109 third- and fourth-grade children signed up for the sessions. The program was to have started this week, but it has been postponed because of a lack of teachers willing to tutor. The district pays $15 a session, and most of the teachers at Redbud Elementary don't have the energy to tutor after working with the children all day. So far, only two fourth-grade teachers have agreed to participate. In some parts of the United States, tutors reportedly earn $150 per hour.

Louisiana voters soundly rejected Amendments 2 and 3 in Tuesday's election. The amendments would have eliminated some sales tax but would have increased state income tax. If they had passed, the state would have raised more than $200 million earmarked for teacher salaries in the public schools and state universities.

It is the twelfth week of school, and many of the fourth graders have not yet been able to complete the assessment program and enter the instructional program of the new $85,500 software package that is supposed to "pinpoint" difficulties. Teachers are grumbling that the district has bought a white elephant. The rest of the school cannot use the computer lab because it is reserved for the fourth graders who go there twice a day for half an hour—once for reading and once for math. The only time the other children get a glimpse of the computer lab is when they walk past it on their way to the portable music classroom.

Fourth Grade

Yesterday was the fourth-grade field trip to Shreveport. The city, with a population of about 300,000, is fifty miles from Redbud. We saw *A Christmas Carol* at the Strand Theater. Only half the fourth graders could afford the $8.50 ticket price. The others were given the day off. Most of the teachers could afford to pay the $2.50 per child to see the *Aladdin* performance, but this time many of the teachers could not come up with $170 so that all the children in their classes could attend.

Mrs. Howe, the bus driver, has decorated the interior of her school bus with more than one hundred photographs of Redbud students who were her passengers at one time or another. Some appear to have been there for many years. Mrs. Howe pointed out a few to me, including one who was killed in the Gulf War and several who are parents of children she presently drives to and from school. She adds a grandmotherly touch to the family feeling of an elementary school.

My bus seatmate was Chalese, a slow learner with few friends. Her eyes grew large as we crossed the Red River and traveled into Shreveport. Chalese told me that she had never seen such tall buildings or such a big river.

The children were awestruck by the theater. Prior to the performance, they could stand, look around, and gaze at the chandeliers, balcony, and box seats. The combination of a bus trip to a city, a fine theater performance, and the majestic beauty of an old theater provided needed enrichment for our Redbud children. If only they all could have gone on the trip.

Third Grade

The children take care of one another. On Tie Day, Redbud Elementary students are allowed to wear men's ties. Chikae brings a tie, but he doesn't know how to tie it. Antinesha ties it for him in a perfect knot. Where did she learn this? Jaheesa's braids are too tight. Shantel takes off Jaheesa's hair bows (barrettes) and loosens Jaheesa's braids. Cherise's ear is bleeding from a too-big earring in her pierced ear. Kanesha removes the earring and gets Cherise a wet paper towel to place on the ear. All of this is accomplished without direction from me. The children frequently exhibit compassion and unselfishness.

The pupils' lack of prior knowledge, at least the type that appears on many standardized tests, is apparent daily. On a test provided by the balanced literacy series that the school is using, all the children incorrectly complete an item. They can pronounce the word *harp*, but they have no idea of what the word means. We look up *harp* in a dictionary, and we are fortunate that an illustration accompanies the definition. In a balanced literacy book selection, the word *recital* is part of the book's title and central to the plot of the story. No child in the class ever has taken a music lesson or a dance lesson, and no child has ever attended a recital. In our language books, the word *opera* appears in an exercise. Again, no child knows the meaning.

The children are having difficulties with irregular plurals. Each morning I put sentences on the blackboard that must be corrected by the class. Today one sentence reads, "i seen many geeses in the skie." The children cannot come up with the plural of *goose*. Attempts include *gooses* and *goses*.

Today the class teaches me a meaning for the word *poor*. We are talking about healthy and unhealthy foods. Antinesha comments, "My cousin eats a lot but he's still poe."

"What's *poe*?" I ask.

"You know like when somebody doesn't have money but this means somebody's skinny," Antinesha replies.

"Oh, *poor*," I say. "I never heard of that meaning of the word." I look it up in a large dictionary that I brought from home. The children are correct. A meaning of *poor* is *emaciated*. "You taught me something new," I tell them.

Leon proudly shows me his new shoes from Wal-Mart: white tennis shoes that are too big. After recess I see him wiping dust off them with a dry paper towel. I tell him that he is smart to take such good care of his new shoes.

Some of the students can tell time, and others cannot. I have those who know how to tell time help those who are having some problems. As I walk around the room offering assistance, I notice that the tutors have drawn lopsided clocks and are showing their tutees how to count by fives and ones to determine the correct time. The tutors are patient with their pupils. Sometimes the children offer better explanations of things to other children than I can.

I bring in a lamp for the children's "library time." Twenty minutes before the children go home each day, we will turn off the overhead lights and turn on the new lamp. Pupils have signed up to read a picture book to the class during this time. Even the children who read below grade level want to take a turn. Manuel bumps the new lamp on the way to the pencil sharpener. "Be careful!" Shantel says to Manuel. "There's no money-back guarantee on lamps."

Jelani and Kanzah ask to get water several times today. Their gums are bleeding. I remind them to tell their grandmothers because they live with them.

I give the class their final test in carrying and regrouping (borrowing). Each child is called to my desk to discuss errors and get some extra help where needed. Wendice does poorly on the borrowing section, missing most of the problems. I ask him if his mother can help him a bit at home. "No," he replies. "When I get home, she drunk."

"Every day?" I inquire.

"Every day she drunk or gone." I tell Wendice that we'll find a helper at school.

When I ask Ms. Dawson about Wendice's home life, she tells me that the mother was a "dopehead" and is still "a drunk." She says, "You'll get no help from there."

Third and Fourth Grades

It is Friday. Redbud High School's football team won a berth in the play-offs. All Redbud schools will be dismissed at 12:30 today to enable fans to travel to Hammond, Louisiana, for the game. Something finally is given higher priority than the LEAP test—a football game.

WEEK 13, NOVEMBER 13–17: HUNDREDS OF OBJECTIVES

Third and Fourth Grades

Our after-school faculty meeting began with a sales pitch for a supplementary teacher retirement program. The spiel was mercifully brief. The remainder of the meeting was spent discussing the children's low LEAP and Iowa Test of Basic Skills scores. Ms. Bridges, the reading specialist, pointed out specific skills that each grade level needed to review or reteach. She and Pam Porter stressed the need for skill mastery before moving on in the curriculum. A teacher stated that this presented a dilemma. "How can we cover the state-mandated curriculum, with its hundreds of objectives, and teach all of them to mastery with only 176 school days?" she inquired. No one had an answer.

Ms. Bridges held up two professional books on teaching reading. She asked for volunteers to lead after-school book discussions on these references. There were no takers. A third-grade teacher said, "We have no more time in our lives for book talks."

Third Grade

We are reviewing the *ai* vowel team in the phonics program we are required to use. The word *waitress* appears on an instructional sheet. The children are able to "sound out" the word, but they do not know what it means. The only restaurant knowledge they have is about fast-food restaurants. I explain that at many restaurants, a waitress asks what you want to eat and brings it to you. You usually do not have to clean up after yourself in restaurants where there are waitresses. I introduce the words *waiter, waitperson, menu, tip,* and *reservations.* Jimmy says, "I saw one of those fancy restaurants on TV. A man had a rag over his arm."

"That's a waiter," I comment, "but a waiter usually doesn't have a cloth over his arm."

"There's a restaurant in Minden with a waitress," Antinesha tells the class. "I went there once. It's called the Golden Fence."

"Do they have menus at the Golden Fence?" I ask.

"No, they got the food you can get written on a big board," she responds.

While reviewing the vowel team *oa,* I learn another meaning of the word *roast* from the third graders. Leon explains, "When you get *roast,* you get hit with a big, wide, thick strap."

"You have to get hit until you get bruises to get *roast,*" Shantel points out. The other children agree.

Third and Fourth Grades

The third- and fourth-grade teachers are in trouble this afternoon. An uncertified teacher tells Ms. Dawson that the cafeteria was too noisy during lunchtime and that the behavior of the third graders, in particular, was "atrocious." This is the same teacher who has displayed a penchant for paddling too many too often too hard and is rumored to be a racial bigot. The third- and fourth-grade teachers are disturbed by such tattletale behavior from one who knows little about teaching children and the human tendency to chat during a meal. Many have commented about this teacher's "sucking up" to Ms. Dawson, the vice principal/disciplinarian. They have heard this teacher remark, "I'd rather error [*sic*] on the side of being too harsh than too lax." This is the same teacher who is looking for classes "on the level of basket weaving" to get certified by the state of Louisiana. It is a sad fact that as more certified, experienced teachers are driven from the profession, they are replaced by uncertified people, some of whom should not be allowed near a classroom of children.

Third Grade

The children take good care of me. I am hoarse today. Jimmy tells me he can make soup and bring it tomorrow. "From the can?" I ask.

"Yes, ma'am," he answers.

Several others say that they are canned-soup makers, too. I am seated on the rug, and the children are around me. I am reading a story about places where wild animals can be found. Randall and Kanesha are gently dusting off the bottoms of my pant legs with their hands. Apparently, I bumped into something, and the dust shows on my black pants.

Mr. Johnson has been at a meeting for two days. Each morning before school begins, in the cafeteria, in the hallways, and each afternoon when school ends, the children in his classes ask about him. Verlin and Gabrielle, in particular, seem concerned.

"Where is he now? Are you sure he's coming back?" they ask repeatedly—even though Mr. Johnson told them his itinerary and showed them his route on a map. Both children want to carry my book bag and cooler to and from my car so they can talk about him. There has been so much teacher turnover at the school that students in our classes ask us every Friday if we will be there the following Monday. The children seem to long for consistency.

Fourth Grade

My amaryllis bloom died while I was on a trip, so I decide to give it a proper Louisiana funeral, complete with dirge. As I march the plant to the wastebasket, mouths fall open. Just as I am about to "bury" it in the wastebasket, Dwayne cries, "Can I have it?"

I tell him he can and add that he can plant it outside when the weather gets warmer. It sits on his desk all day, and he proudly shows other teachers as he heads for the school bus at the end of the day. The children we work with are appreciative of the smallest possession. Whenever our pupils get anything new—even a pencil—they show it to us with pride.

Third Grade

This morning, the eight-year-olds are filled with etymological and medical knowledge and social advice. Kanzah announces that he has diarrhea and must go to the bathroom frequently. I tell the class that this condition can be dangerous because it can cause dehydration. They need to drink fluids if they have it. "It's bad. You can die from it," Manuel says seriously. "That's why they call it *die*-arrhea." The class nods with looks of "I haven't thought about this, but it makes sense."

The discussion turns to ringworm. Nearly every child in the class has had ringworm, and they offer the same medical advice: "Drink a beer."

"When I had it bad," Keaziah tells us, "my mama gave me Bud Light and it went away fast." Other children offer similar testimonials. Mayo Clinic take note.

Cherise asks me if I know how to tell when somebody is growing.

"By measuring them?" I offer.

"No, you can tell when you're growing because there's a hole in the back of your knee, and when that hurts, you're growing," she says confidently.

"I wet the bed sometimes," reports Jaron.

Shantel gives him a disapproving look. "If I did that, I'd keep it to myself," she says.

After lunch, I walk into the gym early to pick up my class. They are trying to make baskets in the one hoop near the main doors. I realize the importance of seeing the whole child—creating, at work, and at play. Wendice, who is often lethargic because of the late hours he keeps, is a whiz on the court. Wendice is tiny for his age. He comes up to me with the comparatively huge basketball, smiles, and says, "This one's for you, Ms. Johnson."

Then he dribbles, aims, and, with all his strength, hurls the basketball. He makes a basket.

Third and Fourth Grades

We are heartened by Peggy Harris's article "'Grassroots' Testing Response" in the November 2000 issue of the *Council Chronicle* published by the National Council of Teachers of English (NCTE). It describes efforts to oppose high-stakes testing, and it summarizes the work of the NCTE Task Force on High-Stakes Testing. The task force is distributing bumper stickers and buttons with the slogan "My Child Is More Than a Test Score." The task force is involved in four other activities:

- Creating political action kits on high-stakes tests
- Preparing a statement opposing high-stakes testing
- Publishing a report card on specific tests in use
- Collecting stories about the effects of high-stakes on teachers and students (NCTE 2000, 1, 5)

Perhaps the voices of professional associations, such as the NCTE and the International Reading Association, will do some good, but we think that only parents writing to their legislators will bring about change.

Pam Porter sends a letter and a copy of the School Report Card for Parents home with the children. The report card shows that Redbud Elementary School has dropped from a school performance score of 44.1 to 41.3. This score labels the school "academically below average" because it falls between 30.1 and 69.3. The Louisiana labels for the schools on the far ends of the continuum are "academically unacceptable schools" with scores of 30 or below and "schools of academic excellence" with scores of 150 or above. The state average for all schools is 77.3. In her letter to parents and guardians, Pam explains that the low score was based on tests given last March and did not include the LEAP test scores of students who attended summer school and then passed their retakes of the LEAP. She also points out that school attendance accounts for 10 percent of the total school score, and she urges parents and guardians to keep their children's attendance high.

We wonder why school officials and politicians across the country seem oblivious to or disinterested in the omnipresent correlation between children living in poverty and low test scores. We are not making excuses—we are stating a fact. In Louisiana, the schools that score at the bottom are in the high-poverty areas of inner-city New Orleans, in the river parishes along the Mississippi delta, and in other pockets of poverty, such as the town of Redbud. The schools that score at the top are the magnet schools and campus lab schools with selective admissions procedures. Other schools performing well are found in the suburbs and areas of affluence. Furthermore, many parents, particularly white parents with the means to do so, send their children to private academies and Christian schools. Most of these schools are exempt from accountability requirements, high-stakes tests, and school labels. More than 80 percent of the students at Redbud Elementary School are African American, but nearly half the residents of Redbud are white. We are reminded of these numbers as we look at photos in the Redbud newspaper. They show scenes from Redbud's sesquicentennial celebration. Few African American faces can be found in the thirty-three pictures of the event. Most of the white parents of school-age children in Redbud send their children to Christian schools and private academies.

Since the voters of Louisiana defeated the package that would have raised the salaries of public school teachers and professors, teachers have begun to take some actions. Teacher picket lines have been seen in cities across the state. Nearly every teacher at Redbud Elementary School signed a petition urging Governor Foster to find a way to increase the salaries of Louisiana teachers, who are among the lowest paid in the nation.

Friday is here, and the dismissal bell rings. Next week is the Thanksgiving holiday. Several of the children linger in classrooms, pretending to be busy. Some tell us that they do not want to go home. After the children finally leave,

Ruth says that this behavior is not uncommon. "They get two meals a day here, they have a schedule, they're safe, and they have people who care. They know they won't get this at home."

WEEK 14, NOVEMBER 27–DECEMBER 1: TEACHERS *WILL* BE HELD ACCOUNTABLE

Third Grade

The children return from the Thanksgiving vacation somewhat subdued. Kanzah, however, is crying. He has a long row of stitches along his jawbone. His friends tell me that he had an encounter with some barbed wire on a fence.

Cherise says that her mouth hurts. "I had a cavity and got my tooth pulled yesterday," she says softly.

"Yesterday was Sunday. Was there a dentist's office open on Sunday?" I ask.

"My grandma pulled it," Cherise replies.

It was a permanent tooth. Now there is a space showing when Cherise smiles.

Fourth Grade

The week begins with an announcement by Nikeya that there is a cockroach on De'Lewis's book bag. De'Lewis jumps up and swats at it. Jamal leaps out of his chair saying, "I'll get it," as he squashes the roach.

Joshua's hand goes up. "Last night I ate some things in bed. Later a cockroach walked across my face. My mama said not to eat in bed."

Yolande has not come to school for more than eight weeks. At first she was rumored to be moving to Baton Rouge; however, she is truant. Each day, students report that Yolande is still in Redbud. I have reported this every morning on the attendance slip. According to school records, Yolande missed sixty-two days last year. The principal notified the truant officer and social services, but nothing seems to bring her back to school. Today, Jaylene announces, "Yolande said she's coming back to class on Monday."

Third Grade

I am on playground duty at 7:15 A.M. When the bell rings, Mrs. Marlow tells me that office personnel have been paging me repeatedly. I usher my class into our classroom, and, coat still on, I hurry to the office. A grandmother and a third grader carrying a Wal-Mart bag of school supplies await me. I greet the child, speak briefly with the grandmother, and escort the child to the class-room. Ms. Tompkins, an in-school suspension substitute, is waiting for me by the classroom door. She reprimands me, in front of my class, about the chil-dren's behavior while I was in the office. I bite my tongue, put wadded paper towels under a leg of a desk to balance it for the new child, and take roll call. Then I take off my coat.

Gerard is the new child. His grandmother tells me that since he left my class in September, he has attended four schools. I emptied his desk a few weeks ago, never thinking that he would return. All day, Gerard stares off into space. He is preoccupied. I think of the times I hear politicians pronounce, "Teachers *will* be held accountable," and then think of Gerard's six beginnings of school before December 1. At the end of the day, I realize what a toll Ger-ard's moving about has taken. He is far behind the children who were on his academic level when he left.

Third and Fourth Grades

It strikes us that since the school year began more than three months ago, we have had no opportunity for extended conversation or discussion with our colleagues. There has been no time during the jam-packed school day. We are with our pupils before the school day begins, during the lunch period, and un-til the buses pull out of the driveway. The only "free time" is the approximately ten minutes the children are at music or physical education. During that time, most teachers wait in line to use the one toilet or wait in line to use the one telephone to return calls to parents or guardians. By the time the buses leave, teachers are drained. Anyone who has spent a full day with a minimum of twenty children, all under the age of ten, will understand this fatigue. Our only opportunities to communicate with other teachers are fleeting comments on the run in the hallway, in the lunchroom, or on the playground. We recall teachers from our earlier classroom experiences who left the profession be-cause there was no time for professional or personal conversation with other adults. We are not referring to the stilted "faculty study groups" proposed by the recent visiting state consultant.

Fourth Grade

Two of my pupils are sick today. Rhonda tells me about her stomachache as the tears roll. Dwayne, with hat pulled far over his head, slumps with a severe headache. Telephone calls to both homes yield no results. Rhonda's mother says that she cannot leave her small child, so Rhonda will just have to stay at school. Dwayne's mother cannot be reached. There is no place in the school where sick children can lie down. This is difficult for teachers. We know that the children are suffering, and we want to help them, but all we can do is offer comforting words.

Third and Fourth Grades

We learn that the school was broken into during the Thanksgiving vacation. The vandals stood on a garbage can and broke into the girls' restroom window. Pam Porter says that the damage was minor. Salt was poured on floors, paint was sprayed in the boys' bathroom, small items were tossed about, and decorations and students' work were torn from the walls.

Fourth Grade

Today our student teachers arrive. They will be with us until February 22. The university that they attend is on the quarter system. Ms. Hammond is a petite African American from the nearby town of Minden. The students seem pleased to have her in our room. Demetrius guesses her age to be fourteen; she is twenty-three.

Third Grade

My student teacher, Ms. Melody Schwartz, is a tall, slender, white twenty-one-year-old. I know Melody because she was a student in my "Diagnosing Reading Difficulties" course last year. I go over the daily routine with Ms. Schwartz and give her the few teacher's manuals that I have. She has the enthusiasm that I frequently see in teachers just beginning their careers.

The students in my class and in Mr. Johnson's class show off for the student teachers. Jimmy tells Ms. Schwartz and me, "They're acting like a bunch of wild animals." From experience, we know that this behavior will diminish as the children become accustomed to the student teachers' presence in the rooms.

Fourth Grade

Our third and fourth graders are true recyclers. They find uses for everything. Each day, I have a plastic bottle of water on my desk. As soon as it is empty, several voices ask, "Can I have your bottle, Mr. Johnson?"

"Sure," I say, "why do you want it?"

"To get some water."

The next day, a child comes to school with frozen water in the bottle. The child drinks it as it slowly melts.

Third Grade

My class routinely asks for discards in the wastebasket. Leaky markers, snips of colored paper, and even used masking tape are desirable items.

Third and Fourth Grades

In the state of Louisiana, a woman named Leslie Jacobs is referred to as "the architect of the school accountability program." She is a member of the Board of Elementary and Secondary Education. An article in the Shreveport *Times* states that the board "has tossed a rope to eighth graders who have run into a brick wall trying to master the LEAP 21 test" (Evans 2000, 1A, 3A). State officials are becoming concerned that many students will drop out of school because of failing the test. The new plan calls for establishing, by school districts, "viable vocational programs for students to leave school ready for the work force" if they fail the LEAP test two years in a row. This policy will, in effect, create a tracking system likely to provide the state with workers for minimum-wage jobs. Mark Miller, Deerborne Parish school superintendent, points out that this plan will pose serious problems for rural districts that lack sufficient resources for existing programs.

An article by David Barham in *The News-Star* of Monroe, Louisiana, quotes Leslie Jacobs: "What do you do with the kids who can't get through the eighth-grade LEAP test?" Her plan would put the failing students in a non–high school track that would "interest the student with job opportunities." Jacobs says that this plan is "a more attractive option than dropping out, but less attractive than high school" (Barham 2000, 1). It apparently has not dawned on Ms. Jacobs that there are other options, such as doing away with high-stakes testing. Something isn't right in a state when officials are willing to consign large numbers of its early adolescents to lives of material poverty. Jacobs was quick to point out that the new plan will not let Louisiana schools off the hook: "These students still count in the school accountability performance score" (3). Once again, poor children in poor schools are going to be getting the short end of the stick.

Third Grade

The temperature is in the thirties when the children arrive today. Some of them are dressed in short-sleeved shirts and shorts. They are not wearing sweaters or jackets, and they shiver in the cold. As I open my classroom door, I see a mess. The vandals have struck again. This time they hit the rooms that had been used for tutoring children after school. These rooms were not locked when the tutoring sessions were dismissed. The contents of my desk are scattered about the floor. I had a few dollars in my desk to supply children with emergency loans. This money is missing. Other teachers find that contents of their desks and files are scattered about.

After the ten-minute morning recess, Gerard tells me that he wants to speak to me privately. The three other children standing near me go to their desks. "What's the problem?" I ask.

"Two boys on the playground are calling me 'Chubs' and 'Pork Chop.'"

"That's terrible," I say. "Who are these boys?"

"I don't know their names. But that's not all," Gerard continues. "They said, 'If you eat another crumb, you'll explode.'"

"You'll have to point them out to me the next time we have recess," I say.

"I'm going to set a trap for them," confides Gerard. "I'll take my trading cards with me, and when they see me playing with them, they'll come near me, and then I can show you who they are."

"That's a fine plan," I respond.

FIVE

DECEMBER

"CLAMP DOWN"

WEEK 15, DECEMBER 4–8: OUT-OF-TOUCH OFFICIALS

Third and Fourth Grades

We realize how out of touch some U.S. Department of Education officials are when we read a quotation in Sunday's newspaper. An assistant secretary of education praised Louisiana for its education reform efforts. "I want to congratulate you on the great progress your state has made in developing the Louisiana Educational Assessment Program for the 21st Century and implementing the Public Education Accountability System. These impressive efforts clearly demonstrate Louisiana's efforts to making sure that all students achieve to challenging standards" ("State School Reform Gets Praise of U.S. Education Secretary" 2000, 2B). The assistant secretary apparently did not hear about the attempted suicide by a Redbud eighth grader who failed the math portion of the LEAP test or about the stressed-out children in fourth grade who can think of nothing but the impending LEAP test and its distressing consequences or about the multitude of teachers leaving the profession because of the pressures on them to teach to the LEAP test or the Iowa test at all grade levels. Nor did he hear about underfunded schools with children who come from every degree of poverty. Nor did he hear about Chalese, Chikae, and the other children with learning disabilities who may never be able to achieve these "challenging standards." It is high time that the bureaucrats in Washington and Baton Rouge get out into the schools for more than a photo-op.

Two former school superintendents, M. Donald Thomas and William L. Bainbridge, understand what the education official does not. In a perceptive article, "The Truth about 'All Children Can Learn'" (Thomas and Bainbridge 2000), they pinpoint the conditions that prevent learning. They sum up the article with these words:

> Yes, all children can learn the basic curriculum of the school if we have the courage to do what is right. We must value all children. We must provide adequate resources for schools, especially for schools in poor and rural areas. We must make judgments based on many variables, and we must eliminate red herrings from worthwhile consideration. (34)

Thomas and Bainbridge plead that every classroom be staffed by a certified teacher with an adequate salary, that every child have adequate health care, and that zero-tolerance measures, such as the Louisiana LEAP test, be discontinued.

Fourth Grade

I begin the day by asking the students to write a two-paragraph description of the highlights of their weekend. Emerald's is particularly tragic:

> My House Fire
> Thing that happened in my life is that my house got burn up. got burn up. First it starting at the top and then it just starting to burn. My close, shoes, and bed, toys and my fish tank. It is sad because my brothers game got burn up. One thing about is that everybody come to help my mom. My grandmother tried to run back in there but my mom hold my grandmother back.
> In my life at my uncle house has been so bad. My cousin always picking on me and they don't like me. My uncle try to make me happy but he cannont make me happy. Things in my life goes bad.

Third and Fourth Grades

On Monday morning, the announcement is made that all teachers are to turn in their lesson plan books and grade books to the office immediately. Late in the day, the books are returned to the teachers by the grade-level representatives. Several plan books contain sticky notes that point out deficiencies. Presumably the inspection was conducted by Pam Porter, but who insisted on the inspection and why are not made clear to the teachers. Several teachers tell each other that their planning system deviates somewhat from the lockstep, clumsy, mandated state formats. "It works for me," says Ruth. "I wish that were good enough." Teachers feel that the unannounced collection of these books is just another instance of monitoring by officials that widens the distance between teachers and administrators. This "pop quiz" mentality suggests that teachers are not trusted to do their job.

There were two more break-ins this week. On Monday night, a window in Mr. Effingham's room was broken, and things were scattered about. The entry point of the most recent break-in has not been discovered. Again, things of value were not taken. The vandals just made a mess. They also went to the Internet and accessed some forbidden sites. Some sort of alarm system is being installed. Several teachers have expressed fears about staying in the building after dark. "I don't want to be here when somebody's creeping around," commented Mrs. Larson.

We receive a memo from Pam Porter stating, among other things, that there will be faculty meetings the next two Monday evenings: December 11 and December 18. Consultants will be at the school to teach us how to do the whole-faculty study groups. Teachers have no voice in this matter.

Fourth Grade

Holiday fever is in the air. Milo confides that he has bought Mrs. Henderson a T-shirt about math. "I think it's too small, though," he says.

"What size tie do you wear, Mr. Johnson?" asks Nikeya.

Third and Fourth Grades

Another warning came today from Ms. Dawson. Teachers are told to "clamp down" on talking in the lunchroom. "Too many teachers are talking to each other when they should be monitoring their students." Teachers who fail to comply are to be "talked to individually."

Northern Louisiana has been experiencing a cold snap this week. Every night, the temperature dips below thirty degrees. Children sit in the hallways after breakfast instead of playing outside before school starts. Some do not wear sweaters or jackets. The weather is too much for the air conditioners/heaters in our classrooms. They freeze up, make clunking noises, and kick out no heat. The custodians have to be called several times to get them working again. Classrooms are chilly most of the week because these window units are not airtight. Large gaps offer a good view of the school yard from the fourth-grade room and views of the driveway from the third-grade classroom. A small bird could easily hop through the gaps.

"A fungus known as 'stachybotrys' was found in several rooms at Redbud Memorial Hospital about a month ago, causing hospital officials to close down one wing of the hospital" (Herring 2000d). Hospital employees had complained because of illness. At Redbud Elementary School, children and teachers take turns having viral infections, colds, skin rashes, and more. Teachers suspect something lurks in the damp, moldy ceiling tiles in our classrooms.

Fourth Grade

The commercial photographers are back to take holiday pictures of those who can afford the $10 to $40 package. Only a few students in each class bring the minimum amount of money. They are allowed to wear "dress-up clothes" rather than school uniforms. Birdia, who is in Ruth's fourth-grade class, comes to school in a baby-blue, frilly, taffeta-like dress. When Ms. Johnson and I tell her how beautiful she looks, she says, "I got it for Easter. My grandpa told me he will bring the picture money later." Ruth tells me that it is unlikely that the grandfather will appear. Birdia's brother, Dario, is in my class. Ruth and I agree to split the cost of the $10 package for a picture of Birdia and Dario together. Recall that Ruth's salary is $24,221. The grandfather never does come to school with the picture money.

On picture days we see the benefits of school uniforms. When the children wear their "very best," we see baggy men's shirts and pants and men's ties on the boys and ill-fitting, hand-me-down, well-worn party dresses on the girls. The clothing jars us and reminds us how little our pupils have in terms of material goods. They are not aware of their poverty now as they move about the room in their finest attire, but they will be as the years pass.

I continue to be struck by the generosity and big hearts of some of the teachers at Redbud Elementary who are among the most poorly paid teachers in the United States. They buy school supplies, pay for theatrical productions, and buy treats; most of all, they give a lot of love to the children.

WEEK 16, DECEMBER 11–15: TEACHING AND LEARNING IN A COLD BUILDING

Third and Fourth Grades

We arrive at school to find that there has been a power outage. We have no heat or lights. The air temperature is twenty-seven degrees—too chilly for the children to go outdoors. They huddle in the hallway, which is warmer than the classrooms. We hear that strong winds have snapped power lines. At 7:55, teachers begin to conduct classes in cold, dark classrooms. Children who have coats keep them on; a few unclaimed sweaters and jackets from years past are distributed to children who are wearing only short-sleeved shirts.

When the power is restored at approximately 9:30, the window heaters begin to chug. They kick out air—first cool, then tepid, then warm. The rooms on the sunny side of the building begin to warm up. Those on the shady side are cold all day.

Fourth Grade

We have learned over the past three months that one of the unpleasant aspects of teaching is dealing with the few pushy or demanding parents. Elias (2000) reported a dramatic increase across the nation in parents assuming adversarial postures toward schools. "There's less respect. Parents are going to school acting like lawyers or agents for their kids" (1D). Pam Porter tells us that the president of the PTO led a small delegation of parents to the superintendent's office. There the parents complained that teachers are too hard on their children, the principal is never available, and teachers don't communicate enough with parents. They demanded permission to visit classrooms unannounced. The superintendent informed them that such visits would violate district and state policy. Recall the parents who sent the note early in the year insisting that no traces of fairies, jack-o'-lanterns, and so on be seen in Redbud Elementary. The same parents now go to Pam Porter to complain about their child's two teachers. They say that Mrs. Henderson didn't give enough help to Kamie in science, causing her to get a B in the subject. I am alleged to have homework policies that violate school rules. As the parents leave the school building, Ms. Dawson hears the father mutter threats about a lawsuit. The tone and tactics of these parents are reprehensible to Mrs. Henderson and me. Such parents, although few in number, are one more reason why some teachers quit the profession.

Third Grade

Kanzah brings aspirin to school. In the morning, he asks me if he can take a tablet because he has a toothache. I ask him if he has gone to a dentist as his grandmother said he would. "No," he says.

Wendice is crying with tooth pain. I send him to the office to call his mother. She picks him up. The next morning, I ask him if he has seen a dentist. "No," he replies.

Third and Fourth Grades

There has been an ice storm warning for late Tuesday night and Wednesday morning. We arise early on Wednesday to check a Shreveport TV station for school closings. No Louisiana closings are reported. By 6:00 A.M., only Caddo Parish, which includes Shreveport, has closed. As we drive in heavy rain toward Redbud, the temperature on our car thermometer shows thirty-one degrees. We wonder when the rain will turn to ice. There are few vehicles moving on Interstate 20, normally busy at any time of the day or night. Highway 9, which runs between Arcadia and Redbud, has almost no traffic. The farther north we go, the heavier the rain becomes. We pull off the road in Athens because the visibility makes it impossible to proceed. Soon the rain diminishes, and we set out again. Now ice forms on our windshield and side mirrors, and we can see the trees bending under the weight of the ice. It is nearly as dark as night.

We get to school, and roll call reveals that more than two hundred students are absent. Shortly after 9:00, the school loses its power, and the rooms quickly become cold. Ice has accumulated on the power lines, and some trees have fallen, bringing the power lines down with them. Pam Porter tries to reach the school board office to request buses for the children. Telephone lines are also down, and she cannot make contact with the board via her cell phone. Pam decides to send all her out-of-town teachers home. Several live thirty to fifty miles from the school. The remaining students are divided among the teachers who live in Redbud. About twenty of us leave the building feeling a mixture of guilt over leaving our pupils with other teachers and annoyance that school was not closed before children or teachers set out from home. We leave in a convoy with Glenda and Nikki, who live in towns off Interstate 20. Ten minutes into our drive home, we hear on the car radio that the superintendent has closed all Deerborne Parish schools. The time is 9:49 A.M.

Fourth Grade

My room gets so cold that I visit Wal-Mart and purchase two electric heaters. I hope that they will provide enough heat to supplement the inadequate window units.

The next morning, I plug in the heaters and immediately blow a fuse. I learn that I will be able to plug in one heater if no computers are in use and nothing else is plugged in. Children and teachers have gotten used to wearing coats and gloves in class this week.

Third Grade

Jaheesa is having problems listening in class. She writes the following apology (edited for spelling) to me and Ms. Schwartz:

> I will not talk on the rug or at my desk. I know I talk but I just can't help myself. I know they say zip your lips and throw away the key. I tried that but it didn't help and they say put your hand on your mouth. But that did not help. Today is my birthday and God knows I do not want to act like this. When I am at home I will talk and my dad says I talk too much. He said if I get a letter from your teachers he said they are not lying because you talk too much at home. I wish I can stop talking. I am sorry that I was talking on the rug.

The children often surprise us with their thoughts and notes. Sometimes they are disjointed and have no apparent source. Roland, without being told to do so, writes a note to Ms. Schwartz and me: "P.E. stands for Physical Education. Mrs. Johnson and Ms. Schwartz are trying to educate your brain to get smarter."

Gerard comes up to my desk. He looks pale and asks if he can go to the restroom. When he returns, he raises his hand. "Can I tell you something?" he asks.

"Sure," I respond.

He comes up to my desk. "I barfed," he whispers.

"Do you want to go home?" I ask.

"There is a good thing and a bad thing if I go home," Gerard states.

"What are those things?" I inquire.

"The good thing is that if I barf again, I'll be at home. The bad thing is that I'll miss my studies."

"I think you had better go home," I tell him. "I'll get your schoolwork together for you, and you can do it if you feel better later."

Gerard goes to the office to call his grandmother to pick him up.

Fourth Grade

Friday morning, a beaming Nikeya brings me a little shopping bag with red tissue paper in it. "What's this?" I ask.

"Open it. It's for you," says Nikeya.

I remove the tissue paper and find a clip-on tie from Wal-Mart. I have worn a tie to school nearly every day this year. Most of them have characters and designs that are appealing to children. I always will treasure this tie from Nikeya—my very first clip-on.

WEEK 17, DECEMBER 18–19:
HOMEMADE CARDS AND SMALL GIFTS

Fourth Grade

There are only one and a half days this week because of winter vacation. It's a good thing because my fourth-grade classroom has no heat, and the temperature outside each morning has been below freezing. One window heater does not turn on at all, and the other blows cool air. It is difficult to learn in the cold. Tuesday morning is devoted to room holiday parties, so I take my fourth graders, carrying their desk chairs, to Ms. Johnson's fairly warm third-grade classroom for a joint party. I decide that if the heaters are not fixed by the time school resumes on January 2, I will ask Pam Porter to find space for my students in the cafeteria or the gymnasium.

Third and Fourth Grades

Several children bring bags of small candy bars and suckers for the holiday party. Each of us receives homemade cards and small gifts from some of the children. We sing songs, pass out presents for the children, and play games that our student teachers have prepared. Then we give each child a plastic kazoo and lead them in a few kazoo tunes before they leave for the holidays.

SIX

JANUARY

TEST PREPARATION—THE PACE QUICKENS

WEEK 18, JANUARY 2–5: STILL NO HEAT

Third and Fourth Grades

New Year's Eve brought northern Louisiana the most snow in fifteen years—between four and six inches in and around Redbud. Nothing moves on New Year's Day, and that afternoon we receive telephone calls informing us that Deerborne Parish schools will be closed on January 2 because of icy roads. Most of the children who attend Redbud Elementary are bused to school whether they live in town or in the country. The weather stays cold, and the parish schools remain closed on January 3. Our first week back after vacation, therefore, is short—Thursday and Friday only.

Students and faculty are filled with stories about the snow. This is the most snow the children ever have seen, and they discover the joys of making snow figures, sledding (on pieces of cardboard), and snowball fights.

Some of our students proudly show us the new shoes and coats they received for Christmas. Many of the coats are much too large for the children, allowing for several years of growth.

The local television weather forecaster says that this is the second-coldest winter in northern Louisiana since such records have been kept (i.e., 1895). Today the temperature is sixteen degrees.

Fourth Grade

My room still has no heat. One window heater does not work at all, and the other continues to blow only cold air. I ask Pam Porter if anything can be done to repair or replace the heaters. The temperature in the room is not above twenty degrees. Later Pam informs me via the intercom that someone will come to replace a heater. The children and I wear coats, hats, and gloves, but it is not possible to concentrate on teaching and learning. Many of the children are ill dressed for such temperatures.

We become a class of vagabonds seeking heat. We spend an hour working in Ms. Johnson's third-grade classroom and some time in the computer lab, which has a little heat. On the way to the lab, we notice that Mrs. Marlow has her third-grade class in the gym. She is trying to teach a lesson while another class noisily is involved in a basketball game. Later we spend time watching educational videos in Ruth Waverly's room. By midday, a new window heater has been installed, but it has insufficient power to make a dent in the cold air. It is meant for a tiny office. A man inspects the heater that blows cold air and gives me the impression that something will be done. At the end of the school day, the room is still frigid.

Third Grade

When I am in my classroom before school begins, the evening custodian appears. For weeks, he has swept around Gerard's desk, which is somewhat leveled by two ancient language arts textbooks propped under a short desk leg. I have sent notes to the office (following the correct procedure for reporting repairs) to no avail. I ask the custodian to fix the leg of the desk. He does so in less than a minute. His shoes stick to the floor of my classroom just as mine do. The promised winter-break mopping of the filthy classroom floors never took place.

Third and Fourth Grades

We note that the New Orleans Saints are going to face the Minnesota Vikings in a second-round playoff game. We never heard from the Saints in response to the children's letters and our letter describing our lack of playground equipment. We didn't even get a football or a photograph of the team. The children have given up asking about the letters.

Third Grade

Wendice is crying. While standing at my desk, he got some chalk dust on his new coat. I brush it off for him. When he goes outside to clean the chalkboard erasers at the end of the day, he takes off his coat before he approaches the chalkboard.

Today is Jelani's birthday. "My daddy is wearing an alarm on his leg," he says, "but he's gonna take it off."

"Why is he going to take it off?" I ask.

"So he can come to Louisiana to see me for my birthday," Jelani answers.

Fourth Grade

My room is warm. I left the new heater on overnight, and the temperature has climbed to the fifties. We can stay in our room today.

Rhonda asks if she can talk with me. "Sure," I say.

"Have I been better?" she asks. "Have I been talking less? I'm on a new medication. Sometimes my mama loses patience with me. My brother is the same way. Mama divorced my dad because he was doing so much drugs. My aunt said if mama had stayed married to him, we wouldn't have anything—not even a house. We would be on the street."

"Where is your dad now?" I inquire.

Rhonda responds, "Oh, he's around. He doesn't really live anywhere. I might not be in school on Monday because he might take me to Monroe or Shreveport just so we can have a day together."

"No problem. I hope you have a great time," I comment.

"Well, it might not happen," she says.

Rhonda is a small white girl who is bright and a good reader. She likes to talk in class and often has her hand in the air. Rhonda seems to call out for extra attention.

WEEK 19, JANUARY 8–12:
"THREE COMPUTERS IN EVERY CLASSROOM"

Third and Fourth Grades

We had read in the Redbud newspaper, the *Guardian-Journal*, the following paragraph:

[The] superintendent . . . told school board members at their regular meeting on December 7, "By the end of next week, there should be three computers in every classroom connected to the Internet, except for fourth and eighth grade, which will have four." (Herring 2000a, 1)

A month has passed since that school board meeting, and there are no computers connected to the Internet in Room B, third grade (there was a connection to one computer, but the connection is no longer working), and there are only three connected to the Internet in fourth grade, Room H.

Third Grade

In social studies, we are discussing early European settlers in America.
"Why did the Pilgrims come to America?" I ask.
"Because they wanted a Thanksgiving dinner," replies Chikae in all seriousness.
Manuel wants to move his desk from the front of the room to the back. He writes me a note:

> I want to be where Kelvin is because I dont want to talk and give my teachers a headache. And I dont want to go to Ms. Dawson. I want to learn something. I dont want to be stupid. because you do not no anything when you are stupid. Thats why I want to move.

Third and Fourth Grades

After school, a faculty meeting is held to discuss new lesson plan formats being proposed by someone. We are not sure who this person is, but a few teachers say the formats are the brainchild of a central office supervisor. Each format is two pages in length per day. They deal with shared reading, guided reading, workstations, writing, handwriting, spelling, phonics, math, and science/social studies. Kim Bridges, the reading specialist, would like the faculty to vote on which format they would prefer to use. One requires more writing by the teacher than the other, but the other is more detailed. Several teachers are heard asking each other, "What's wrong with the plan that we have been using all year?" It is suggested that the different formats be tried out for a couple of weeks before a faculty vote is taken. One second-grade teacher turns to us and asks, "Why can't they just leave us alone?" We are told that during the recent inspection of our lesson plan books, it was noted that some teachers are writing their plans in different ways. The insistence now is for uniformity of lesson plan writing.

Kim Bridges also teaches us a new procedure and new rubric for evaluating our students' writing. We had been asked to bring samples of our students' written work. During the meeting, we use the new rubric to score that work. Under the rubric's stringent guidelines, most samples the faculty examines receive Fs.

Pam Porter has some announcements to make. "Do not count absences for December 14, 15, 18, and 19. Dress codes for students and teachers will be strictly enforced. Be sure to review the dress code for teachers in the faculty handbook. Some grade books didn't list the skill being taught when I checked them. You must list the skills and the total points possible. Every teacher must have one writing grade per week in the grade book. We need you to come to the PTO meeting on January 22. Finally, there are only forty-three more school days until the LEAP test and the Iowa test."

Fourth Grade

Emerald asks to speak with me. "I saw my daddy this weekend. He at Warton."

"Oh, I hear that Warton is pretty nice," I say.

Emerald continues, "He don't work there, he in there. He didn't pay child support to my mama. He gave me a letter, and I have it in my folder. Do you want to see it?"

"Sure, if you want me to," I answer.

The letter is two pages in length and gives evidence of a writer who is barely literate. He tells about incidents at Warton, tells Emerald how much he loves her, and promises that things will be different when he gets out. Emerald, her mother, and three brothers are still living with an uncle's family because the trailer they bought after their house fire is not yet ready for occupancy.

Milo recently has been put on Ritalin. He has lost his vivacity. He sits quietly at his desk and seems to be completely preoccupied and drowsy. I will call his mother to ask why he needs to be on the drug.

Rhonda informs me that her dad didn't show up to take her to Monroe or Shreveport for the father–daughter day they had planned. "I suppose he got tied up. But I had fun at my aunt's house," Rhonda says.

Third Grade

Jelani's father did not cross state lines to attend his son's birthday celebration.

Roland comes up to my desk. "I went in my pants," he whispers.

"Do you want to call your mother?" I ask.

"Yes, but I can't go home because if I don't have perfect attendance, I can't get the money at the end of the year."

Roland's mother arrives with a change of pants for him. He stays in school the rest of the day. He is too ill to work and sleeps at his desk.

Fourth Grade

My writing assignment asks children to describe the most wonderful room they can imagine. It can be a room in a house, a school, or anywhere, but they must use their imagination. Verlin writes the following:

> My Game Room
> Once I imagine that I had a game room. I had a pool table, checkers, and chessboard, and my own TV with cable. My playstation, nintendo, and my VCR.
> I will invite my friends over and play with my stuff. I will have a sofa and a resting chair. My game room will be large and cozy. My mom will be tired of hearing noise.
> One day I hope I do have a game room. I will watch TV all day, that is if I don't get in trouble. I hope my dream do come true.

This is what Rhonda writes:

> My Wonderful Room
> I have a large bedroom with my own bathroom. The walls are painted light purple and the carpet is a darker shade of purple. I have a white bed with a canopy. The bedspread is lavendar and white checked. My dresser and my desk are white to match my bed. My curtains are white with ruffles.
> There is a window seat where I can put my toys. I have shelves around the top of my walls where I keep my stuffed animals. There is a night stand by the bed with my clock and telephone.
> My stereo is set up against one wall. My TV sits beside my stereo. There is a collection of my CDs and movies. This is my dream room.

My students can only dream about bedrooms and game rooms that are a reality for some American children. Perhaps they see such rooms on television; I know they see them in a few of their storybooks.

Third Grade

As a writing assignment, I ask the children what I should tell my university students about being good teachers when I return to university teaching next year. Here are a few of their suggestions (edited for spelling):

"If people are bad give them a warning or send them to the principal."
(Haden)

"You have to be smart. You can't fool around. You care about your kids."
(Manuel)

"You can tell them it's a hard job." (Kelvin)

"Have self-control. It is also nice to be a class act." (Shantel)

"She should tell them how some people behave and some don't."
(Roland)

"Never be kind to the bad students." (Antinesha)

Fourth Grade

Next Monday is Dr. Martin Luther King Jr. Day. There will be no school.
We read a picture book about Dr. King's life to our classes. The fourth-grade
students particularly are interested when they are told what it was like on the
day Dr. King was murdered. I was a professor at the University of Wisconsin
during that time. I describe how everyone poured into the streets—students,
faculty, townspeople—and joined a procession of sorrow that marched up State
Street to the state capitol.

"Why did they kill him?" asks Tyler, a white boy. "He was for peace and
love."

I tell the class about the turbulent times after the assassination of President
John F. Kennedy and presidential candidate Robert F. Kennedy. Most of my
pupils were born in 1990–1991, so the events of the 1960s seem incomprehen-
sibly long ago to them. Verlin says, "Here's one good thing: We're different colors in this class, but everybody likes each other. That's what Dr. King wanted."

WEEK 20, JANUARY 16–19: PREPARING FOR HIGH-STAKES TESTS

Third Grade

We are reading a story in our balanced literacy series about a family (father, mother, and child) who arrive at an airport, check in, and proceed to the
departure gates. "How many of you have been to an airport?" I inquire. Three
students raise their hands.

"My stepdad took me on an airplane," says Jaron. "They sold hot dogs at
the airport."

"I was on an airplane when I was little," adds Shantel. "I don't remember
it, and it's a good thing, too. I'm afraid of heights."

"I kinda was at an airport," offers Manuel. "We drove past one once."

My pupils, except for one, have no prior knowledge of baggage tags, check-in procedures, security measures, airport design, "tugs" that push planes back, or in-flight and landing procedures.

We continue to be troubled by many of the storybooks in the reading series that Redbud adopted. They are about family vacations to out-of-town places, children at summer camps, music lessons, and other events and activities with which most of our students have had no experience.

Fourth Grade

The class roster continues to change. I have lost LaTonya, Danika, and Kamie, and soon I will lose Malcolm. Kamie's father, who objected to Halloween activities at Redbud Elementary, sent her to a private Christian school. The other three pupils have moved or will move to other states.

Today is report card day. Yolande is not present. Her report card shows that she has missed forty-eight days of school. She isn't ill; she just isn't coming to school. I have phoned Yolande's grandmother, and so has Ms. Dawson. The absences have been reported to the truancy officer. Yolande had the same high absentee rate in third grade and had to repeat the grade. No sensible person could hold teachers accountable for something out of their control, but that's exactly what some aspects of accountability do. Absentee rates are figured into a school score and reported on a school report card.

Verlin makes the honor roll again and pleads, "Please, Mr. Johnson, don't write on my report card that I talk too much. Then my mama will buy me something at Super Wal-Mart."

I write, "Verlin's talking contributes to our class discussions."

Third and Fourth Grades

We are becoming immune to the filth and odors in which we work. Our student teachers frequently comment on the condition of the building. Ms. Hammond says, "I could never teach in this dirty school."

Classroom floors go unmopped and sometimes unswept. It is not uncommon to see a teacher pushing a broom or squatting to scrub a section of the floor. The boys' bathroom has an overpowering urine smell that permeates the hallway. The girls' bathroom sinks are caked with dirt. The school has three custodians who double as bus drivers and cafeteria workers. One reportedly also works as an orderly at the Redbud hospital.

Third Grade

Haden has a headache, but, despite the throbbing, he cannot stay awake. "Do you want to call home?" I ask.

"I can't. They're at work."

"Can you call someone at work to pick you up? You seem very sick."

"I am sick, but I'm not supposed to call anybody," he murmurs.

I ask another teacher why some parents or guardians would want a sick child to sit at his or her desk all day rather than be at home in bed.

"It's poverty," is the answer from the veteran. "The parent can't afford to lose a day's pay or can't afford a babysitter, so the child sits in school."

In connection with our social studies lessons, my student teacher, Ms. Schwartz, wants to take the children to the local Dodge Museum for a field trip. The cost is fifty cents per child. Gerard becomes upset.

"I can't go," he cries. "I'm not smart and so I won't get a good report card and then I won't get the fifty cents."

Immediately Jaheesa tells Gerard that she has fifty cents he can have. Jimmy assures Gerard that he, too, has fifty cents at home and will bring it so Gerard can go on the field trip with the class.

The realities of high-stakes testing hit home today for the children, Ms. Schwartz, and me. We give a section of a practice standardized reading test. The children have forty-five minutes to read six selections and answer twenty questions. The items are designed to test skills such as main idea/details, sequence, cause and effect, character analysis, and so on. The test results are miserable. Only six children "pass" the test. If this had been the high-stakes LEAP test after summer remediation, fourteen of the children in my class would have to repeat the grade. The most surprising thing about the results is that three of my top readers did not pass. They are among the few who read at grade level, but this certainly was not apparent with their scores of 15 percent, 15 percent, and 10 percent. And the practice test is for second grade—not third grade.

Ms. Schwartz and I try to figure out what happened. Antinesha tells us that she did poorly because she had to take care of her baby sister all night. "I have to change her and feed her," she says. Other children misnumber many of their answers and therefore score low. Most of the children lack the prior knowledge to fully comprehend the selections. Several of the special education children who take the test lack the basic skills to complete even one section.

Some of the children were staring into space during the testing time, preoccupied with childhood daydreams or more serious thoughts. It is difficult to convince children that the results of high-stakes tests can alter their lives when many still believe in Santa Claus.

Third and Fourth Grades

We are heartened by the findings presented in *Education Week*'s (2001) annual *Quality Counts* report:

> Teachers are generally opposed to making decisions about student promotion or graduation based solely on state tests. Only 11 percent of teachers would support a policy to require that all students pass tests before moving up to the next grade; 88 percent said teachers and principals should consider test scores along with grades and their own individual assessments of students.... Sixty-seven percent of teachers said their teaching had become "somewhat" or "far too much" focused on state tests. And 66 percent said they were concentrating on tested information to the detriment of other important areas of learning. Seventy-nine percent of those surveyed had instructed their classes in such test-taking skills as pacing and filling in bubbles to answer multiple-choice questions. (20)

Why don't politicians, state department officials, and high-level administrators listen to the wisdom of the teachers? Teachers are with their children five days a week. They know the unnecessary stress brought about by the consequences of failing a test. They know that filling in bubbles will not help the students get through life. They know how the curriculum has been gutted of meaningful learning experiences such as art, oral expression, and other aspects of an education that can't be measured with a paper-and-pencil test.

Fourth Grade

Verlin informs me that he has not yet gone to Super Wal-Mart to find a small gift for his good report card. "My mama doesn't get paid until next Friday," he reports. "She says that we don't have enough for lunch money and a present, so we got to spend the money on food. When she gets paid, then she'll buy me something."

Today is Malcolm's last day at Redbud Elementary. He is moving to North Carolina. We sing "For He's a Jolly Good Fellow" and ask him to write to us. Malcolm says, "My birthday is February 7."

When one of my pupils has a birthday, I give a dollar to the child, who can then go first in the lunch line. Malcolm doesn't want to miss out just because he is moving. We break into a round of "Happy Birthday," I give Malcolm a dollar, and he goes first to lunch.

Ms. Hammond is upset. She asked the class to return a homework assignment with a parent or guardian's signature. Garrison Wright returns his signed, "Mr. Garrison."

WEEK 21, JANUARY 22–26: TEST TENSION BUILDS

Fourth Grade

The LEAP test frenzy is increasing. Every teacher gets a memorandum that reads,

> The State Department of Education is providing all schools a grant for re-mediation of all fourth grade students. They will pay teachers and/or tutors to teach students in a ratio of 5:1, and will provide a scripted guide and all materials. This is the first time any guide has been provided that is consistent with the LEAP test.
>
> As you can see with a ratio of five students to one teacher, we will need at least eighteen teachers/tutors at this school alone. We are planning to hold these classes on Monday and Wednesday since the Title I classes are already on Tuesday and Thursday. This will give fourth graders an opportunity to attend all sessions.
>
> Those working in this program will be paid by the hour an amount determined by the central office. If you will teach in this program let me know IMMEDIATELY since we must start as soon as we are able. This will continue until the week before the LEAP tests.

Students eligible for this new tutoring program are those who scored below the thirty-first percentile on the third-grade Iowa test. That totals more than ninety of the 120 fourth-grade students at Redbud Elementary. The "scripted materials" supposedly were written so that anyone with two years of college could do the tutoring. Many questions arise. Why did this pronouncement come only thirty-two school days before the LEAP test? Who wrote the scripted lessons? How much did this cost the state? Why are groups limited to five students? Where will the district find another eighteen people to tutor when there are already eight faculty members tutoring on Tuesdays and Thursdays? Will it ever dawn on State of Louisiana officials that the simplest, most sensible, and most humane thing to do would be to drop the LEAP test and thereby stop this scrambling for last-minute band-aids and quick fixes? Give the savings to the schools so that the teachers can purchase needed materials and supplies.

The $85,500 computer program that was going to "pinpoint" and "remediate" the skill needs of these same fourth graders is a lemon. Half the time the program doesn't work at all, and when it does work, it is a painfully slow collection of drill-and-practice routines. The fourth-grade teachers now skip most of their assigned computer times.

Fourth-grade teachers are given a stack of ninety-four-page Iowa test prac-tice booklets to use with our students before the March 12 LEAP test begins. To do so would consume dozens of hours of instructional time. Why are fourth graders being asked to practice for the Iowa test when they will be taking the LEAP test? The school's name should be changed to Redbud Test Preparation Center so that it more accurately depicts what goes on inside its walls.

Third and Fourth Grades

We receive a memo from the central office informing us of procedures to follow if we want to recommend students for art instruction. The form in-cludes the following seven evaluative statements about a student being consid-ered for the art class:

> Draws more than his/her peers.
> Draws better than his/her peers.
> Volunteers to do art or art-like activities.
> Deferred to by other students when drawing or making objects.
> Brings drawings or art made at home to school.
> Sets high standards of quality for his/her artwork.
> Reacts with interest and excitement to art activities and information.

Each statement is rated from 1 (seldom or never) to 5 (almost always). Each statement that receives a score of 4 or 5 must be supported by two ex-amples of the student's work, two statements of support (presumably written by the teacher), or one statement and one example. "In other words, when you are finished, there must be a TOTAL of 14 examples and statements. HINT: They will not accept drawings of cartoon characters such as Mickey Mouse, Donald Duck, or Pokemon, etc." The memo points out that a student must have a score of 34 or 35 to "continue to the next level."

We would like to recommend all our students for art. They need aesthetic experiences and outlets for their creativity. To recommend the sixty-six stu-dents in our combined classes would require writing 924 statements or assem-bling 924 pieces of student art or some combination of the two. The com-pleted "art screening instrument" and accompanying documentation for each child must be submitted by next Friday. We have been told by the veteran teachers that only fifteen students of the 611 enrolled in Redbud Elementary can be admitted to art class.

A 5:30 A.M., Shreveport morning television show features a Bossier City, Louisiana, school that has won a School Spirit Award. Scores of happy-appearing, jumping, shouting white children are in the school gym. They are waving large, oblong balloons. The school principal is interviewed. He exudes pride about the School Spirit Award and comments on achieving the school of academic distinction ranking. He points out that his school is in the top 1 percent of all the schools in the entire state. He credits bright students, fine teachers, and devoted parents. The camera scans the school playground, which is equipped with all the latest play structures. Inside the school building, the viewer is shown eager-looking children reading books. The principal praises their "great PTO," which just had a fund-raiser and bought a new state-of-the-art playground structure for the children to use at recess.

We know this school. It is fairly new and well maintained, and it serves a neighborhood of subdivisions with expensive homes. One of the teachers there told us that the principal likes to brag about the school's being a neighborhood school—not a magnet school like other schools of academic distinction. "But look at the neighborhood. Look at the beautiful homes. We should be a school of distinction. The children have everything at home," she reported. It is apparent to all American teachers that schools serving children of affluence, with few exceptions, have a much easier job than schools serving children of poverty. It is the schools of affluence that usually have the highest test scores, get the highest rankings, and receive kudos in local newspapers. They get all the goodies.

Third Grade

This same morning as we drive toward school, we notice that Jaheesa is not standing at her usual bus spot on Dr. Martin Luther King Jr. Street. Instead, she stands two blocks further on. In science class, we are talking about movement of seeds, animals (i.e., migration), and humans. Modes of transportation are discussed (e.g., train travel). Wendice says, "I walk along the train tracks and see crackheads." I tell him that walking along train tracks is dangerous and that he should cease the practice.

"Stay away from crackheads, too," I add. "They can do bad things to people."

"Somebody killed a woman last night," says Jaheesa, "right by where I live." A roomful of hands go up. Most of the children have heard about the murder. "The killer did this," Jaheesa reports. She draws her finger from one ear, across her throat, to the other ear.

The brutally murdered woman was forty-nine years old. A Shreveport television station interviewed the victim's neighbors, who exhibited fear because the murderer had not been apprehended. One neighbor told the reporter, "What scares us is that it is somebody among us." Our pupils at Redbud Elementary School always have much more on their minds and in their lives than academic skills. The murdered woman is the grandmother of a child in my third-grade class.

WEEK 22, JANUARY 29–FEBRUARY 2

Third and Fourth Grades

A headline of a front-page article in the January 29, 2001, edition of the Monroe, Louisiana, *News-Star* states, "Teachers get locked down but paid up: Educators bust out of schools for better pay." The article reports, "Glenda Joshua had to go to prison to get her freedom. The former public school teacher was frustrated with low pay and overcrowded classrooms, so she sentenced herself to teaching in the criminal justice system" (O'Brien 2001). The article points out that the starting teacher salary in Louisiana's criminal justice system is $36,400 and that teachers with twenty to twenty-five years or more of experience can earn up to $62,000. That compares with a starting salary in Redbud of $23,515 and a maximum for a teacher with twenty-five years of experience and a Ph.D. of $34,904.

The principal, Ally Williams of the Swanson Correctional Center for Youth, notes that he gets inquiries every week from teachers. His teaching staff is 100 percent certified, and class sizes are small. "We are obligated to work 260 days versus 180 days out of the year," Williams said. "We made more money because of that."

"There is no turnover here," Williams said. "When they come here, they never go back to public schools. Discipline out here is better than in the public schools. We don't tolerate a lot of things that go on on the streets" (O'Brien 2001, 1).

Something is wrong in Louisiana when teachers would rather teach inside a prison than inside a public school.

All Redbud Elementary teachers receive the following memorandum:

Teachers,

Try using the lesson plans given to you at the last faculty meeting for a week.

Review the two lesson plans and give your grade rep feedback (sections most useful, changes that may need to be made to better fit your grade level, etc.). We will meet with the grade reps next week to discuss the plans.

Third Grade

I take my paycheck to the local bank. The teller deposits it and makes the unsolicited remark, "That's not much money for a month's work." She should know. She sees a lot of monthly paychecks.

The children are resourceful. I finally receive a new pencil sharpener. The electric one that I bought for the class at the beginning of the year is now held together with many strips of masking tape and makes an ominous, high-pitched sound each time it is used. The electrical outlet is distant from the sharpener, and several children have accidentally knocked the sharpener to the floor when stepping over the stretched cord. The custodian installs the new manual sharpener on top of an old wooden cabinet. The first child to use the sharpener tells the class and me that the handle is on the wrong way. To use the sharpener, the child must crank the handle toward herself with her left hand. Several of the children know the solution to the problem. Jaheesa demonstrates. She squeezes around to the back of the cabinet so she can sharpen her pencil with her right hand moving the handle away from her. Too bad this type of problem solving isn't on the Iowa or LEAP test.

Ms. Schwartz and I take the class to the public library. We are somewhat apprehensive because even though the library is only a couple of blocks from the school building, we must walk, and there is a murderer on the loose. We give detailed instructions to the children. Ms. Schwartz leads the tight formation of pupils, and I, scanning in all directions, bring up the rear.

Fourth Grade

My fourth graders get excited when a packet of letters comes from their pen pals in a Chicago suburb. Today, everyone gets a letter except Rashand. Each child in my room writes a letter to his or her pen pal. Rashand writes this plea (edited for spelling):

> I need a new pen pal because I never receive any letter. Thats why I needed a new pen pal. I wanted a friend that I wanted to tell about the science fair and other things. And he could tell me what he's done and ask me when is my Birthday and tell me his. We could write more letters and show pictures or send them. Thank you for getting me a new pen pal.
>
> Rashand

Tony responds to a question from his northern pen pal by writing, "Now I am going to tell you a little thing. I don't stay with my mom, but I stay at my Grandmas house."

Many children write about favorite foods and games and what they like best about school. Only four of my pupils send pictures in response to requests from their suburban pen pals. Most of my class members simply do not have pictures of themselves. Dawnyetta brings a smiling photo of herself in second grade, and Emerald brings two dog-eared photos. One is a picture of her playing with dolls when she was in first grade. The other is a snapshot of a young woman in a white dress holding some flowers. On the bottom is written, "mother wedding day."

Third Grade

The children need a little brushing up on former presidents and traditional American symbols. When given a group of uncolored pictures for the month of February, Chikae colors Abraham Lincoln black, Antinesha colors a bald eagle green, and Manuel says, "I don't know Jack about this bell, but it looks like somebody dropped it." It is a picture of the Liberty Bell.

Fourth Grade

Earvin isn't in school today. Rachael and Lynette, who live near him, report that his house was on fire yesterday. "The outside is still standing, but the inside got all burned out. Somebody was cooking on the stove," reports Rachael.

I ask if the family is okay. Lynette volunteers, "Earvin's mama had a new baby a month ago, but they are all okay. But everything got all burned up." Mrs. Henderson and I will look into getting clothing for Earvin. Rachael and Lynette don't know where Earvin and his family are living. This is the second of my fourth graders to lose everything in a house fire.

Third Grade

Wendice hands me the following note:

Dear mr Bloomfield I womt my sons to ride your bus 44 to the boys and girls Club ever day
Nate and Wendice

I identify the handwriting as Kanesha's. I give the children a stern lecture on writing notes and pretending that they come from a parent or guardian. We talk about forgery. The children give several examples of people they have heard about who forge checks. The next morning, I find the following note on my desk from Kanesha:

> Dear Mrs. Johnson I am very very sorry. I had worte that note but I will not do it no more if he tell me to I am going to say no becase I do not wont to get in toubble by Miss. Dawson
>
> Will you for give me Mrs. Johnson please

Third and Fourth Grades

Each morning when we arrive at school, we see the cars of the veteran teachers: Mrs. Larson, Mrs. Quigley, and Mrs. Waverly. They always are the first to arrive and the last to leave. They participate in after-school tutoring—now four days a week. Their days begin at 7:00 A.M., when the doors open, and end close to 5:00 P.M.—except when there are meetings or when they attend additional university classes or professional development programs. These teachers are the backbone of Redbud Elementary School. These are the teachers who are especially galled when they hear politicians speak of support for "vouchers for students in failing Title I schools that do not improve their students' performance after three years. Such schools would be required to give a portion of their federal aid to students to enable them to attend another school, whether public or private" (Robelen 2001, 10, 42). These veteran teachers at Redbud can work no harder than they now do. They are dedicated, skillful teachers whom any school would be happy to have. These teachers perform heroically in helping children upward from a weak foundation, but schoolwide scores on a standardized test largely miss their hard work. Sometimes progress is measured in baby steps—not leaps. The implication of the voucher proposal, however, is that these teachers are failing their students.

There are many flaws in the proposed voucher plan. Proponents of vouchers do not recognize that many private schools will not want children of poverty. It takes a special adult to get physically close to children who don't always smell good, have skin rashes and open sores, wear dirty clothing, and have bleeding gums. It takes a special adult to get emotionally close to children who are unruly because of traumatic life conditions. It takes a special adult to come to work daily with the specter of poverty hanging over the classroom and to face the concomitant offshoots of poverty: poor nutrition, lack of medical care, inadequate housing, crime, and despair. Will parents and guardians who currently send their children to private schools to escape the problems we see daily welcome streetwise children of poverty to their sons' and daughters' safe havens?

In Louisiana, a $1,500 voucher, the amount proposed per child, would cover only one-third to one-half of the tuition of a private school. Who will pay the rest? The parents and guardians cannot afford the remaining amount. Why do some people assume that private school teachers are so much better than public school teachers that they can do what we cannot do?

SEVEN

FEBRUARY

PEP RALLIES FOR TESTS

WEEK 23, FEBRUARY 5–9

Third Grade

Something is on Randall's mind. When the class is given a creative writing assignment, he slams down his right hand on his desktop. Ms. Schwartz is working with the class, so I call Randall to a quiet corner of the classroom where there are two chairs.

"What's the problem, Randall?" I inquire.

"I can't write anything," Randall says huffily.

"Yes, you can. You've got a good brain," I reply as I point to his head.

"You think somebody who got all Cs and a D on his report card has a good brain?" he asks.

"I know you can improve your grades, Randall. I know the work that you can do when you want to. Is something bothering you?"

"I need a therapist," he confides.

"Why?" I ask.

"Because I can't sleep. I was up until 10:00 last night thinking about my new stepdad. I don't like him and he don't like me."

"Is he hurting you?" I inquire.

"He's not hitting me, but he watches war movies all the time and he makes me watch them. When somebody gets blown up, he laughs and says, 'They got him! They got him!' I don't think kids should watch that stuff."

"Can you tell him you'd rather read a book?" I suggest.

"He don't want me to read. But I have a little book hidden under my bed. Sometimes I can read that if it's not too dark."

The talk veers into areas that I promise to keep confidential. He says, "If you tell any of it, I'll get a whipping."

Randall seems to be calmer and goes back to his desk. Later in the day, however, I notice that he is staring off into space through teary eyes.

Fourth Grade

Earlier in the year, some students were disciplined for teasing Dario for smelling bad. He lives with his extended family in an old shotgun house in the country. Teachers say that the family may not have hot water. Today Dario's body and clothing odors are so strong that it is necessary to call him out of class. Ms. Dawson telephones the grandfather to take Dario home for a bath and a change of clothes. Dario is a bright boy and one of the best readers in my class. He is pleasant to everyone, and he doesn't seem to realize the extent of his family's poverty. I don't know if this continuing problem of a lack of cleanliness reflects a parental disregard of hygiene or some other factor.

Earvin is back in school this week. He tells me that his family lost almost everything in their house fire. "Now we are living with my aunt," Earvin reports in his soft voice and with his usual shy smile. He may be small in size, but he is big in courage.

All fourth graders take a "practice" LEAP test constructed from discarded test items from the past two years. I have seven students who go to special education each day because of low achievement. They, too, must take the actual LEAP test next month—even though several of them will not be able to read a word on it. Chalese, a nonreader, looks at her practice test and randomly draws lines that connect numbers. How can state officials such as Leslie Jacobs, a frequent spokesperson for the Board of Elementary and Secondary Education, require children with severe learning disabilities to sit through five days of an examination they cannot pass? Chalese's feelings of hopelessness are written on her face as she stares at today's practice test.

Third and Fourth Grades

Redbud police have arrested and charged a twenty-nine-year-old man in connection with the murder of the forty-nine-year-old grandmother. He lives one block from the murder scene, which some say is a crackhouse. The accused man has a son at Redbud Elementary School. The police suspect that other people may be involved in the crime.

Third Grade

Wendice smells strongly of cigarette smoke. The children tell me that they have seen Wendice smoking. I call him outside the classroom. "Wendice, are you smoking cigarettes?" I ask.
"Yes, ma'am," he replies.
"But you're only nine years old. Where do you get them?"
"My brother sticks them in my mouth."
"Tell him to stop," I say firmly. "By the way, you aren't working as hard as you should be," I point out.
"I know. I'm lazy," he states matter-of-factly.
At the end of the day, Wendice puts a note on my desk:

I love you
Mrs. Johnson
I'm very sorry
What I did
Bad thing
Not Working

Third and Fourth Grades

The Louisiana Department of Education has announced that any non-public or home-schooled students who plan to enroll in the public school system in grades 5 or 9 for the 2001–2002 school year must pass the LEAP test given in March. Those who remain in private schools or will continue to be home-schooled are exempt from the LEAP. Pam Porter, the principal, tells us that this policy is intended to keep public school students from transferring to a private school for a year to avoid taking the test.

Today the school holds two pep rallies. The first is for children in grades 1, 2, and 3, who will take the Iowa Test of Basic Skills next month. The children are brought into the gymnasium and are seated on the floor by grade level. They look so tiny and trusting. The first speaker, Mayor David Duncan, tells the children that a very important day is coming up. It is important for them and the school. "What day am I talking about?" he asks the children.

"Valentine's Day," a small voice responds. Many little heads nod in agreement. It is a poignant reminder that we are working with children. The oldest among them, with the exceptions of those who have been retained, has been on Earth only nine years.

The second pep rally is for fourth graders. Pam Porter begins by speaking about the LEAP test that the students will take on five consecutive days, March 12–16. She stresses the importance of each person's score to themselves but also to the school's rating. Next a panel of fifth graders who passed the LEAP test last spring present their tips:

"Stay calm. If you don't know one, go on to the next one."

"Get lots of rest and eat a good breakfast."

"Study hard every day."

"Listen to the directions."

"Don't be afraid of the test."

The mayor of Redbud, David Duncan, is the next speaker. He gives an inspirational speech. He tells the students how much he believes in them and their abilities. As a graduate of Redbud Elementary School, Redbud junior and senior high, and Grambling State University, Mr. Duncan is a positive role model for the children. He knows many of the fourth graders by name. Mr. Duncan is the youngest African American mayor in Louisiana.

Ms. Bridges, the reading specialist, is a superb storyteller. She enthralls the group with her yarn about Chester, a boy who is afraid to take tests. Ms. Dawson and two teachers have small roles in Ms. Bridges's story, and the 110 fourth graders howl with laughter. The pep rally ends with more words of encouragement from Pam Porter. Everyone leaves the gym in good spirits, having participated in a new phenomenon in American education: pep rallies for high-stakes tests.

Third Grade

Ms. Schwartz has been working with the children on adjectives. For a writing exercise, she tells them to write a paragraph with adjectives that describe themselves. Shantel writes,

> My name is Shantel. I am very smart. I can read very good right now I look like a monster. I mean look at me. Look at my hair. I have a head ful of curly fries that my grandma did. It is ugly. I hate it. I mean she can do better than this.

WEEK 24, FEBRUARY 12–16: TEST TROUBLES IN TEXAS

Third and Fourth Grades

On the weekend, we read an article in the February 2001 *Reading Teacher* titled "High-Stakes Testing in Reading: Today in Texas, Tomorrow?" The authors report the results of a survey of two hundred Texas teachers. One of the findings examined the effects of the Texas Assessment of Academic Skills (TAAS) on students:

> According to teachers, many students experience headaches and stomachaches while taking the TAAS. A surprising number are anxious, irritable, or aggressive. The data are troubling because discomfort and illness during the TAAS undermine students' test performance, further polluting the scores and decreasing their validity. It seems likely that low-scoring students would be the ones most negatively affected, which puts at-risk students in more jeopardy during TAAS testing. (Hoffman, Assaf, and Paris 2001, 487)

Three of the teachers surveyed by the researchers made these comments:

> I am very sad that education has stooped to the low level of measuring performance with standardized testing and Texas has taken it even lower with their TAAS. We know what works in education—we just seem to ignore the research and keep on banging our heads against the "TAAS wall" and retention walls.

> Please support teachers more than ever. Our children are hurting more than ever. If there was ever a time to change, it is now. Give teachers back their classrooms. Let them teach and spend quality time with their students. They need us!

> I believe that TAAS interferes with the very nature of our job. The pressure from administrators to increase campus scores leaves teachers little time for real instruction. My heart breaks to see so many teachers "just surviving." I believe that our solution is just to support each other because the public has no real concept of the situation. (Hoffman et al. 2001, 490)

Louisiana's accountability system is much more draconian. At this writing, Louisiana is the only state in the nation that mandates that fourth and eighth graders can fail the grade by failing the test. In the spring of 2000, when the policy went into effect, more than one-third of fourth and eighth graders in Louisiana failed the test.

We worry that our Redbud pupils will suffer the same problems being reported by the Texas teachers, only in greater degrees. In the Texas survey, 47 percent of students were reported to often or always develop headaches, 40 percent had upset stomachs, 38 percent showed irritability, 35 percent displayed increased aggression, 34 percent "froze up," and 29 percent vomited while taking the TAAS test (Hoffman et al. 2001, 487).

Fourth Grade

It is Monday morning of Valentine's Day week, and the children are eager to tell stories of "romance." The 4-H Club held a Valentine's dance on Saturday from 6:00 to 8:00 P.M. Detailed stories about who danced with whom spring from the mouths of volunteers: LaDelle danced with Rashand, Perry with Melissa, and Jaylene with Demetrius until another girl cut in. Joshua boasts that he danced with five girls. Nikeya is said to have worn a long, purple skirt. Antron stayed by the concession stand all evening, turning down invitations to dance. Settling down to schoolwork comes more slowly than usual today.

Fourth-grade teachers are asked to send home a booklet for each student's parent or guardian. Titled "Reaching for Results: LEAP 21, Grade 4" (Picard 2001), the twenty-four-page booklet contains sample mathematics and language/reading questions as well as sample student responses to writing prompts. Before listing ten test-taking tips, the booklet includes seven pages under the heading "Questions and Answers: Louisiana 'High-Stakes' Testing—*The Facts*." Two of the questions and answers are the following:

Q: Does "high-stakes" testing work?

A: Research from Texas and Chicago shows that Louisiana's policy—one of retention plus remediation—will work. In Texas, a study tracked 35,000 children who failed the state test in the 3rd grade. Some were retained; others were promoted. By the 5th grade, the students who were retained were achieving higher scores on state tests than students who were promoted. The study found that giving students the help they needed was what made the difference. Louisiana's policy combines retention with extra help for students. Some of the efforts include:

early intervention (K–3 reading and math programs) so we can fix problems early,
summer school,
after-school or Saturday tutoring,
smaller class sizes and transitional 4th-grade classes, and
incentives for teachers and schools to help these students.

These answers are misleading. No citations are provided for the research, and Texas won't even begin a policy of retaining all third graders who have failed the TAAS for two more years. So, which third graders who failed were retained, and why were others promoted in Texas? Furthermore, by the time the failed third graders reached fifth grade, they were a year older than the ones who had been promoted despite failing the test.

How does a K–3 reading and math program address the needs of retained fourth graders who failed the LEAP test? Are summer school and after-school tutoring programs "extra help" or punishment? Is it educationally sound to require students to give up their summer for several more weeks of test preparation drills? Who decides what is taught during these tutoring sessions? At Redbud Elementary School, we have seen no signs of smaller class sizes, transitional fourth-grade classes, or incentives for teachers.

> Q: With such an emphasis on testing, won't teachers "teach to the test" and ignore other topics important to the overall education of students?
> A: It is a fact that tests drive instruction. However, if the tests measure what students should know and be able to do, then it is appropriate that teachers incorporate LEAP 21–type work into their daily teaching.

The second question and answer imply that the LEAP test does measure "what students should know and be able to do." One might question whether tests measuring such state standards as the following are developmentally appropriate for fourth-grade children:

> Strand E: ECONOMICS: Interdependence and decision making
> Standard: Students develop an understanding of fundamental economic concepts as they apply to the interdependence and decision making of individuals, households, businesses, and governments in the United States and the world.

How many adults understand the notions of supply, demand, and scarcity; how the stock market works; or the causes and effects of inflation and recession? How many American adults know about foreign economic systems? Are adults aware of the fundamental concepts that undergird world economic interdependence? Most of our fourth graders never have been more than fifty miles from home. Where is the developmentally appropriate curriculum that would assist teachers in helping students grasp these economic complexities? We wonder who actually wrote these standards and what their experiences are with children.

Third Grade

Randall comes up to my desk. He looks especially disheveled this morning. "My mom and dad were fighting again last night," he tells me. "I was hiding under my bed. One of these days, I know I'm gonna hear a 'pow.'" Randall pulls an imaginary trigger on an imaginary gun.

Third and Fourth Grades

After lunch, all classes are called by grade to the gym. As the students file in, they are greeted by flashing lights and bouncy music. Standing in front with Pam Porter is a stylish gentleman in a coat and tie. The four large tables behind the man are covered with a black tarp, and the image of an order form fills a large projection screen. The children are subjected to a world-class sales pitch to sell "gifts" from a glossy, multicolored catalog. The catalog items include wind chimes, chocolates, magazines, candles, picture frames, stuffed animals, and more. Prices range from $4.50 to $19.95. The goal is for each student and parent or guardian to sell at least ten items or more between now and February 26. Doing so, the children are told, will earn the school a lot of money for new computers and software. Then the pitchman, like a magician, snatches the tarp to reveal the prizes the children can earn for reaching their quotas. The children gasp at the riches displayed on the table. He demonstrates a few: a small, handheld, battery-operated fan that can be used on hot days; a portable radio in the shape of a cell phone; and a lava lamp look-alike with swishing antennae. He begins his pitch by asking how many children can sell one hundred gifts. Every hand goes up. "We're not asking you to sell one hundred or even fifty or thirty—just ten. Sell only to family and people you know very well. Don't go out at night or knock on strangers' doors. Just sell to your relatives. They don't have to live in Redbud. They can be anywhere in the United States. How many of you can sell ten gifts by the twenty-sixth?"

Every hand goes up. Each class walks out in time to the peppy music as the strobe lights flash. Apparently, poor schools must subject children to this kind of pressure to obtain needed equipment that more affluent schools already have. If each of the four hundred children in grades 1 to 4 were to sell ten "gifts," that would amount to more than one "gift" for every adult and child in Redbud. Such unrealistic goals ensure failure for the children.

Fourth Grade

Yolande is back in school. She lives with her grandmother, who has adopted her. Yolande has missed more than seventy consecutive days of school this year. The Families in Need Service has an intervention this morning.

Yolande must either return to school or be removed from her home. Yolande is accompanied by her grandmother who says, "I will support you, Mr. Johnson."

In the classroom, the students give Yolande welcoming applause. Despite efforts by the school and the parish truant officer, she has been roaming the streets for the past three months. This repeats her pattern from last year, when she was a second-year third grader. As the day goes on, it becomes clear that Yolande is considerably behind her classmates in reading and writing skills.

WEEK 25, FEBRUARY 19–23

Third and Fourth Grades

There was no school on Monday because of the Presidents' Day holiday. Tuesday is a professional development day for the district faculty. Professors from a nearby university present sessions throughout the day. The morning begins with coffee and soft drinks in the corridor outside the high school auditorium. As we move toward the auditorium with our drinks in hand, we are stopped by Ms. Manzer, the elementary supervisor, who says, "No. No drinks in the auditorium. I had to help clean up the last time we had one of these. The mess was worse than junior high schoolers make." We quickly gulp our drinks, find a wastebasket, and head toward the auditorium. Mr. Green, the secondary supervisor, is the emcee. He introduces an associate dean from the university and Superintendent Miller. They give a few words of welcome and provide an overview of the day. Then Mr. Green informs the teachers that bells will ring so that sessions may begin and end on time. He reminds teachers to sign the attendance sheet if they have not done so.

One of us attends a session called "Teacher Collaborations." There are only two attendees at the presentation, and there are two presenters. One of the presenters suggests that the poor attendance makes his point that teachers aren't interested in collaboration and that many don't even know what it is. He doesn't seem to consider that teachers find other session topics of more immediate interest (e.g., dealing with stress, legal issues for educators, improving mathematics scores, and books for the elementary teacher).

The session is a nonstop insult to teachers. The presenters' handout states that some teachers "do not possess sharing skills, protect their autonomy and independence, lack a sense of efficacy, equate avoiding collaboration with avoiding conflict, and view it (i.e., collaboration) as little more than 'window dressing.'" An attendee points out that the teachers we work with want to collaborate but that there is no time during the day. One of the presenters glibly says, "Do it during your lunch hour."

"We must eat with our children and we have only twenty minutes to get their hands washed, get them in line, have them eat, line them up, and march them back to the main building to use the restroom and get to music or phy. ed."

"Well then do it after school," the presenter says.

"Most of the teachers tutor after school, have papers to grade and lesson plans to review, and several have an hour to drive before they get home," is the response.

"Hire substitute teachers," says the increasingly annoyed presenter.

"There's no money to hire subs," replies the attendee.

"Collaborate on a Saturday. I work on Saturdays," the presenter shoots back.

Other remarks from the presenters include, "Teachers are bickering and not listening to one another. Teachers' thinking is conditioned. Men in our study said that the women in their school don't have anything in common with them." And with hands flapping like an agitated fowl, "Teachers are teachers and kids are kids." In our experience, we have not found these over-generalizations to be accurate. The session is little more than a contemptuous view of teachers delivered in a haughty fashion.

Comments on the remaining presentations, with only one other exception, are favorable. Teachers report that the sessions are better than most they attended in previous years. The other exception is a session titled "Improving Reading Skills." This presenter antagonizes her audience by using language suitable for a kindergarten class, by demonstrating insipid ideas for extending reading experiences (without citing any sources), and by ending the session twenty minutes early. The presenter's lack of experience as a classroom teacher is evident, and her session would be useful to critics of education who call the profession "rinky-dink."

A note in teachers' mailboxes reminds us that the high school cheerleaders will be at Redbud Elementary on March 2 to judge the winning cheer for each grade. These are not cheers for a sports team. These are cheers for the Iowa test and the LEAP test. The cheerleaders will select the best cheers from grades 1, 2, and 3 and the three top cheers from grade 4. All these winning cheers will be presented in another pep rally on March 9—the Friday before testing week.

Fourth Grade

My homeroom students take a break from their academic studies to prepare their cheer. It is performed to the cadence of a rap:

"LEAP Test Cheer"
We're from Mr. Johnson's homeroom
We are the best

We're not afraid
Of that old LEAP test.
We have studied
We have learned
We have lots of energy to burn.
So bring on the LEAP
We are ready
We'll do our best
To stay cool and steady.
We're from Mr. Johnson's homeroom
We are the best
We're not afraid
Of that old LEAP test.

Third Grade

I had to fly out of town on personal business, and when I return to the classroom, the children are particularly noisy. Kelvin says loudly, "Be quiet, class. You should be glad Ms. Johnson's back. The plane could have run out of gas."

"Or somebody could have taken her hostage," adds Jimmy.

The third-grade classes will be taking a field trip to Shreveport in March. The cost per child, for transportation, admission to a science museum, and lunch, is $11.00. "That's too much money," says Cherise. I know that several Redbud third graders will not be able to afford the field trip.

Fourth Grade

Thursday is the last day that our student teacher, Ms. Hammond, is with us. This African American soon-to-be teacher has been a role model for the children. She is strong, talented, and caring. We have a little party with refreshments, and each child stands up and says a few words. Ms. Hammond's eyes are not dry for long. Jatoyia sings her rendition of a farewell song that puts a lump in everyone's throat. Each student presents Ms. Hammond with a colorful, homemade good-bye card. Here are texts of three:

> Dear. Ms. Hammond
> I will miss you so much if you leve. I mite evening cry until all of my tears are gone. Your the best stundent teacher i every had.
> One of your stundents,
> Nikeya
> P.S. Please come back a visit

Dear Ms. Hammond

I will miss you very much when you become a teacher you will be a good teacher and you can write real good. Please come see us and bring us some more red beans and rice you was a nice teacher.

P.s. Your very smart and beatifuls
Love,
Rhonda

Dear Ms. Hammond,

When I think of you I think about the fun we had together. Every night on my knees and pray I think about you was the most perfect student teacher we ever had and when you leave I will cry because that how much I love you. You is the best teacher! We will miss you!

Shonora

Ms. Hammond will not apply for a position at Redbud Elementary School because the starting salary in Minden, her hometown twenty miles away, is $6,000 higher.

Third Grade

Ms. Schwartz, our student teacher, also is leaving. She is getting married next month, and her surname will be Tremain. Antinesha writes in a card to Ms. Schwartz, "Mr. Tremain you have a good wife." Haden writes,

Mrs. Schwartz. Will you for give me for atticing bad in I hope you come in visit us and thank you for doing good shuff for us and thank you for teach us how to do math have a wedding you and Mr. Tremain and write back to us I'm going to miss you.

Jelani, a student in my class, has his picture in the local newspaper for being rescued from a fire. The caption under the photograph states,

Turshken Haskell of Redbud became an unsuspecting hero on Monday, February 19, when he saved the lives of eight people when their house caught fire while they were sleeping. Haskell was on his way to work just after 6 a.m. when he noticed a cloud of smoke at 677 Azalea Street. He kicked in the door and woke up 62-year-old Keela Spencer, then helped her get everyone out of the house. Minutes later the roof fell in. The Redbud

Fire Department could not save the house or the contents, but kept the damage down on neighboring houses. (Herring 2001b, 7)

Teachers bring Wal-Mart plastic bags of clothing and other items to my room for Jelani and his siblings. This is the third student in our homerooms who has lost everything in home fires this school year: Emerald, Earvin, and now Jelani.

WEEK 26, FEBRUARY 26–MARCH 2: "I WISH YOU PRAY FOR US ON THE BIG LEAP TEST"

Third and Fourth Grades

While driving through a Shreveport business area during the weekend, we spot a sign outside a commercial building that reads, "The Reading Center Can Help Students Prepare for the LEAP or Iowa." "More help for those who have the money," one of us mumbles.

Third Grade

One of the children asks me why we are taking the Iowa test. "Does anyone in the class know why?" I ask.

"The nation wants to see how smart we are here," replies Chikae.

"I'm not from Louisiana. I'm from Shreveport," notes Leon.

"Shreveport is a city in Louisiana," I point out.

"We take the test because the Iowa people want us to take it. They think they're so perfect," says Wendice.

"I think Iowa signed a contract with the government," suggests Antinesha. "The Louisiana test was too easy."

"I heard somebody named John in Iowa made the Louisiana test harder," Jaron tells us.

"They probably did," Gerard replies. "My grandma said she took a test that was so easy anybody could pass it. It had a picture of a tiger, a car, and a rhino, and the test said, 'Which one is a tiger?'"

"That really is easy," I add. "What if Redbud Elementary School doesn't do well on the Iowa test?" I ask.

Kanesha responds quickly, "Take the Louisiana test."

Third and Fourth Grades

Some relatives and friends send school supplies to the classes. The children write thank-you notes to the group. Here are some excerpts:

Dear Jim, Monica, Sharon, and Natasha,

Thank you for the supplies you gave us. You're such nice people. Not all people are nice.

Your friend
Derek

Dear Jim, Monica, Sharon, and Natasha,

I don't have much to say but let me get to the piont. Frist let me thank you for sent us the supplies. Mr. Johnson said that he told you that we are low on supplies. the wole class will have to thank him. We have a tset in two week and if we don't past it we will not go to the 5th gread. I hope everybodied past the Leap tset I got to go. Thank you for the boxful.

from Damien

Dear Jim Monica, Sharon and Natasha,

Think you for giving us the gift. You are a true friend. If you need anthing from us just come to the school and we will be there as soon you come in Mr. Johnson room. . . . We got a big leap test come up. Do your school have leap test. If we don't pass it we will be right there seting in the same sete again.

Thank you
Earvin

Dear Jim, Monica, Shawn, and Natesty,

Thank you for the wonderful Valentine gifts. I hope you can come and see us one day. God bless you forgiving us these great gifts. I will use the gift carefully in every way I can. I like the wonderful gift again and thank for being there. I wish you pray for us on the Big Leap test.

Love,
Rachael

Dear Jim, Monica, Sharon, and Natasha,

Thank you so much for the school supplies. We really needed them. I'm sure we will use alot. The pencil will be helpful on the Leap Test. If you are wondering the Leap Test is a test all 4th graders take. We study for it all year then it hits us in the face. Also my name Ashley. I am 10 years old and, my birthday is Dec. 11, 1990. I have three brothers and no sisters. But now you all have become a part of my family. I'll never forget you.

Your friend,
Ashley

Third and Fourth Grades

We read an article by Mark Walsh in *Education Week* about the British publisher, Pearson PLE, which has become a major force in American education. Within recent years, the publisher has bought all of Simon & Schuster's education assets as well as National Computer Systems, Inc., which is the nation's leading scorer of K–12 tests. Walsh states,

> As envisioned by the company, students will use Pearson textbooks and take tests produced and scored by the company. Teachers and administrators will track student achievement on Pearson school software. And parents will check on their children's progress on a school Web site developed by Pearson. (Walsh 2001, 8)

In the article, Peter Jovanovich, chief executive of Pearson Education, pointed out that now there are just five major school publishers, whereas twenty years ago there were twenty large U.S. school publishers. The article concludes with the observation that Wall Street believes publishers such as Pearson will benefit from the federal school accountability agenda:

> Mr. Jovanovich made the same point at the recent New York City gathering, displaying for analysts a quote from the President that called for state testing and school-by-school report cards. Said the Pearson executive: "This almost reads like our business plan." (Walsh 2001, 8)

One can imagine the lobbying power that such publishing giants could bring to bear in Washington and in state and local governments. In an article titled "Scholars Say High-Stakes Tests Deserve a Failing Grade," Miller (2001) notes that high-stakes testing suits the political imperatives behind accountability:

> Poor results in the beginning are desirable for policy makers who want to show they have had an effect. . . . The resulting overly rosy picture that is painted by short-term gains observed in most new testing programs gives the impression of improvement right on schedule for the next election. (A15)

This alliance, which merges the self-interests of politicians and state officials with those of big business, is unsettling. In both cases, children and teachers seem to be the targets of external pressure and influence. What may be good for votes and corporate bottom lines may not be so good for the future of the children we teach every day.

Fourth Grade

Tony tells me that he was in Baton Rouge on Saturday. "Oh, what did you do there?" I ask.

"Went to see my daddy with my grandma. We go a lot."

Tony's father is in Angola, Louisiana's maximum-security prison.

"Will he be there much longer?" I inquire.

"A long time. He might never get out. I look like him."

"Well then he must be a handsome guy like you," I say, "and it's good that you can see him often." One of the Redbud Elementary School teachers tells me that Tony's father is serving a life sentence for murder.

The pending LEAP test is beginning to show its effects on some of my students. Dario, who has not been ill all year, tells me every day that he has a bad stomachache. Carlonna tells me the same thing. Rashand tells me that he is so nervous he doesn't know what to do. Rashand failed the LEAP test last spring and summer and is now in fourth grade for the second time. I try to reassure him that he is a bright, capable boy who can easily pass the test this time if he will just relax and stop worrying about it.

Third and Fourth Grades

Today, class cheers are judged by the Redbud High School cheerleaders. First, second, and third graders perform Iowa test cheers; fourth graders perform LEAP test cheers. The winning classes will perform their cheers at the all-school test rally next Friday.

Third Grade

I'm getting closer to having an Internet connection in my classroom. An unidentified woman appears during class time to examine a computer. She reports, "You got a mouse problem here."

I say, "What's wrong with the mouse?"

She replies, "Not that mouse. A real mouse. It chewed through your cable. I'll get you a new one."

"Thanks," I say.

EIGHT

MARCH

TEST-DAY TRAUMAS

WEEK 27, MARCH 5–9

Fourth Grade

The morning begins with my homeroom students unexpectedly standing
and singing the "Happy Birthday" song led by Letrinette. Each child gives
me a homemade, self-designed birthday card. Dawnyetta's card says,

> Dear: Mr. Johsnon,
>   Happy Birthday I hope you have fun on your specail day. Thank you so
> much for teach us. I hope everyby pass the leap Test. But one more I didn't
> get you noting for your Birthday. But I will try really hard to pass the
> Leaptest just for you. Happy Birthday.

Dawnyetta failed the LEAP test last spring and summer, so she is in her
second year as a fourth grader. Later in the day, third graders bring me cards,
including one from Manuel that reads,

> Dear Mr. Johnson
>   I hope you have a better birthday than I did. HAPPY BIRTHDAY

127

One can only wonder what kind of a birthday Manuel had.

Fourth-grade teachers meet to review logistics for next week's LEAP test. Mrs. Larson and Mrs. Waverly, the two veterans among us, walk us through the process. We learn that testing will occur from 8:00 to 12:00 every morning or longer if any students need more time. The LEAP is not a timed test. We are given a sixty-eight-page test administration manual for fourth grade and are told that we must sign the oath of security and confidentiality statement, which also must be signed by the school test coordinator and the school principal. The penalty for breach of security is stipulated in the manual:

> Any teachers or other school personnel who breach test security or allow breaches in test security shall be disciplined in accordance with the provisions of R.S. 17:416 et seq., R.S. 17:441 et seq., policy and regulations adopted by the Board of Elementary and Secondary Education, and any and all laws that may be enacted by the Louisiana Legislature. (Louisiana Department of Education 2001a, inside cover)

We don't have any idea what the disciplinary actions are, but we think they must be severe.

We learn that the tests are kept secure at all times from everyone—including the teachers. Even during the administration of the test next week, teachers are not to look at the questions in the student test booklets—just at the administrator's manual—out of fear, perhaps, that we will help a student with a question. We are to walk around the room, checking to see if they are filling in their answer-sheet bubbles properly and sequentially, but we must do this without peeking at any student's test booklet. We are warned by the veterans that state inspectors could appear in our classrooms at any time to see that we are following the guidelines to the letter. No inspectors came last year, we are told. The security surrounding the LEAP test vaguely reminds me of my training exercises in the U.S. Army many years ago. I hope that I won't be handcuffed and led out of my classroom by state inspectors for accidentally letting my eyes fall on a student's test booklet.

Third Grade

I had to sign a sheet acknowledging that I took possession of a sixty-nine-page *Louisiana Statewide Norm-Referenced Testing Program: 2001 Test Administration Manual Grade 3: Iowa Tests of Basic Skills Form M* (Louisiana Department of Education 2001b). The manual contains a test administrator's security agreement, which I have to sign. As with the LEAP test, the security agreement also must be signed by the school test administrator and the principal. The manual contains the same warning about "breach of test security" that is included with the LEAP test. As I wade through the myriad rules and regulations in the evening, I note that even an "erasure analysis" policy is in force. Apparently, someone or something will examine the number of erasures and will note which incorrect answers are changed to correct answers.

There's more. Mrs. Marlow, a third-grade teacher, gives me the "answer folders" for the children in my classroom. Each contains a bar code and preprinted information. For the students who did not attend Redbud Elementary last year, I must supply Social Security numbers, birth dates, and other information. Each answer folder requires that my first initial and first four letters of my last name be printed under two sections that report the child's present math instructor and science instructor. Then I must fill in these ten bubbles with my number 2 pencil for each child: two hundred bubbles just for this section of the answer folder.

There's still more. On another day, Mrs. Marlow brings me an eight-page Deerborne Parish test security policy handout. The following excerpt reflects the tone and content of the handout:

> In the event the test booklets or answer documents are determined to be missing while in possession of the school, the school test coordinator shall immediately notify by telephone the District Test Coordinator. The designated school district personnel shall investigate the cause of the discrepancy and provide the Louisiana Department of Education with a report of the investigation within thirty (30) calendar days of the initiation of the investigation. At a minimum, the report shall include the nature of the situation, the time and place of occurrence, and the names of the persons involved in or witnesses to the occurrence. Officials from the Louisiana Department of Education are authorized to conduct additional investigations. (Louisiana Department of Education 2001b, 5)

With the test materials under lock and key and all the signing for manuals and the security oaths, it would take a more clever person than I to circumvent these procedures. I think back to my earlier years as a classroom teacher when giving a standardized test meant that I could use it as one measure of how my students were doing in comparison to other third graders across the country. It revealed some of my pupils' strengths and weaknesses—but I actually already knew them. Parents, teachers, and administrators understood that the tests were just one indicator of a child's progress. The message to teachers today is that people in positions of authority in state governments do not trust them. This seems to be another by-product of the accountability movement.

Third and Fourth Grades

Susan T. Herring, editor of Redbud's *Guardian-Journal*, describes a report issued by a team of experts with the Louisiana Small Town Program. The experts found that the biggest threat to Redbud is drugs. Their report stated that three illegal drugs are in common use: marijuana, crack cocaine, and methamphetamine. It also said the illegal use of alcohol and tobacco by minors was "extremely common, with some 80–90% of Redbud teenagers consuming alcohol. Some children as young as 9 years old were found to be using drugs and alcohol, and they estimated about 90% of all burglaries and violent crime in Redbud were related to drug use" (Herring 2001a, 1).

Most nine-year-olds are in third grade.

Third Grade

Mrs. LeGrande is looking for additional Iowa test prep booklets. I tell her that I have only enough for my class. She says, "Mrs. Quigley is really upset and she got on me because she has no booklets."

"I can share with another teacher," I say. "I thought there were enough for everyone."

This is the first rift I've seen among my colleagues since I have been at Redbud Elementary School. The pressure on teachers for the students to perform has manifested itself in faculty irritability. Mrs. Quigley is ordinarily easygoing and accommodating. Her remarks are out of character. The mood of the school and dispositions of some teachers have changed.

I test my pupils on several sections of the Iowa test prep booklet. During the test, Gerard comes up to my desk and asks, "Can you die of lead poisoning? I poked myself with my pencil."

"That's graphite in your pencil and you won't die," I tell him. "Now finish your test. You're being timed."

After the practice test has been completed, Kanzah comes up to my desk and asks if he can call home. "I went in my pants during the test," he says.

The results of the practice test are dismal. When I return the children's answer sheets to them, they see papers filled with red marks. "What happened?" I ask. "Only a couple of people did well on this."

"I don't know the words," replies Kelvin.

"I can sound them out," adds Jaheesa, "but I don't know what they mean."

"I can't read the math problems," comments Sam. "I'm good in math but not if there's words."

Third and Fourth Grades

We have worked hard with our pupils since last August, but we cannot seem to make up for lost experiences and large deficits in linguistic maturation. The language acquisition research of Eve Clark, professor at Stanford University, shows that children, on average, learn about ten new words a day beginning around age two. This gives them a speaking/listening vocabulary of fourteen thousand words by the time they are six years old (Clark 1993). According to Carolyn Kesslem, an experienced kindergarten teacher at Redbud Elementary, that's far from the case with the children at our school. Carolyn tells us, "They come to school lacking an understanding of even the most basic concepts. Many don't know what an apple is. They haven't been to grocery stores. An apple is more than something to eat. It can represent a circle. A lowercase *a* has a circle."

It is well established that preschool children acquire their vocabulary through verbal interactions with adults (Aitchison 1994; Ingram 1992; Pinker 1994). Ms. Kesslem tells us about Dario, my fourth grader who lives with his mother, grandfather, and two siblings. Before starting school, Dario and his siblings were locked in their trailer every time the adults left home. When he started school, he could barely speak and became panicky when he found himself alone in a room. Carolyn says that many of the children have television as their primary companion before entering Redbud Elementary School. Watching television is a passive—not interactive—activity.

Third Grade

Five sturdy boxes are delivered to my classroom. Inside the boxes are twenty new children's dictionaries. The pupils cannot believe their good fortune. There are colored pictures and contemporary entry words. What a difference some updated teaching materials will make.

Fourth Grade

LEAP test saturation continues across the fourth-grade classes. Oral language activities disappeared from our curriculum weeks ago. Social studies and science get merely a mention these days. Written language and math are the high-stakes test subjects. Any child who fails either of these tests must attend summer school and try again. If they don't pass the summer retake, they stay in grade 4 for another year.

The children are exhausted from all of the skill-and-drill overkill of the past weeks. They are not their usual ebullient selves. They are jittery and smile infrequently. There are more arguments and more physical confrontations among pupils. Students and teachers alike are showing the signs of stress. Little Jatoyia, a fourth-grade repeater who will take the LEAP test for the third time, says, "I want this LEAP over."

Third Grade

It's Friday afternoon, a few minutes from dismissal. Chikae raises his hand. "Can I bring my rabbit's foot to school to help me on the Iowa test on Monday?"

"Yes, you may," I say.

"No rabbits' feet" is one rule I did not find in the test manuals.

WEEK 28, MARCH 12–16: TEST WEEK

Third and Fourth Grades

Severe thunderstorms passed through Redbud last night. Many of the children, while exiting the school buses, tell us that they've been awake since 4:00 A.M. Some say they are afraid of storms.

As we enter our classrooms, we each are greeted by a double-decker appliance standing in front of one of the windows. It resembles a caboose tipped on end. Over the weekend, unbeknownst to teachers, someone installed new heating/air-conditioning units. Teachers were not consulted about the placement of these giants. In the third-grade classroom, a table holding two "down" computers has been pushed toward the middle of the room to make way for the contraption. In each room, the thermostats are above windows where they can be affected most by outside temperatures. We are somewhat intimidated by the units, which are six feet, eight inches tall, and one and a half feet wide. We don't know how to operate them. Teachers later report that as they passed out standardized test booklets, pupils could not keep their eyes off the mysterious mechanical strangers in their rooms. "They may as well have put a potbellied stove right in the middle of each classroom," comments Mrs. Larson.

Third Grade

After morning housekeeping duties, the school test coordinator brings me the Iowa test booklets. I must sign for them. I pass out the coded answer folders and read from the script in the administrator's booklet. As the children begin the first timed test, Kelvin vomits in his hands and runs to the bathroom. He does not complete the first section. I must document this. Gerard takes one look at the first section and begins to cry. He picks up his pencil and, between sobs, randomly fills in bubbles on the answer folder. I cannot comfort or encourage the children. I must read the words printed in boldface in my administrator's manual. Throughout the morning, I notice that even my best reader cannot complete the test sections in the time allotted. When the first day's test sections are finished, the test coordinator collects my stack and answer folders. Again I must sign my name to indicate that the materials have been collected. Then they are locked up in a location unknown to me.

Fourth Grade

The morning LEAP test consists of two parts. Part 1 asks students to write a descriptive essay of 100 to 150 words. They may use a dictionary and a thesaurus. Part 2 requires that the children use resource materials such as a table of contents, glossary, copyright page, and more. Each test counts for 20 percent of their total language score.

Before the children entered the classroom this morning, I placed a small pile of books by the desk of each student. This gives them something to read when they finish the test without going to the bookshelf. A few completers riffle through the books; LaDelle, Joshua, and Milo put their heads on their desks and fall asleep.

In the afternoon, the teachers compare notes about how things went. Each teacher mentions that several children finished the resources part of the test in a few minutes. "The child just went down the answer page filling in bubbles" is a recurring comment. Teachers report that numerous students wanted to ask questions about the two "constructed response" questions. Teachers are not allowed to look at the test questions, so we only can surmise that these two questions must be particularly difficult or ambiguously worded. Mrs. Waverly observes, "I've worked so hard with them all year, and some just raced through the test without even reading the material or thinking. I'm frustrated." The consensus among fourth-grade teachers is that a number of the pupils just seem to want to get the test behind them.

Third and Fourth Grades

Before school starts, the teachers' attention is briefly diverted from the Iowa and LEAP test administration under way. Immediately after the Pledge of

Allegiance, the intercom announces, "Teachers, grade reps will pick up your lesson plan books and grade books now. Thank you." This unannounced inspection of our planning and record keeping, amid all the test pressures, comes as a surprise. "I didn't even do a plan for this week," says Mrs. Waverly, "because all we're doing is the LEAP test. My plan book is at home." Others are worried because they've been following test prep booklets all week and do not have grades for the academic subjects in their grade books. The collection of these materials is another blow to teachers' sense of professionalism. Once again we're being monitored.

Third Grade

On the second morning of the Iowa test, the vacuum cleaner is whining in the hallway. The machine occasionally bumps our battered classroom door. After I turn in my plan book and grade book to the grade-level rep, I note that Sam has started to cry. "What's wrong, Sam?" I ask.

He sobs, "My dog got hit by a diesel last night and I had to bury him." Other children comfort Sam with tales of pets that have died. This seems to help. Now I must sign for and pass out the test booklets, or I will be behind schedule. Haden falls asleep between test sections. It is difficult to awaken him to continue with the testing. While the children are on a ten-minute recess, I hurry to the teacher's room to locate a form. Mrs. Marlow seems glad to see me. She is standing next to a cumbersome cart on wheels. The cart holds several closed boxes. "Will you watch these while I use the bathroom?" she asks.

"Sure," I reply. "Is there anything good in them?"

"The Iowa test booklets," she answers. "I'm not supposed to leave them unattended, but I can't get this big cart in the bathroom with me. I tried. There isn't room for me and the cart." I agree to guard the boxes for the few moments that she is in the restroom.

Third and Fourth Grades

In the evening, we receive an e-mail from a friend who teaches in Shreveport. He reports that during the day, he had been visited by a state LEAP test inspector who spent two hours in his classroom watching him administer the test to his special education students. What was the inspector looking for? What is the inspector's background in measurement and special education? This kind of needless monitoring hastens teachers' departures from the profession. If only the state inspector could have spent those two hours tutoring a child.

Fourth Grade

In the afternoon, when LEAP testing is finished for the day, I read a book to the children that gives some little-known facts about the U.S. presidents. "President Andrew Jackson didn't learn to read until he was fourteen," I tell the pupils.

A small voice from the back of the room pipes up, "He must have been dumb."

Perry asks if he can keep the LEAP test booklet when we're finished. "That is forbidden," I respond. "Everything must be returned to the state." We have completed the English language and math sections of the test by Wednesday. Mrs. Waverly, the fourth-grade test coordinator, spends hours collating the tests and answer booklets and matching their code numbers with a master list to be certain that everything is accounted for. Each day these test materials must be locked up until they are sent to the state. "Do you get paid extra for this?" I ask her.

"Of course not," she answers. The only people who don't seem to get paid for the extra work are the teachers. The test developers, publishers, vendors, and scoring firms are cleaning up. So are the private test preparation enterprises for the well-to-do and the writers of test prep booklets and software sold to the schools.

Third Grade

It is the last day of the Iowa test. As the pupils fill in answer-folder bubbles, a child sneezes. "Bless you," says a chorus of third-grade voices. The voices remind me that in the stark, serious realm of standardized testing where our pupils, our teachers, and our schools will be judged without compassion, I am working with children.

While I was not watching, Antinesha used a pen instead of a number 2 pencil for some answers in a test section. I must report this to the test coordinator. When I do, she says, "I'll have to call the state to find out what to do."

Antinesha is crying. "Why did you use a pen instead of the pencils?"

"Because these pencils aren't any good. You can't erase good with them, either."

"You didn't finish a lot of the test. Is something bothering you?" I inquire.

"My grandpa fell and hurt his leg last night and has to have surgery." Antinesha is close to her grandfather. Her father does not live with her, and she never mentions him.

Fourth Grade

After each of the four subject-matter tests on the LEAP, students answer a fifteen-item multiple-choice questionnaire. For some reason, the manual directs teachers to read these questions aloud—even though we were not allowed to look at the test questions. I surmise that they want to make certain these questions are answered by everyone because several of them gather data about the teachers. Questions ask children how often they use the library for pleasure or research (we have no library at Redbud Elementary), whether they receive comments from their teachers about their writing and suggestions for improving their writing, and how often their teachers explain in writing how their social studies work will be graded. The state appears to be using young children to snoop on teachers.

The LEAP test finally ends at midday on Friday. The children are exhausted and relieved that it is over. Rashand says, "Mr. Johnson, my brain hurts." Dwayne, De'Lewis, LaDelle, and Nikeya smile for the first time all week.

"Will you grade these this weekend?" inquires Jaylene. Students seem shocked to know that they will have to wait six or eight weeks before learning whether they passed.

Mrs. Larson, the foundation of the fourth grade, has organized a "field day" this afternoon to celebrate the completion of the LEAP. With the help of about thirty parent volunteers and the fourth-grade teachers, the children rotate among eleven game stations. The games include football toss, relay race, potato race, tug-of-war, drop the clothespin, and others. Following the games, everyone receives a can of soda, a bag of potato chips, and a piece of candy. We teachers are thrilled to see the children being children again: running, laughing, and having a good time.

Third Grade

The children must complete a questionnaire at the end of the Iowa test. The test administrator's manual tells me that I can read the questions and choices to the pupils. Some of the questions ask about computers in their homes (most of my pupils have no computer), calculators (we have no calculators in my classroom, and most have none at home), library use (we have no school library), and attitudes toward art (we have no art classes). This is one section of the Iowa that all the children can complete confidently.

I collect the answer folders, math scratch paper (which must be turned in to the test coordinator), and test booklets. I tell the children that we now are finished with the test. "Thank you, Lord," says Wendice.

WEEK 29, MARCH 19–23: THE TESTING NEVER ENDS

Fourth Grade

Yolande, who has been absent nearly ninety days this year, missed three of the five LEAP test days. This week she has missed the two makeup days. The State Department of Education is called about this matter. Their response is that Yolande will get a zero on the LEAP test, and this zero will be part of the calculation of Redbud Elementary School's rating. Yolande lives with her grandmother, who has adopted her but seems to have little control over her. The school has reported the situation to social services numerous times.

My students are in a bad mood this week. They argue and fight. After five days of LEAP testing last week, this week they face three days of Iowa testing. The Iowa testing is mandated not by the state but rather by Superintendent Miller, who wants to compare Redbud Elementary fourth graders with those at Hines Elementary, another school in the parish. All this testing has produced increased agitation and anger. Everyone's nerves are frayed, including the fourth-grade teachers'. I hope that spring break next week will have a calming effect because we have learned that following the vacation there will be two more days of LEAP testing. Its purpose is to "field-test" next year's LEAP test.

Third Grade

Several staff members are in a state of near panic, especially Pam Porter, our principal, and Mrs. Marlow, the third-grade test coordinator. A third-grade Iowa test booklet is missing during the "official count" of the test materials being readied for the Department of Education in Baton Rouge. This is taken seriously. The rumor is that the state will send someone to Redbud Elementary to give polygraph tests to determine who took the book. This is yet another manifestation of the paranoia about test security. Why should anyone care if a booklet is missing? The testing is over. What market value could an old Iowa test possibly have? Classrooms are being inspected. Trash in the Dumpsters is being opened, and Mrs. Marlow, wearing latex gloves, examines it piece by piece. We have never seen anything like this in all our years in education. This is another offshoot of high-stakes testing and the labeling of children and schools.

One of Jimmy's teeth broke off. Leon has a wet paper towel applied to a sore tooth, and Cherise has a bleeding lower gum around a tooth.

During math class, Randall sits so that the soles of his shoes are visible to me. The toe areas on both shoes are worn through. Fragments of dirty white socks can be seen as well as some bare toes. I don't know how long his shoes have lacked bottoms.

Fourth Grade

On the second day of the Iowa testing, Letrinette, who is one of the best students in my homeroom, slams her pencil down and says, "Please, Mr. Johnson, can't we just stop taking these tests?" Her face is contorted as if in physical pain.

"Just one more day," I assure her. "Tomorrow they'll all be over, and then we'll have a one-week break." I don't have the heart to tell my pupils that two days of LEAP pilot testing will occur on the Monday and Tuesday after the break.

Mrs. Larson continues to enlist community support for our fourth-grade students. She arrives at school at the end of the week with several large boxes of potato chips. Mrs. Larson has convinced the local Brookshires to contribute the chips. She also got cans of soda and boxes of candy from Deerborne Electric. This afternoon, the students will have a treat to signify the end of another round of testing.

Third Grade

Mrs. Newburg, a special education teacher, has given Jelani an individualized diagnostic reading test. She tells me that Jelani has climbed from the kindergarten level at the beginning of the year to a current second-grade level. This remarkable gain will not show up on the Iowa test. He remains below grade level.

Pam Porter calls me to her office. A man is sitting in the corner of the room. She says that he is waiting to collect the Iowa test materials. She also tells me that she has received word about the child who used a pen for some items on the test. I must recopy all the child's answers using a pencil. Pam is too kind to tell me to do this immediately, but the man in her office is hint enough. I take the child's test to my room and a blank answer folder. I must have a witness watch me and check my accuracy and honesty—even though I do not have a test booklet. After the dismissal bell rings, I fill in 427 bubbles with a witness at my side.

Fourth Grade

Several friends and relatives have contributed money to buy art supplies for the children of Redbud Elementary. Huge boxes filled with tempera paint, finger paint, sidewalk chalk, watercolors, colored pencils, scissors, modeling clay, and more have arrived. We will soon have time to use the supplies with testing skill and drill almost behind us. The students write thank-you notes to the contributors:

Dear Chris and Shelley,
 Thanks for the glue, the scissors, and the other wonderful stuff.
 We enjoy all the art supplies. One day come and visit us. We have two teachers. They are Mr. Johnson and Mrs. Avalon [my new student teacher]. They work us hard and the art supplies give us a brake. In school last week we took the Leap test. It is a test that sees if we past the fourth grade. I like test but not that one. Bye and thanks again.
 Sincerely,
 Letrinette

Dear Kirk and Laura,
 I would like to thank you for all the hard work you did for us. If you didn't pitch in we wouldn't know what we will do. Any time we have stuff in the classroom it always come up missing. We don't like that. We want our classroom to be just like other classrooms.
 When you have free time may you come visit us. On Apr: 17, I will be 10 years old. I hope I have a good time on Sunday. Last week we had the Leap test. We had to take it Monday March 12 through the 16. Most people thought Science was the hardest. Then most people thout math was the easiest. I would like to thank you again. Thank you! Thank you! and Thank . . . you! . . .
 Yours truley,
 LaDelle

The LEAP test continues to be evident in nearly everything the pupils write.

Third Grade

A Redbud law firm donates money so that several third graders can go on our field trip to a science museum in Shreveport. As we ride down Interstate 20 in the school bus, life is good. The pupils tell me "why did the chicken cross the road" jokes, sing to themselves, and squeal with delight as eighteen-wheeler drivers honk their air horns. The children are amazed by the sights and sounds of downtown Shreveport. They crane their necks and point their fingers in all directions. If only our benefactors could see the joy in their faces.

Third and Fourth Grades

The Louisiana house and senate passed legislation to increase taxes on riverboat casinos to pay for teacher salary raises. An article in the *Times* by Dan Turner states, "'We were at a point in our educational system that, if we didn't do something, we were going to be a backwater state forever,' Governor Mike Foster said, explaining his willingness to use gambling money for education" (Turner 2001, 1A). So next fall, the teachers will begin to receive their $2,000 pay increases.

The *Ruston Daily Leader* reports that far more fourth- and eighth-grade students repeated a grade in 2000–2001 than in the previous year:

> Cecil J. Picard, state superintendent of education, said the high number of students held back showed that the test did what it was designed to do: Identify students who need to improve basic skills. One goal of LEAP is to halt so-called "social promotion" or passing students who cannot handle the work. "We're sorry to see the high number of students held back this year, but are pleased that high-stakes testing is doing what was intended and that students are now getting help," said Picard. ("Officials" 2001, 1)

A new euphemism has been coined: "being held back" in place of "failing." And failure is interpreted as success. The article indicates that 17 percent of fourth graders were held back, the number varying by parish. For example, in Orleans Parish (New Orleans), 40 percent of fourth graders were held back. The actual number of students who failed the grade is probably higher because the statistics released did not take into account students who left the state or switched to private schools. We await the news from this month's LEAP testing to see how many more "successes" will be revealed. If we were in charge, we would not be happy about these large failure rates. Instead of examining teachers, we would be reviewing the test itself and the entire testing policy. We would be putting all the accountability money into preschool education and adequately staffing classrooms and giving teachers the instructional resources that they need.

At the end of the week, two newsletters are in our school mailboxes. Redbud Elementary School's *Balanced Literacy Newsletter* (March 21, 2001) contains the following comment:

> Survival
> We did it! We survived *the tests*. Even with all the tears and upset stomachs, we survived. Now maybe we can get back to teaching kids. (1)

The other newsletter is an eight-page tricolor brochure, *Reaching for Results*, from the Louisiana Department of Education (2001c) printed at a cost of $7,400. In the brochure, Superintendent Picard is quoted: "Our students are performing better. Our teachers have never worked harder. If we stay the course, Louisiana's future has never looked brighter, but we must stay the course" (7).

Mrs. Waverly holds up *Reaching for Results* and asks a group of teachers, "Did you see the cost of this? If we had $7,400, we could buy a decent copy machine. Then our kids could read better because they wouldn't have to strain their eyes trying to decipher the faint purple ditto sheets we are forced to use."

NINE

APRIL

FREEDOM TO TEACH AND LEARN

WEEK 30, APRIL 2–6

Third and Fourth Grades

The week begins the day after April Fool's Day, and the children are filled with tricks. We are told that we have spiders crawling on our heads, worms on our legs, and roaches in our ears. As funny as the pupils find these gags, we know that they aren't beyond the realm of possibility.

Fourth Grade

The children tell stories of their various escapades during spring break. Joshua boasts about all the fish he caught in Lake Deerborne. Perry and Derek recount several successful squirrel hunting expeditions in nearby woods. LaDelle received a surprise birthday party attended by her cousin Antron and other family and friends. The stories could have continued all day. Our pupils are first-rate storytellers, and they enjoy hearing as well as telling a good tale. We begin rehearsals for a play developed by Ms. Avalon, my new student teacher. It is based on a parody of the Three Little Pigs. The play is a "courtroom drama" with a judge, bailiff, lawyers, witnesses, defendants, and a jury. Everyone in class has a part. Later in the week, we present the play to the other fourth-grade classes who find great humor in the play and especially the verdict when the wolf is found innocent of all charges. The play grew out of a social studies discussion of trial courts and appellate courts. I have been surprised by how much the pupils know about legal matters. They report watching several courtroom shows on television.

Third and Fourth Grades

A faculty meeting is held after school on Monday. The school must participate in a Louisiana Department of Education–mandated self-analysis. We are told that we will follow the School Analysis Model (SAM) (Louisiana Department of Education 2005) provided by the state. A teacher committee is charged with disseminating and tabulating questionnaires and arranging for faculty focus group discussions. An administrator from the district explains that we must do this because we probably will be designated a "school-improvement school." This is a bad label. It incorporates three levels. In level 1, changes will be required. We don't yet know what those changes will be, but they might include the reassignment of teachers within the district. In level 2, which is worse, "distinguished educators" will be sent to the school to turn things around. If we are designated a level 3 school, the bottom of the barrel, the state government will make changes for us, which could include closing down Redbud Elementary. "Where will 611 children go then?" a teacher asks.

"I don't know," the administrator responds. "It could be a veiled threat." The teachers are given a sixty-item questionnaire to complete by the following day. All teachers must sign for the questionnaire when they receive it, and they must sign again when they turn it in the following day between 2:30 and 3:30 P.M. Although the questionnaire is anonymous, a teacher/monitor has been assigned to a room to receive the questionnaires and signatures. Some of the items on the questionnaire are ambiguous, and a response would require clarification, but no room is provided for comments. For example, "Students at this school can do better school work than other students." Other students where? Does the item mean our students could do better if provided the requisite resources for teaching and learning? Does it mean they can do better than students at an even poorer school (if there is one)? At a selective magnet school or laboratory school? Of what use could such opinions be when they are suffused in such ambiguity?

An article in the *Times* ("Orleans Plan Would Dismiss Uncertified Teachers" 2001) describes the plans of the Orleans Parish (New Orleans) school board to comply with the state's accountability program. Orleans Parish had forty-seven schools ranked as "academically unacceptable." The problems they face were documented:

> Nonetheless, there is no way the school system will have enough seats in its better-performing schools to provide true choice for 17,000 students now at unacceptable schools. . . . If students still want to leave unacceptable schools, they can participate in a lottery for about 650 seats. (6B)

We wonder what is going to happen to the other 16,350 students sitting in these unacceptable schools in New Orleans who don't win the lottery. The accountability mavens have a lot of issues that need revisiting.

The Orleans Parish school board also "plans to get rid of all uncertified teachers in its eight lowest-performing schools and offer $8,000 more per year to attract new principals to those campuses next year" ("Orleans Plan Would Dismiss Uncertified Teachers" 2001, 6B). Perhaps the board should consider giving some of that extra money to the hardworking teachers they presently have or to the new teachers they must find to replace the dismissed, uncertified teachers.

Fourth Grade

Letrinette brings a baseball-size snow globe to my desk. It is an underwater scene with a mermaid. The glass is broken, and the liquid and most of the glitter are gone. "I got this from my auntie, but it broke in my backpack," she comments with sad eyes.

"It's beautiful," I tell her. "Wrap it carefully, and maybe you can get a new globe for it." All day the broken globe sits on Letrinette's desk covered with a paper towel. I often see her peeking under the towel at her possession.

We have noticed all year that children rarely bring things to show. Perhaps it is because they have so few material things that they can show. We also have noted that when the pupils are given small gifts from us, they immediately hide them in coats or bury them in backpacks. They do not display the gifts for other children to see.

Two days of LEAP test "field testing" are mandated now by the state. My students have lost all zest and simply go through the motions of taking these tests of reading, writing, proofreading, and using reference materials. They have been taking standardized tests since March 12. While the children are writing, I thumb through the administrator's manual. The purpose of this test is to determine the best items to include on the LEAP test for next year. A statement on the manual says that the cost for printing it was only $2,560; however, it also indicates that eight forms of the LEAP test are being field-tested in grades 4, 8, and 10. That's a total of $61,440 just for printing field test administrators' manuals. This does not include the cost of each thirty-six-page student test booklet. The manual states that a Minnesota company, Data Recognition Corporation, conducted the "development and implementation of educational assessment procedures" for the Louisiana Department of Education, Division of Student Standards and Assessment. We have no clear picture of the total fees paid by the State of Louisiana to the Data Recognition Corporation. We have been told by a state legislator that Louisiana will spend more than $56 million each year on its accountability testing program. We can't begin to estimate the additional costs being paid by school districts for expensive electronic and print materials purchased in the hopes that students will get higher test scores. This troubles us in a school that has no hot water for the children, no library, no playground equipment, no art classes, a shortage of textbooks for each child, and uncertified teachers in some of the classrooms.

Third Grade

I read the book *Follow the Drinking Gourd* to the class. It is a story about how slaves escaped to freedom by looking for the Big Dipper (the Drinking Gourd) pointing toward the North Star. The children are intrigued by the story and are surprised to learn that stars can make a shape. I introduce the word "constellation" to them. I go to the donated encyclopedia set to look for examples. The "constellation" entry is text only. I still do not have an Internet connection. I try to draw a few constellations on the chalkboard. I do not want to be resentful, but I think of a well-funded laboratory school in a nearby town that can turn children away. Parents must apply to send their children to the school. Some parents put their children on the waiting list when they are born. There is a planetarium adjacent to the school building. This school is labeled a "school of academic achievement" by the state.

Leon falls asleep during math class. Shantel, who sits next to him, suddenly swats his arm. "What's the matter?" I ask.

"Leon's got a roach on his arm." I get my flyswatter.

While I am on recess duty, one of my pupils comes to me and tells me that his mother has left home and that she hates him. Another of my pupils is standing by me. "Don't worry, it's okay," he tells the distraught child. "My daddy hates me. He hasn't seen me or talked to me since I was six months old." He puts his arm around the upset child. There is no school counselor at Redbud; the children and I have assumed that role.

WEEK 31, APRIL 9–12: RICH KIDS, POOR KIDS

Third and Fourth Grades

Every day in Redbud, Louisiana, we are surrounded by the sights, sounds, smells, and feel of poverty. We have come to know our students and their parents and guardians, and often we are struck by their humanity—their generosity and caring for others despite their material deprivation. We find it difficult to feel sympathetic toward a family we read about in the Saturday *New York Times* (Yardley 2001). The reporter describes an Austin, Texas, family that lives in a $667,000 four-bedroom home. The surgeon husband/father earns about $300,000 per year. The wife/mother spends her time "chasing children and ferrying them to schools, doctors, and soccer games" (A8). The family spends about $26,000 a year for a nanny. The physician became concerned about family finances and assigned his office manager the task of running the family budget. The manager now gives the mom an allowance every other week. "We have a good life," she added, "and yet we still have the same struggles as other people. I feel like a lot of the time we are treading water." When school closed for spring break, "everybody I know went to Colorado and Utah. We drove to San Antonio for the day and took the baby to the zoo" (A8). The couple gave the reporter a tour through an area filled with mansions. "The message was clear: They are rich, not us" (A1). The family is looking for another home but is "having a hard time finding a five-bedroom house in a neighborhood they like for less than $1 million" (A8).

Author and social critic bell hooks (2000) explained the feelings of deprivation experienced by the well-off:

> A number of "rich" individuals I interviewed emphatically expressed that they did not see themselves as rich. They would point to friends and colleagues who have billions. In all cases, they judged their class status by those who had more rather than those who had less. . . . If privileged people feel "lack," there is no reason they should feel accountable to those who are truly needy. (76)

As long as individuals with means can feel deprived by looking at those who have more, we may never expect generosity or understanding for the American children who attend a school like Redbud Elementary. Something tells us that most of the mansion crowd does not care one whit if our pupils have a library or hot water in their school.

Third Grade

Leon cannot seem to stay awake today. "What time did you go to bed last night?" I ask.

"I went to sleep at 2:30," he responds.

"That's too late for you. What were you doing until 2:30 in the morning?" I inquire.

Leon says, "I couldn't sleep because it was too noisy. River Bottom always is noisy when it gets hot outside."

Third and Fourth Grades

Ms. Dawson calls each grade level into the gym to give a lecture to the children about their behavior. The pupils have spring fever. They are becoming increasingly restless. Spats and tattles are on the rise. Ms. Dawson is trying to keep the lid on. As a part of her lecture, she asks several children to stand as she reviews the school's dress code. The children, relieved to be dressed according to code, are heartbreaking. We have become inured to our pupils' clothing. We don't notice the hand-me-down men's pants that some of the third and fourth graders wear. We are so accustomed to holes in shirts, socks, and shoes that they have become part of the uniform. Our perceptions have changed. It is only when we see the children from a distance—spatially and psychologically—that we notice the condition of their clothing. Many are pitiful to look at. Children of affluence would consider some of our pupils' clothing rags, or they would buy expensive take-offs on the baggy pants, tops with holes, skirts faded from too many washings, and oversized shoes. We know what is under our students' attire: courage, resilience, and expectations that everything will turn out all right.

We have found that art projects have a soothing effect on the children. Teachers who want to integrate art into the curriculum must buy the supplies out of their own pockets. There is no budget for materials. This year, Redbud Elementary is a bit more fortunate because of art supplies we have received from contributors. Today we combine our classes and have them paint rocks that they have found in their neighborhoods. The medium is tempera paint, and the message is to create any object—real or imaginary—from the rocks. The children are intrigued with the process of applying paint to a variety of surfaces. The room is silent as all concentrate on the project. Their works of art include a piece of pizza, a cave, a whale, a ladybug, a hillside with flowers and a snake, a rat, a racing car, and more. The pupils take great care with the paint and brushes—not a drop of paint is wasted, and the brushes are thoroughly cleaned. Word spreads quickly throughout the school about the art project. Teachers and administrators visit the classroom to view the works of art and congratulate the artists. As they finish their works and put them on the drying tables, the students chatter about the lucky people who will receive these treasures. "My mama's getting this one because she likes turtles," says Milo with a smile.

"My asteroid is for my brother," adds Dwayne.

"I made this one for you, Mr. Johnson," offers Earvin. It is a rock with a red "J" on a black background. Even though Earvin just lost everything in a house fire, he is willing to part with something that he made with pride.

Third Grade

We are completing our daily oral language exercises. We talk about the difference between language that might be used at home and language that is used in school and "in public." Jimmy says, "My uncle was kicked out of a fancy restaurant because he used home talk."

"Really?" I asked.

"Yes, ma'am. He was on his honeymoon, and he said stuff he'd say at home, so they kicked him out."

Fourth Grade

The class has received a new batch of letters from their Illinois pen pals. They spend time composing, proofreading, and revising their responses. Here are a few excerpts:

Dear Julie,
  I am Milo. My birthday is July 15. I am 10. I have brown hair green eyes. I have two dog's Killer and Rough. Do you know youre REAL DADDY? I'm going to meet mine next weekend. Well I got to go
Bye.
Your friend,
Milo
P.S. I can't send a picture yet.

Dear Dan,
  Hi. It's me Verlin. This Saturday, my mom is getting married. I will be so happy for the first time for my mom to get married. Yesterday I got a new shirt. In summer I will try to write you.
Your pen pal,
Verlin

Dear Jasmine,

We had to take the Leap Test. But you didn't have to. I wish I could stay up there. When I grow up I want to be a teacher. To show how smart I am. What do you want to be when you grow up? How is the weather? P.S. I hope you have a good spring break.

Your pen pal,
LaDelle

The Illinois pen pals never responded to the letters.

WEEK 32, APRIL 17–20:
HOW POVERTY RELATES TO TEST SCORES

Third Grade

Today I'm disgusted with no one in particular but with conditions in general. The time off for religious holidays has removed me from the harsh world of Redbud Elementary for a few days. Now it hits me hard. Jelani has been ill all day with a high fever. He has tried to reach someone at home repeatedly, but there has been no answer. There is no place for him to lie down, and there is no school nurse. She is at Redbud Elementary School on Tuesday mornings only. Mrs. Tomah, my second-semester student teacher, dampens a coarse, brown paper towel soaked with cold water and applies the towel to Jelani's forehead. He stays slumped over at his desk all day.

There is a bright spot today. We finally got our Internet connection—five weeks before the end of the school year.

Third and Fourth Grades

Eighty-year-old relatives visit Redbud Elementary this week. The Wisconsin couple are pen pals of our third and fourth graders. They have exchanged news about weather, native plants, and animal migration patterns. They have compared life in a northern, midwestern state with that in northwestern Louisiana. Our pupils have learned some physical geography from their pen pals.

The children are thrilled to meet the couple "in person." They wangle extra help and attention from the guests and must be reminded by us not to "swarm" the couple. In each classroom, we have a question-and-answer session for the visitors. Randall asks, "Do you know how to make pigs-in-a-blanket?"

"Have you ever been bear hunting?" inquires Nikeya.

"Are you afraid to fly?" Wendice asks, and "Can you stay until the end of the year?"

Leon says, "I will spend my money if you will fly back to visit us again."

"How much money do you have?" I ask Leon.

"Eighty-one cents," he replies.

The children are premier escorts. They take the couple by the arms to the playground and to the lunchroom. They empty the guests' hot-lunch trays when their meals are finished.

The guests, who had not been in public schools in decades, were rattled by what they witnessed. They were upset by the condition of the building and the lack of basic instructional materials. "The people in Washington should see this school," commented one. The guests also were struck by the grueling day that classroom teachers put in. "They're treated like peons. They don't even get a lunch break," the guests noted. These observations were made by two people who lived through the Great Depression and fought and had brothers in World War II. They know about hardships and lack. It takes a lot to jar them. Redbud Elementary did.

Fourth Grade

It is getting increasingly difficult to keep the pupils motivated. The LEAP test is over, and they seem to have lost their steam. "Why do we have to keep studying social studies? The test is over," states Jaylene.

"Mr. Johnson, we're tired of writing all the time," whines Antron. Spring is turning to summer. The temperatures reach the eighties; the children want to be outdoors.

The faculty has a number of things planned to try to hold student interest: a Young Authors competition, a trip to the Dodge Museum, a field day of races, and a field trip to Shreveport paid for by Deerborne Electric, the fourth-grade sponsor.

"When will we hear about the LEAP test results?" Verlin asks every day. It has been a month since they took the tests. This long period of waiting for results is stressful to children and teachers. It is a time of anxiety with the undercurrent of potential failure ever present. The children do not know if they will be going to junior high school or if they will be returning to Redbud Elementary next year to be in class with the present third graders.

Third Grade

Jaron proudly shows me his new pair of shoes. The poorly made shoes are several sizes too big for him. "They make me taller," says the smiling, diminutive child. All day he trips and stumbles in the ill-fitting shoes.

Third and Fourth Grades

Wagner and Vander Ark (2001) illuminate a major problem with using high-stakes tests, particularly in low-income schools that serve minorities:

> In too many schools, the curriculum has been reduced to "test prep." An increased focus on teaching to the test further undermines many students' motivation to learn and will likely accelerate the flight of good teachers and principals from the schools that serve the neediest children. The reason many of the best educators are tempted to leave the profession is that they know that bad schools can hide behind good test scores, and good schools don't necessarily have the best test results. (56, 40)

We have found Redbud Elementary to be a good school with not-so-good test scores for all the reasons described in this book.

Third Grade

Manuel reports, "I got my haircut last night and some guy came into the barber shop and almost fell down. He had one of those big ol' cans of beer with him. I mean a *big* ol' can of beer."

"That's a forty-ouncer," comments Leon.

"My uncle got drunk and hit my aunt and she started smoking again," says Kelvin.

"I pour my daddy's beer out and break up his cigarettes and throw them in the tall grass," Sam adds.

Gerard says, "I saw this TV show once where a man kept drinking and a body part—I don't remember which one—broke. They had to bury him."

WEEK 33, APRIL 23–27: END-OF-THE-YEAR PAPERWORK

Third and Fourth Grades

The children write thank-you notes to a university dean who came to Redbud Elementary to read to the children. Here are some excerpts:

> Dear Dean Simmons,
> Hi, I'm Ashley. Thank you so much for the story you read to us. Also thank you for the pencils, ballons, beads, and candy. I really enjoyed the story.
> I pulled my tooth yesterday. It was hanging by a root.

Dear Dean Simmons,

We thank you for everything you give us. I'm happy you came all way to Redbud to read us a story about the tooth fairy. You remember when you read that story the other day my tooth fall I put it under my pillow but the tooth fairy didn't come.

Your friendly,
Shonora Sanders

Dear Dean Simmons,

I am new I don't know you so I'm trying to let you know me. . . . I really wished that I moved here when you come. . . . I really would write a thank you but I didn't get the stuff.

Your friend,
Nicole Bartley

Third Grade

Wendice has been missing for several days. Some of the children report that he is fishing for crawfish. "Well, isn't that just grand," states a disgusted Chikae.

"I heard his mama say, 'It's your future,'" reports Leon. "So he can do whatever he wants. He rolls around on the grass a lot."

Third and Fourth Grades

The paperwork mounts as the year draws to a close. The first "instrument" for teachers to complete is a welcome one: the faculty needs assessment form on which teachers list school strengths, weaknesses, school improvement actions, and school improvement barriers. It is the first time teachers' opinions have been solicited by the state since we began teaching at Redbud Elementary. We hope that the information will reach Baton Rouge. A slip of paper accompanying the instrument states, "The needs assessments should be turned in tomorrow in the resource room between 2:30 and 3:30. Each staff member will initial beside their name as they turn in their needs assessment. This will serve as documentation that all needs assessments were completed." This is one form that certainly doesn't need monitoring for completion.

The next instruments that we are handed during the day aren't so easily completed. They are the Louisiana Department of Education (2005) SAM student questionnaires. The questionnaires are to be completed at a specified time on a specified day. Fifty-five minutes of the school day are allotted for student responses. The intention of some of the statements appears to be "checking up" on teachers. For example,

8. I am good in math because of my teachers.
9. My teachers use many different activities to make learning fun and exciting.
12. The rules at this school are enforced fairly by my teachers.
14. I am good in social studies because of my teachers.
15. My teachers teach me things I use away from school.
22. I am good in reading because of my teachers.
23. My teachers use activities that require me to think while using my hands.
27. My teachers keep other students from bothering me while I do my school work.
29. I am good in science because of my teachers.
30. My teachers encourage me to do extra school work to help improve my grades.
34. I am good in writing because of my teachers.
35. My teachers test what I know in different ways (not just using pen-and-paper).

The students must fill in the appropriate bubbles on the questionnaire with a number 2 pencil if they "strongly disagree," "disagree," "agree," or "strongly agree" with the statements. "Do not know" is another option. Many of the statements require explanations. In statement 6, for example ("I can achieve in school at or above the level of other students in the nation"), "achieve" must be defined. Statement 7 ("I will attend some form of higher education after graduating from high school, e.g., college, junior college, technical school) necessitates providing definitions for "junior college" and "technical school." The word "administrators" has to be defined by us in statement 11 ("Administrators help me when I am having problems in my classes").

Some children get lost on the visually complex form and simply fill in bubbles under one option (e.g., "disagree"). The classroom teacher must tally all of the responses. We each count 740 marks and then send all questionnaires and final counts to our grade reps.

Each teacher must send home a Louisiana Department of Education SAM parent questionnaire with every child. Statements include the following:

6. Administrators willingly provide assistance to me about my child's teacher.

10. This school does a good job teaching my child social studies.

14. Classroom rules are enforced fairly by most of my child's teachers.

17. This school does a good job in teaching my child to read well.

23. Most of my child's teachers encourage him/her to do extra work to improve his/her grades.

24. This school does a good job teaching my child science.

29. This school does a good job teaching my child to write well.

36. This school does a good job in teaching my child mathematics.

As with the student questionnaire, parents are to fill in bubbles for "strongly disagree," "disagree," "agree," "strongly agree," or "do not know" responses. Accompanying the parent questionnaires are the following directions to teachers:

> Please staple the parent note on the front. Make a list of students who received the questionnaires and the ones who returned them. . . . Each grade must have at least 33% returned or we will need to send additional questionnaires before they can be tallied and turned in.

Only a handful of parent questionnaires are returned. One child reports that her mother cannot read the form. Another says that his mother doesn't understand it.

Some of our pupils are taken out of our classrooms to be interviewed by the school improvement team. They apparently are asked a series of questions about their teachers. "What did they ask you?" we inquire. "We aren't supposed to tell you," says Gerard. "But I didn't understand some of the questions."

Perry chimes in, "They ask if you treated all students the same way and if we could go on the Internet." We are troubled by a system that asks students to report on their teachers. Recall that the fourth-grade students were asked questions about their teachers on all parts of the LEAP test. Third graders had similar questions at the end of the Iowa test. Parents and guardians were asked to report on teachers in the parent questionnaires. The persistent state monitoring of teacher behavior becomes demoralizing.

Third Grade

Several children report that on the playground they heard one of the pupils in my class say he was going to bring a .45 (i.e., a gun) to school. This child is taken to Ms. Dawson. He is suspended and must go before a board for a hearing. I don't know when he will return to my classroom.

I am called to the special education portable classroom to meet with a parent at 2:00 P.M. to discuss her son's placement for next year. The special education teacher and I wait for thirty minutes. The mother does not show up.

Leon looks particularly glum this morning. "What's wrong?" I ask.

"My cousin drown yesterday," Leon replies.

In the headlines of the local newspaper, I note that Leon's cousin was only twenty-five years old. He was fishing when the accident occurred.

TEN

MAY

"I DON'T WANT TO SPEND
MY TIME ON PAPERWORK"

WEEK 34, APRIL 30–MAY 4

Third Grade

While on 7:15–7:55 A.M. recess duty, I notice that some of the third-grade girls have discovered a use for a large log on the playground. They have designated it a volleyball "net." The girls serve and return a tiny multicolored rubber ball.

We are reading a story about a boy who is ashamed of his father because the man dresses in unconventional clothes. He wears a hat with cloth antlers and drives a "flower-power" van. The boy lies to his father so that the father will not show up at a school event and embarrass the child.

"I haven't seen a van like that since the '50s," says nine-year-old Antinesha.

"His dad acts like a dodo," points out Manuel.

"Well, the boy shouldn't tell lies," lectures Shantel. "He'll get lie bumps on his tongue."

"What are lie bumps?" I ask. Several children stick out their tongues and point to the bumps.

"If you lie, your teeth can separate, too," adds Roland.

"Just look at that space between Keaziah's teeth," says Jaheesa. "He tells lies and his teeth are spreading apart in the front."

"If he stops telling lies, though, they'll grow back together," says Roland reassuringly.

Mrs. Tomah, my second-semester student teacher, is talking about local and state governments. "What does the governor of our state do?" she asks the class.

"He gets money from the rich people and gives it to the poor people," states Randall.

"He catches people who rob banks," offers Kanesha.

Shantel says, "He answers phone calls and pushes buttons on his phone."

Fourth Grade

We are updating cumulative folders based on information sheets that parents/guardians complete in September and again in April. Changes must be recorded on the "cumulative card" that is located in a small file box in the office. Then the forms must be filed in the folders that are kept in a large file cabinet in the office. Neither cumulative cards nor folders can leave the school office.

More than half my fourth graders had a change of address, telephone number, or both between September and April. This is in addition to Malcolm, Emerald, and LaTonya, who moved out of the district. In September, Derek's information had been signed by his mother and included the notation "may only be picked up by his mother." In April, Derek's father signed the form and noted, "Derek is *not* to be picked up by his mother!" These kinds of notations are found on many of the information forms. Some say that they don't want anyone in the family to pick up the child without showing identification.

End-of-year tensions continue to mount, and name-calling is on the increase. Saying "your mother has AIDS" earns Victavius three days of in-school suspension. I am asked daily if I know the LEAP test results.

Third and Fourth Grades

Pupils in grades 1 to 4 are asked to participate in a schoolwide writing contest, the Young Authors' Showcase. Here is the work of two of our students:

Rhyme Time
by Roland

Once upon a time no one knew a rhyme. Until a boy was born in the corn with a horn. He said, "Horn, corn, and born all rhyme." "What a time for a rhyme," said a man. "I'll give you 20 dimes if you teach me all the rhymes." So he did as a kid. Soon he was an adult. But a mean man made rhyme a crime. Even lime slime was illegal because it was a rhyme. The ocean was a freedom potion. They all knew where to go.

Butterfly
by Manuel

A little color in the air.
It has no useless wings to spare.
But a butterfly is very fair.
A little color in the air.

Fourth Grade

Milo has been excited all week because today he will see his real dad for the first time since he was six weeks old. His father lives in western Texas and will fly to Shreveport and then drive to Redbud. In class, the students write stories in which they use some figurative language. Milo's anticipation about meeting his father is reflected in his writing.

The Big Box
Ritten by Milo Thomas

One day I was sitting at the kitchen table eating when the U.P.S. drove up. Then went outside to get it. I put it on my mama's bed. I was on pins and needles for my mama to get home so I could see what was in it. She was shoping. So I went fishing and came back with a turtle and a brim, but my mama still wasen't back. I started to get butterflies in my stomoch. So then I went to a friend's house. Where we played the 64.

Boy I have to say I had ants in my pants. Then my friend and I made stuff. Then I saw my mama. I went home as fast as I could. Then I said Mama! Mama! The U.P.S. came. Is it the stuff daddy bought me? Huh, is it. My mama said Hold youre horses, son. Boy was I on pins and needles.

When she opened it my mouth dropped. I gazed into the box. It held $100 Glove, 21.99 batting Gloves, two 5.00 balls, and some Cleets. I loved it. This is the best stuff I ever had. I said to myself.

Third Grade

We must administer the DRA (developmental reading assessment) to each student again. This is required by the state. Mrs. Tomah works with the class as I individually test each child. In a story that Gerard reads, we discuss the main idea. "It's like my daddy says," comments Gerard. "You can't judge a cover by its book."

"That's 'You can't judge a book by its cover,'" I point out. "What does that mean?"

"Well, it's like this kid I know. He's got a big mold on his face and a wart on his finger. I saw his feet, too. He's got a corn and athlete's foot. But he's got a lot of girlfriends."

"He must be a nice person," I comment.

While on playground duty, my student teacher tells me some disturbing news: she doesn't want to teach in a public school next year. When I ask her about her decision, she says, "I don't want to spend my time on all the paperwork, and I don't want somebody looking over my shoulder all the time. As a first-year teacher, they'll really watch me."

I cannot refute Mrs. Tomah's statements, but her choice is a terrible loss for public education. She is one of the best beginning teachers I have seen. She cares about children, teaches well-planned lessons, and goes the extra mile to see that each child is making progress. If she were to teach at Redbud Elementary, she could help children that others might not reach. If she stayed in public education ten years, she could shape at least two hundred young lives. She tells me that she will take a position, if available, at a private academy for a salary of about $12,000 rather than deal with state bureaucracy and accountability. What a waste.

I ask Mrs. Newburg about the classification of my special education students. She tells me that one is classified as learning disabled and four are mildly mentally disabled. These children have worked diligently all year but are not approaching grade level. Their Iowa test scores will be factored into Redbud Elementary's scores for its rating by the state.

It is Friday. There are just a few moments left before the children leave for the weekend. Mrs. Tomah asks the class if they want to sing a song. Two volunteers, Cherise and Antinesha, go to the front of the classroom to lead the singers. "What would you like to sing?" Mrs. Tomah inquires.

"Silent Night," Antinesha replies. All the third graders, sitting in the afternoon sunshine coming in the windows on an eighty-four-degree day, sing "Silent Night."

WEEK 35, MAY 7–11: LEARNING THE LEAP TEST RESULTS

Third and Fourth Grades

The teacher shortage is becoming critical in Redbud and in other towns in Louisiana. We learn that the Deerborne Parish school board has approved a tuition contract with a nearby university. The plan will pay the tuition of junior and senior education majors who will agree to teach in Deerborne Parish one semester for every quarter of tuition paid. Thus, if two years of tuition are paid, the new teacher must teach in the parish for three years. This is an attempt to get certified teachers into the classroom.

Fourth Grade

Milo bubbles over with news about his weekend with his biological father. "I don't look anything like my real daddy, but we kind of talk alike," Milo reports. "We spent all day Saturday fishing and talking. Yesterday morning he had to go back to Texas. But I'll get to visit him in Texas in the summer."

Third Grade

After lunch, a university supervisor is coming to observe Mrs. Tomah's teaching ability. I tell the children that part of her grade will be based on how well she can handle the class, so they should be on their best behavior.

"What if we have to throw up?" inquires Leon seriously.

"Then you may leave without asking," I say. "Now we'd better tidy up this room before she gets here. There's a lot of mud on the floor from the playground."

Jimmy and Kanzah grab brooms. "We can't have it too clean in here, or she'll think something's fishy," Jimmy points out.

Third and Fourth Grades

As a part of the school improvement plan, one of us has to complete a form titled School Analysis Model (Louisiana Department of Education 2005) Instructional Staff Interview Protocol. It is the basis of a teacher interview conducted by the school improvement team. Items on the form include "What new and innovative teaching strategies have you implemented at this school? Explain the staff expectations for you and other teachers at your school. How do your current classroom assessment practices align with assessment strategies in *LEAP/GEE for the 21st Century*? How are curricular issues being addressed in response to the new School Accountability System?" These questions are fairly easy to answer. "We teach for the test" answers all four of them. Another item is, "Explain your role in budgeting fiscal resources (e.g., determining the amount of money spent for Open House refreshments)." This one is really simple to answer. We have no budget for refreshments or for virtually anything else. When asked, "How does your school's policy address children who are excessively absent and/or potential dropouts?" one of us must answer, "Not well. Yolande has been absent more than one hundred school days this year." We wish that instead of being asked questions such as these, we would have been asked, "What can the district or the state do to help you in your teaching? What supplies and materials do you need?"

We run across some figures, given to us by a professor at a local university, that compared last year's LEAP test performance categories and scores. The figures included the percentage of students on free lunch, the percentage of minority students, and the percentage of students in special education. The comparisons were striking. For example, a school of academic distinction in Bossier Parish (score 126.6 percent) had 10.9 percent on free lunch, 8.1 percent minority students, and 8.8 percent in special education. A laboratory school in Lincoln Parish rated a school of academic achievement (score 123.5 percent) had 0 percent on free lunch, 12.4 percent minority students, and 3.6 percent in special education. Last year, Redbud Elementary School, in contrast, a below-average school (score 44.1 percent), had 88.1 percent on free lunch (not including those on reduced lunch), 79.1 percent minority students, and 16.4 percent in special education. We look at other schools and see the same pattern—the schools with the highest percentages of students on free lunch, the highest percentages of minority students, and the highest percentages of students in special education achieved the lowest scores on the LEAP test. Even a cursory examination of these statistics for the north-central region of Louisiana shows that no school with a large percentage of free lunch students, special education students, and minority students scored high enough to achieve a label of above average. These results stem directly from poverty and its associated ills: lack of medical care, poor nutrition, drug and alcohol abuse, difficulty in finding decent-paying jobs because of little education, and racism.

The African American students in our classes are as bright as any children with whom we have worked, but they have unequal opportunities. Any citizen who paid a brief visit to Redbud Elementary would confirm this. In addition, several private schools, whose students are almost all white, are exempt from the LEAP tests. The pattern is unmistakable. Why put children, teachers, and state coffers through all the stress and expense of testing? Why not put the money where it can do some good? Don't send in experts to tell teachers and administrators what they already know. Permit the districts to use the money saved from testing for additional teachers, teacher assistants, and materials.

Third Grade

While on 7:15 A.M. playground duty, Mrs. Quigley and I notice a third grader standing alone some distance from the other children and too close to the outside fence. We motion for him to join the other boys on the playground. "I'm worried about that child," comments Mrs. Quigley. "He's essentially homeless. He's moved around from one relative to another. Right now he's living with an aunt. He says his daddy is somewhere in California."

"Where's his mother?" I ask.

"In the pen for drugs," Mrs. Quigley replies.

Fourth Grade

I take advantage of the presence of a student teacher by scheduling individual conferences with my students. This is nearly impossible to do without a second adult in the classroom to help with the instructional load. During the conferences, I encourage the children to do their best when they get to junior high and high school and to strive for a college education. Shonora tells me, "It's hard for me to do homework at my house."

"Why is that?" I inquire.

"Because so many people be living there. My mama, her friend Dennis, my two uncles, my cousin, my sister, and me. My two uncles don't work. One wants a job, but the other just stand around all day. Sometimes it just be too noisy for homework."

I suggest that she try to get her homework finished in school or go to the Boys and Girls Club where tutoring is available. During these conferences, I learn that only eleven of my forty-four pupils have computers with an Internet connection and that a mere five have a magazine subscription.

Third Grade

The pupils make cards for Mother's Day. Some of the children don't live with their mothers, so they make cards for the female adult with whom they live. Wendice is crying. I walk over to his desk. "Why are you crying, Wendice? Are you sick?"

"No, ma'am," he answers.

"Do you need help with your card?" I ask.

"No, ma'am. I don't want to make a card for my mother."

"Why not?"

"Because I don't like her," he sniffs.

"Are you sure? Mother's Day comes only once a year," I remind him.

"I don't like her and I don't want to make a card for her."

"How about that nice grandma of yours who lives in the country?"

"Okay, I'll make one for her," Wendice says reluctantly.

Gerard tells me at lunch, "When I get out of high school, I'm going straight to the army."

"That can help you pay for college," I remark.

"Yeah, I want to go to college so I can be one of them lawyers."

"Do you think you'll be rich when you grow up?"

"If I get in that lawyer business I will be. I heard they make $4,000 a year."

"When you're making that kind of money, don't forget about your old third-grade teacher," I say. He smiles.

Third and Fourth Grades

An article by Mark Stricherz in *Education Week* describes the pressure being put on schools in Louisiana, especially the fifty-seven schools that are labeled academically unacceptable based on the LEAP and Iowa test scores. Fifty-one of the fifty-seven schools are in New Orleans. Leslie R. Jacobs is "the state board member who is known as the architect of initiatives designed to improve Louisiana's worst schools" (Stricherz 2001, 37). Jacobs said, "The number-one social value to me this program sends is a message to students they will no longer be promoted for seat time. They have to learn something" (34). The article points out that both Jacobs and Alphonse G. Davis, former Marine Corps colonel and chief executive of the New Orleans schools, "choose to send their children to private schools" (36). We find it incomprehensible that a superintendent of public schools and a member of a state board of elementary and secondary education would not send their children to the public schools that they steer. The Davis and Jacobs families can avoid the dictates of Louisiana's accountability system.

In describing her accountability plan, Jacobs said, "I'd like to say it was based on research. It wasn't. . . . But it was common sense to me, from serving on the New Orleans school board and going into schools that, if a student lacked these skills, we were not helping this child if we were continuing to promote them" (Stricherz 2001, 37). Ms. Jacobs's "common sense" may not agree with notions of "common sense" held by others—for instance, the common sense of those who teach in underfunded schools every day.

Fourth Grade

The fourth-grade teachers are summoned to Pam Porter's office at 1:30 P.M. on Friday. Aides are sent to watch our classes. The LEAP results have been released. We learn that fifty-four of our 118 fourth graders have failed the LEAP and must attend summer school. If they fail to pass a retake of the exam, they will have to repeat the fourth grade. Fourteen of the fifty-four children are special education students. Pam and two veteran teachers are heartened by the improvement over the 2000 results. In 2000, 61 percent of Redbud fourth graders failed the math test, and this year 42 percent failed. In 2000, 56 percent of Redbud fourth graders failed the English language arts test, and this year 32 percent failed.

In Louisiana in 2001, 18 percent of fourth graders failed the English language arts test, 24 percent failed math, 16 percent failed science, and 22 percent failed social studies. In 2003, students must score at the basic level of achievement in order to pass the LEAP test. This year, students who scored approaching basic passed the test. The percentage of fourth graders in Louisiana who did not achieve at the basic level in 2001 included 42 percent in English language arts, 47 percent in math, 49 percent in science, and 45 percent in social studies. If the 2003 criteria had been in place, nearly half of all fourth graders would have failed. It seems clear that the test should be examined more closely—not the children and teachers of Louisiana.

But these are just numbers. Each number represents a child. Fifty-four Redbud Elementary School children must now, at best, give up their summer to prepare and try again and, at worst, spend another year in fourth grade. The teachers sit stunned as we think about the individuals in our classes who have been with us all year and now have failed. We feel as if we are failures. What could we have done differently? What could I have done to help Dwayne, Shonora, and Dianne? How am I going to tell them?

WEEK 36, MAY 14–18: WHEN 40,000 CHILDREN ARE FAILED

Fourth Grade

Over the weekend, I analyze the list of students who failed the LEAP test. We have not yet been informed of the performances of those who passed the test. I discover that six children in my homeroom have failed the English language arts test. Four of the six are in special education, and one is Yolande, who has been truant more than one hundred days this year. Three others, Dario,

Tyler, and Derek, failed the math test as well. Derek's math score was 280, and 282 is a passing score. His self-concept is damaged, and the summer he planned to spend fishing with his father is ruined by two points. In my other class, eight children failed the English language arts test—three of whom are special education students. An additional five students failed the math test as well. Andrenna scored 280, and Danielle, who failed both parts of the LEAP test in 2000, has scored 279—three points from a pass.

I am filled with anger at the state bureaucrats and politicians who designed and mandated this uncompromising accountability system. Our Redbud pupils have so many strikes against them. They often are sick. They have rotting teeth and cry because of severe toothaches. Many come from dysfunctional homes. They are ill-clad and wear ill-fitting shoes. Several do not get enough food or enough rest. They live with acute poverty in substandard homes, often surrounded by drug dealers and users and drunks. The harsh accountability system imposed by the state kicks them further. I'm not opposed to testing. Well-designed tests can give educators useful information. Ideally, the results would inform districts about needs for remediation. Tests should be used to enlighten, not to torment.

Hasten and Brumble (2001) discuss some of the results of the LEAP test:

> As they did last year, roughly one-third of Louisiana's fourth- and eighth graders have flunked one or both parts of a state assessment of basic skills. But state education officials say there is good news ahead. "The news on the fourth grade is wonderful," said Leslie Jacobs, a member of the Board of Elementary and Secondary Education who pushed the testing program—an integral part of the state's overall school reform package that measures students and schools and assigns penalties for failure. (1A)

Jacobs may think that the news is wonderful, but we're sure it's not going to be wonderful to the 17,988 fourth graders and 21,529 eighth graders who failed the spring 2001 LEAP test. Nearly forty thousand students will have to attend summer school and attempt the test again if they have any hopes of passing on to the next grade. I wish that Ms. Jacobs, State Superintendent Cecil Picard, and other state officials would be with us in Redbud to break the news to De'Lewis, Danielle, Andrenna, and all the other children.

Fourth-grade teachers decide that each of us will inform the students of the results in whatever way seems least hurtful. I decide to call my entire class out of the classroom into the hallway, one at a time, in alphabetical order. My first student is Dario. I tell him that he has passed the English language arts portion of the LEAP but will have to attend summer school because he failed the math portion. He cries quietly. "My papa [grandfather] gonna be mad at me. He will beat me."

"I'm sure that if you work very hard from June 4 to July 12 you will pass it this summer, Dario," I tell him. "Don't be discouraged. Just be determined to do your best." He reenters the classroom. My words sound hollow to me. How can he not be discouraged? I am discouraged. He just has had five weeks of summer jerked away from him and maybe all of next year.

My next pupil is Jamal, a special education student. In addition to his speech problems, he has severe learning disabilities. I must inform Jamal that he has failed the English language arts and math portions of the test. I plead with him to go to summer school. In Louisiana, special education students must take the LEAP test. If they fail, they must attend summer school and take the LEAP test again. Then they are promoted to fifth grade whether or not they pass the second test. Most of these children don't have a chance to pass the test. Why take away the children's summer and make them sit through the test again when the results mean nothing?

Next comes Jaylene, who has passed both parts of the test and will go on to fifth grade. "Do you mean it? I passed?" She jumps and screams. I tell her to try not to show her joy when she returns to the classroom because children who didn't pass feel bad.

This process continues until I have informed my twelve students who passed, five of my six students who failed English language arts and math (Yolande, of course, is absent), and three others who failed the math portion but passed English. Ms. Avalon, my student teacher, remains in the classroom, reading a story to the class. When I reenter my classroom, most of the children are crying. Those who passed are hugging those who failed and are comforting them. LaDelle tells Chalese, "You'll do fine in summer, Chal." Chalese also has severe learning disabilities. She can barely read. This scene is repeated in the hallway and in the four other fourth-grade classrooms. One little girl in the room next door tells her friend, "I'm going to kill myself." The teachers are as choked with emotion as the students. This trauma will not be experienced in the private elementary schools in the state.

Third Grade

After school, while the children are sitting in the hallway waiting for their buses to be called, it is nearly silent. The pupils have not been this quiet all year. Sounds of fourth graders crying carry down to where my third graders sit.

"Why are all those kids crying?" asks Jaron.

"They flunked," says Keaziah softly.

I walk down to the fourth-grade classrooms. I try to console inconsolable children. The pitiful scene is too much for me. I walk back to my third graders.

Fourth Grade

I have playground duty on Tuesday mornings from 7:15 to 7:55 following the children's school breakfast. I notice that the fourth graders who have failed the LEAP test are congregating in small groups as though they no longer feel a part of the fourth grade. They cling to me, both figuratively and literally, as they tell me about what happened at home the night before. They ask about summer school. "Will I be in your room?" asks Chalese. Our school will end on June 1—about two weeks from now. For the children who failed the LEAP, summer school will begin the following week.

Third and Fourth Grades

We are struck by how the decisions of teachers—those who work with the children 176 days (1,232 hours) during the course of a school year—are ignored. Who better to evaluate a student's progress than a certified, experienced teacher who sees all aspects of a child's academic work? We teachers know our students' abilities better than any standardized test score can reveal. We know which children are ready to move to the next grade. We teachers are the experts, but our expertise is brushed aside by the accountability processes. Some politicians say that the tests are an effort to break the cycle of poverty. This is nonsense to us in the classrooms. Memorizing and cramming for tests do not constitute an education. They help no one. They are not measures of critical comprehension or extrapolation, two qualities of an education that will serve students in their adult years. There is no art in our curriculum. Speaking and listening activities have been downplayed because they are not measured on the Iowa or LEAP tests, and science and social studies have taken a backseat to language and math cramming. Some officials and administrators beam with pride because test scores have risen. All this means, however, is that teachers have become better at teaching for the test.

Third Grade

The school nurse comes today. I take four of my pupils to her. Jelani has been complaining of stomach pains for two weeks. I have sent him home, but he returns with the same symptoms. He cries and sleeps most of the time he is in school. Cherise, Kanzah, and Jaron have decayed teeth and bleeding gums. Perhaps a strongly worded letter from the nurse will get the children some help. Leon has persistent nosebleeds, but I have already sent him home for the day. I could not stop the bleeding.

In reading class, we are talking about people overcoming problems. Antinesha tells the class, "My best friend, Alani, has overcome problems. Her real mother went to jail, and her second mother got in a car wreck. But Alani is still okay."

"I've overcome problems," adds Kelvin. "My real dad choked and kicked my mama. One day he didn't come home from work and he never came back."

"My uncle got drunk and fell out," reports Cherise.

"What does 'fell out' mean?" I ask.

"It means to fall over," says Mrs. Tomah.

"Has he overcome that problem?" I ask.

"No, he's still drinking," Cherise replies.

Third and Fourth Grades

Mrs. Sauk is angry. One of her second graders has been living in a pop-up trailer in the middle of the woods. The family has no running water or electricity. Mrs. Sauk says that the child bathes in a nearby stream and that the family cooks meals over an open fire. She can't get anyone to help the family.

WEEK 37, MAY 21–25

Third and Fourth Grades

We are handed a number of end-of-year checklists and forms. The most formidable is a four-page, single-spaced checklist that covers attendance, grade books, greenback registers, cumulative cards, promotion and retention lists (new forms), DRA folders, summer storage, and more. Here are just a few excerpts from one checklist:

Greenback Register

- Fill in *completely* on each student in your homeroom (use *black ink* only).
- Update addresses if there has been a change. Make sure the office has a copy of any address changes (in writing).

- There must be a birth certificate number and a social security number.
- Contact the parent if this information is not available in the office. Report cards will be held until this information is provided.
- The "date entered" for this school year will be August 21, 2000, unless a student was added to your roll later in the year.
- The "date leaving" will be the last day of school, May 31, 2001, unless the student was dropped earlier in the year. The "reason" will be *end of school*. [Note: Each teacher has to write "end of school" in a small space twenty or more times].
- Show 1st and 2nd semester averages as percentages and the final average as a percentage *and* a grade.
- Indicate whether student promoted or is retained (if student is retained, highlight "retained in grade" in yellow).
- Indicate reason for retention (pupil progression plan, attendance, etc.). *This is very important.* Greenbacks are permanent records.
- Use "reinforcements" on both sides of greenback pages.

Cumulative Cards
Front of Cards

- Update all information on the front of the card from student update sheets (use pencil on top/front of card so information can be changed as needed and black ink on the rest of the card).
- Date entered August 21, 2000. Date left May 31. This will vary if students entered late or were dropped. Put failures in the front with a paper clip, and then put a rubber band around the entire set of cum cards.
- Indicate promoted because of pupil progression plan (two years in the same grade) or retained because of pupil progression plan (failing grades), attendance, etc. on cum cards.

Back of Card

- Write teacher's name above the column where you record grades.
- Write student's name on back of cum card if not already written there.
- Fill in the session and grade at the top.
- Draw 2 lines down the middle of the column and put 1st semester (%), 2nd semester (%), and final grade (% and letter grade).
- Put final GPA at the bottom (from report card).

- Do not write "overage" at the bottom. This would be promoting due to pupil progression plan. If you think you have a student that will promote due to being overage, check with the principal.
- Check with grade reps after you fill out 1st card to make sure it is correct before finishing the rest.
  [Note: Cumulative cards are not allowed to be taken out of the school office.]

Promotion and Retention Lists (new forms)

- List the names of students on the promotion (yellow) *or* retention (white) list with last name first, in alphabetical order. Turn in to grade rep by May 25.
- Put red star by name to indicate extreme behavior problems or write note on back if certain students do not need to be together next year, etc.
- Highlight the students who were in the grade for the 2nd time *this year* in pink.
- Indicate black female with BF, white female with WF, etc.
- Indicate students who received speech services with SP and students who receive special education services with SE.
- Indicate SBL referral if you referred student this year.
- DRA scores for grades for grades 1–3 only.
- Fill in IOWA information for grades 1–3. [Note: This includes Iowa reading score, Iowa language score, Iowa math score, and Iowa composite for each child.]

In addition to these three sections, this end-of-school checklist includes three directives related to attendance, two related to grade books, four related to report cards, two related to textbooks, one each related to DRA folders and teacher address form, nine related to summer storage (e.g., "Do not leave money or candy/food in your room over the summer"), and nine under the heading "miscellaneous" (e.g., "Tag the furniture in your room in some way so it will be returned to the correct room after the floors are waxed this summer; some teachers use colored dot stickers—different color for each teacher in that grade").

Fourth Grade

It is our student teacher's last day. We have a surprise good-bye party for her. Pupils pass out paper towels, napkins, popcorn, potato chips, and cookies.

They sing a rousing, off-key rendition of "For She's a Jolly Good Woman." Ja-toyia comes to the front of the room to sing a solo. I notice that Ms. Avalon is beginning to swallow hard. Each student comes forward to present her with a handmade farewell card and offer a few words. Rachael says, "I love you, Ms. Avalon. I know I have been a bad girl, but I will miss you so much." With that, Ms. Avalon's tears begin to flow. All at once, the students are out of their seats "swarming" her with hugs and comforting words. Now her tears turn to sobs. I develop a lump in my throat as I realize that in two short weeks, I'll be say-ing my farewells to these loving and endearing fourth-grade children with whom I have spent an entire school year.

Third and Fourth Grades

Julie Blair (2001) reported in *Education Week* that

lawmakers in Iowa discarded their traditional teacher-compensation system last week and voted to replace it with one that would pay educators based on their performance in the classroom and students' achievement, rather than on the number of years spent teaching. (1)

We know that if this practice becomes widespread, teachers will run for the wealthy suburbs so they have a chance of making a living wage. Surely no one would want to teach at Redbud Elementary or in similar schools in the United States where students lack the advantages that elevate test scores. The article quotes Lew W. Finch, superintendent of schools in Cedar Rapids, Iowa, a district with eighteen thousand students:

I have yet to talk to a teacher that believes that this new plan will help re-tain people in the profession. In fact, many of the teachers believe that it will force them to leave the district, and they certainly don't see it as a selling point. (24–25)

Fourth Grade

Louisiana Governor Mike Foster (2001), in a guest column boasting about improved test results, states,

We need to give credit where credit is due—members of the Board of El-ementary and Secondary Education (BESE) and Superintendent of Educa-tion Cecil Picard have worked closely with my administration to put this program together. Now is the time for us to redouble our efforts to support and strengthen our school accountability program. . . . Please call your state representative and senator today and urge them to join me in staying the course with our school accountability program. . . . We must also soundly defeat any measure to weaken our high-stakes testing on any level. (7A)

No credit is given to teachers. Small wonder that teachers who have worked so hard all year to help their pupils learn are feeling so disheartened.

We think politicians should be held accountable for the condition of schools today. They are the ones who make the laws and control the purse strings. Politicians are the people who create the circumstances under which teachers must teach and children must learn. We can think of no other professionals who are held as accountable as teachers. Physicians are not held accountable for patients who are not cured or die prematurely. We don't hold lawyers accountable for clients who end up in prison. Social workers are not held accountable for clients who can't get jobs. We don't hold dentists accountable for patients who develop cavities or gum disease. Teachers are an easy target, and teacher-bashing is all too common among state and school district officials and policymakers across the nation. We saw dedicated teachers work small miracles with their pupils every day we were on the faculty at Redbud Elementary School. Would it hurt the people in power to say, "Teachers, you have done an excellent job bringing these children along as far as you have"?

THE FINAL WEEK: MAY 28–JUNE 1

Fourth Grade

Today is Memorial Day. For most of the nation, it is a holiday with ceremonies, parades, and picnics. At Redbud Elementary, it is a school day that had been scheduled as a full day. We learned last week that Superintendent Miller decided to dismiss school at noon today for all teachers and students in recognition of our improved LEAP test scores. After the morning Pledge of Allegiance, we march to the high school auditorium for honors day. The fourth graders are dressed in white shirts and navy blue pants, shorts, or skirts. Jamal told me that he didn't own a white top, so I bring him one of mine—many sizes too big. With sleeves rolled up several times and the shirt tucked in, he looks fine. Jamal beams when I tell him that the white shirt is a gift. "I'll grow into it," he says without his usual hesitation.

Mrs. Quigley of the third grade has prepared more than four hundred certificates. Today they are awarded to individual children for such achievements

as being on the honor roll, having perfect attendance, winning the drug awareness poster or essay contest, being the most improved student in each class, and
more. The program concludes with 110 fourth graders who assemble in the
front of the auditorium to sing two songs: "Late for the Bus Stop" and "America the Beautiful." More than one parent and teacher brush away tears as they
watch these smiling, hope-filled, mostly African American children sing in har-
mony about the wonderfulness of America.

There is a small reception after the program for the children who made
the honor roll. Each child gets a sandwich, a cold drink, cake, and ice cream.
Parents, guardians, teachers, and other pupils are not included because of a limited budget. We hear from a teacher that a parent has asked Pam Porter for any
sandwiches that are left over. She needs them to feed her children. Pam gives
the mother the leftover sandwiches.

Third Grade

During a discussion of occupations, Manuel states that he wants to be a
judge. "My daddy says they make about a million just for sending people to
jail." Several hands go up. Many of the pupils tell about relatives who either
have been or are in jail. "My stepdad is in jail for selling crack," says one. Another child offers, "My real daddy is in jail for putting a gun to somebody's
head." A third child explains that his uncle was involved in an armed robbery.
A fourth talks about a relative who has been arrested more than once for
drunken driving.

Kelvin tells the class that he wants to be singer. "Maybe you'll be rich if
you become a famous singer," I say.

"No," he replies, "because if I get rich, I'll make a store for people, and
I'll give food away."

Third and Fourth Grades

The remaining days are half days to give teachers the afternoons to attend
meetings and wrap up their paperwork. Thursday is the last school day for the
children. We ask them to write about something they really wish for. Here are
some of their wishes (edited for spelling) for themselves or the world:

Gerard: "I wish I could stop my mom from marrying that jerk Howard."
Sam: "Don't fight, don't chew tobacco."
Rachael: "A black President and a black White House."
Garrison: "If people stop doing drugs and selling them."

Carlonna: "We could keep all of the drug dealers off the street."

Shonora: "Take a way beer and alcohol."

Nikeya: "Stop killing folks."

Derek: "A person that would take drugs away from everybody."

LaDelle: "We can pull together and stop all the violence and drugs."

Rashand: "Stop wars and save children from starvation."

Jatoyia: "Stop shooting and stop drinking beer and don't do drugs and let the world be free and clean and safe."

Dwayne: "By giving people joy and peace."

Damien: "If they will stop giving the LEAP test."

We also ask the children to write down suggestions to teachers. Here is a sampling:

Andrenna: "Tell the kids that you are the boss."

Manuel: "You should never let a child go wild."

Chikae: "Do not throw away expensive paper."

Antinesha: "Make sure that you don't have a killer in your classroom."

Nicole: "Be fair to all of the people. Don't make everybody get in trouble if it was only three or five people."

Danielle: "Make them control their temper."

Graham: "We would like for them to give their hardest and bestest work they can do."

Victavius: "If students don't want to work put them out and the students who want to work teach them."

Shantel: "If they don't listen flunk them."

Kanesha: "Just paddle them give them 20 licks. That will fix them up good."

Haden: "Don't let people run to the bathroom because they will play."

Cherise: "They're counting on you. Teach them everything that you know. Teach them everything they need to know."

Ashley: "Make sure you make learning fun so kids will enjoy it and learn more."

Jaron: "Do not suspend a kid because then they got a day off."

Randall: "Do not be mean to a student or you might destroy their dreams."

We spend the last few days doing art projects with our classes. The children make self-portraits using construction paper, yarn, markers, and colored pencils. We make chalk drawings with sidewalk chalk and construction paper.

We make butterflies from coffee filters daubed with water colors. The children are never more quiet or more engaged than when working with art materials.

Thursday is our last day with the children, and we spend the time cleaning desks and chalkboards, gathering and stacking books, and just talking. We bring small farewell gifts to the children—yo-yos, bubble makers, assorted balls. We dispense the last of our stickers, wall hangings, and remaining school supplies. We accompany them to lunch for the last time at 11:15 where they eat wieners on bread with barbecue sauce, french fries, lettuce salad, and canned pear halves. All teachers stand with their classes as they await the buses and exchange best wishes, hugs, humor, and not a few tears. And then they are gone.

Third Grade

A week ago, Riverside Publishing recalled all of the Iowa Test of Basic Skills results in Louisiana because they "include misleading information. . . . In all, about 230,000 students in grades three, five, six, seven and nine took the tests in March" ("Publisher Recalls State's Iowa Results" 2001, 4A). Pam Porter informs the third-grade teachers that she has learned we will not get the third-grade results back until sometime in June. This will be too late for the teachers to enclose the results with the report cards or to enter the information on the student promotion and retention lists or the cumulative cards. We do not know how our students have done on the tests as we leave Redbud Elementary for the year.

Fourth Grade

Mrs. Larson, several other district teachers, and fifty-four fourth graders from Redbud Elementary School will return to the building next week to begin LEAP remediation summer school. The outside temperature reaches into the nineties most days now, but these fifty-four students will not be going to Lake Deerborne or to the Redbud public pool to swim. They'll come instead to intensive test preparation activities before they take the LEAP test another time in July. Altogether in Deerborne Parish, ninety-six fourth graders failed the LEAP test and will attend summer school.

Third and Fourth Grades

We shake our heads as we read in the newspapers this week that both branches of Congress had approved President George W. Bush's plan to test all public school students in grades 3 to 8 every year. We know that this testing will accomplish little good for anyone except to give employment to those in the bureaucratic fiefdoms that are sure to spring up with this additional testing. It will give profits to the corporations that rush to the trough and market print and electronic materials and tutoring services with promises of help in preparing the millions of children who will be forced to take these tests.

We recall the days when we taught children years ago. School districts used standardized tests to see how well they were doing. But there was no mania surrounding them. They were used as indicators of progress. No one taught for the test—it never would have dawned on anyone to do so. There were no high stakes attached to the results in the form of either reward or punishment for children, teachers, or schools based on test scores. We hope those times are not gone forever. A U.S. Department of Education official stated, "Anyone who is against annual testing of children is an apologist for a broken system of education that dismisses certain children and classes of children as unteachable" (*Education Week* 2001, 25). We don't think that any child is unteachable, but we know the disservice high-stakes testing does to many poor, mostly minority children in American schools. The testing robs children of the time that would otherwise be devoted to teaching and learning.

Fourth Grade

Students who will attend summer school from my homeroom because they failed English language or math or both are Dario, Jamal, Chalese, Derek, Yolande, Antron, Dwayne, and Tyler. The students from Mrs. Henderson's homeroom, my other class, who must attend are Garrison, Tony, Demetrius, Shonora, Nikos, Travis, Andrenna, Earvin, Gregory, Dianne, and Rhonda. I wonder how many of these children will pass the retake of the LEAP test.

De'Lewis, Danielle, and Lynette also failed the LEAP test this spring, but they will be promoted to fifth grade because they already have spent two years in fourth grade. Dawnyetta, Jatoyia, Victavius, Damien, Rashand, and Milo are repeat fourth graders who passed the LEAP test this time and will go on to fifth grade. Milo will be able to go to Texas this summer to go fishing with his biological father instead of going to summer school.

The appearance of our classes changed during the year. In fourth grade, Rachael and Tyler transferred to our school late last fall and stayed. Pauline, Danika, and Latonya transferred in, stayed for a while, and then left. Malcolm moved to North Carolina, and Emerald moved to a new trailer home in a nearby town after her house was destroyed by fire. Lynette, Danielle, Damien, and De'Lewis became more settled—less jumpy. Verlin and Graham continued to talk just as much at the end of the year as at the beginning. Both of these bright boys, along with Letrinette, LaDelle, Nikeya, Ashley, and Melissa and others, can go far in life if they get the right breaks. They are among the brightest students I have taught of any age. Two fourth-grade student teachers, Ms. Hammond and Mrs. Avalon, have come and gone, leaving their imprints on the children and taking valuable experiences into their teaching careers.

The third graders continue to be authorities on medical diagnoses and remedies as well as on national politics, economics, and virtually everything else. Two of my pupils, Jaheesa and Gerard, have told me that they will move away from Redbud this summer. One of my student teachers, Mrs. Tremain (née Schwartz), has decided to teach at Redbud Elementary School next year. She will teach third grade in the same classroom where she did her student teaching. She should do well because she knows the realities of working at Redbud Elementary, and she understands the children's needs. One of my pupils will be returning to third grade; he was absent too many days for the district to allow him to be promoted.

There are some gifts that will travel with us as we leave Redbud Elementary School. They were earned by our special education students for good work or given to us by our regular education pupils who have so little themselves. The gifts include a few plastic lizards, a rubber ball with rubber spikes, and smudged, wrinkled stickers with the backing still attached—junk to the casual observer, priceless to us. On Friday, we say our thanks and good-byes to the teachers and administrators who have been so much a part of our life for the past ten months. We promise to visit the school in the fall and to stay in contact via e-mail and telephone. As we depart Redbud, headed for White Lightning Road, we wave to some Redbud acquaintances who sit on the porches of their un-air-conditioned mobile homes. We have been transformed forever by our year as classroom teachers at Redbud Elementary School.

ELEVEN

HOW CAN WE BUILD
A BETTER FUTURE?

RECOMMENDATIONS FOR POLICY CHANGE

A textbook titled *Louisiana: Adventures in Time and Place*, which is used in Louisiana elementary schools, includes a discussion of the unequal treatment of African Americans during the period of segregation:

> However, most of the places set aside for black Americans were not as nice as those for white Americans. Schools for black children were usually very different from those for white children. Schools for black children were usually smaller and in poor condition. Many were rundown buildings with one room and no chalkboards. African American schools rarely had libraries. African American children often used the textbooks and equipment that had been thrown out by the white schools. This unfair difference in the treatment of people is called discrimination [dis kri muh NAY shun]. Discrimination kept African Americans in Louisiana from getting a good education. (Banks et al. 1998, 101)

Redbud Elementary School is not a small school, but in many other ways it resembles the school described in the previous quotation, as do many mostly African American schools in poor rural communities and in low-income urban neighborhoods.

Michael Harrington, in his classic *The Other America: Poverty in the United States* (1962), stated,

> After one reads the facts, either there are anger and shame, or there are not. And, as usual, the fate of the poor hangs upon the decision of the better-off. If this anger and shame are not forthcoming, someone can write a book about the other America a generation from now and it will be the same, or worse. (159)

In April 2001, Representative Chaka Fattah (D-Pa.) introduced a bill to equalize school funding. Fattah stated, "If no child is to be left behind then all children must be given an equal opportunity to compete. . . . Unfortunately, our method of school finance creates and maintains a very unequal system" (Raspberry 2001, 3B). In his article "Let States Equalize Education," Raspberry also cited Donald Anderson, the executive director of the National Community Development Organization:

> A plea for accountability is almost mocking. How can poor school districts achieve the same level of progress when they have no funds to upgrade staff, improve student/teacher ratios, upgrade their facilities or to provide such equipment as computers? (3B)

These underfunded schools are invariably the schools that are labeled "unacceptable," "below average," or "inadequate" by school accountability systems. It is time to stop labeling and start funding. It is hurtful to children and teachers who try so hard but whose results don't show up on the tests used to label and punish. The ZIP code of a community serves as an indicator of which schools will do the best and the worst on a standardized test. Testing for accountability purposes is superfluous. Money should be diverted from tests to the schools with the greatest financial needs. Roza (2001) predicts a gloomy future for poor schools:

> Picture the cycle: A high-poverty school starts with a complex student population. Poor performance gives the school a bad rap. The best teachers (and principals) opt to work elsewhere, and the school experiences ever-escalating staff turnover. High turnover continues to take its toll as parents have few relationships with school staff members, programs lack coherency, and the faculty is perpetually inexperienced. The school's reputation continues to dive, and as the teacher pool shrinks, it becomes even harder to hire qualified teachers for this school. In this kind of spiral, it really doesn't matter how much you put into reorganization, accountability, or other reforms. The bottom line is that the school still needs proficient teachers to teach the

kids. Without a good, stable teaching force, the school has almost no chance
of recovery. (56)

It is well established that tests, even the best of them, provide only a small
amount of evidence to judge what pupils are learning and how well schools
are doing their jobs. Teacher observations and appraisals of their pupils' work
and achievement certainly are equally as valid as test scores. Evaluations about
daily and unit work, as well as course grades in school subjects, offer additional
information about the child's learning. States that use test scores to compare
the performance of students, schools, or districts with others in the state do not
take into account the poverty levels and family problems that permeate some
schools. Such comparisons do not take into account the vastly different tax
bases and per-pupil expenditures that favor some schools significantly more
than others. Common sense tells us it is unrealistic to compare children from
high-poverty homes with children of affluence. Accountability designs, if they
are to be meaningful and just, must provide the money necessary to equalize
the opportunities of the many students in need. Too often, the hard work done
by teachers in low-performing schools goes unrecognized and in some in-
stances is punished. School- and teacher-bashing by politicians and some in the
media often dog the schools with the greatest needs. Perhaps this is because
they are easy targets that lack the means of fighting back.

WHAT TEACHERS NEED

State and district administrators and policymakers must unburden teachers of
the unnecessary paperwork and the administrative pronouncements that in-
hibit creative instruction. Teachers need to have the freedom to teach and to
make decisions. They must be relieved of the stresses of satisfying the whims
of bureaucrats and the vote-hungry motivation of elected officials. Teaching is
such an overwhelming undertaking for the pittance paid that some of the best
teachers are being driven away. It is not sensible to require teachers to spend
hours—sometimes days—noting the standards and benchmarks, as well as the
activity, modification, and assessment codes, on their weekly lesson plans. Doing so ensures nothing except frustration and wasted time that could have been
put into planning solid instructional activities.

State and district administrators and policymakers must recognize their
responsibilities in providing the instructional materials and tools that teachers
need to do their jobs. One of our Redbud colleagues had to write an eight-
page grant proposal to get addition, subtraction, multiplication, and division

flash cards and other supplies that should have been provided in her classroom. The proposal had to include an abstract, a demographic profile of the school, major project goals, objectives, and anticipated, and measurable results; a narrative description, documentation of need, description of collaborative partners, and an action plan; and, finally, the list of supplies, manufacturers, and cost. Consider how much time it took to prepare the proposal and how the time might have been better spent.

Teachers need to have a lunch period—as most working Americans already do—free from the job. Requiring elementary school teachers to go from seven or eight in the morning until three to four in the afternoon with perhaps a ten-minute break would be considered sweatshop hours in most businesses. Compare the teachers' lack of a lunch break with a grievance filed by the letter carriers' union in Des Moines, Iowa, that stated that "carriers shouldn't be told when to go to lunch" (Brooks 2001, A1). Redbud teachers wouldn't mind being told when to go to lunch if they could go to lunch without working as they ate.

It bears repeating that most teachers are overworked and underpaid for the responsibilities they have. Teachers deserve the same work breaks accorded to other American workers. They cannot even use the restroom when they need to. Who will watch the children for whom they are legally responsible? The job is so intense that twenty-two-year-olds tell us they fall asleep immediately when they get home from school. We have two recommendations: employ lunchroom supervisors and assign a paraprofessional to each classroom.

Children of poverty must be enrolled in a fully funded nursery school and preschool if they are to compete with other children on standardized tests. At Redbud Elementary, we noted that by the third grade, most children who were behind their peers had already given up on school. Some third graders were caring for their preschool siblings—sometimes before the start of school and sometimes after midnight. Children's lack of background knowledge hinders efforts beyond the preschool to teach grade-level curriculum:

> Language is the basic, major tool with which we think and learn. . . . In many homes children grow up with little or no language teaching except listening to adults with poor language. No one reads to the child: no one reads at all. When these children go to school at 5 or 6 years of age they are already four years behind and they rarely catch up. . . . [We must] as a society, face this problem and actively intervene by providing excellent health care, infant intervention programs, parent training programs, day care and preschool programs. (Torrans 2001, 9A)

Lord cited a study conducted by a University of Wisconsin–Madison professor. For fifteen years the researcher tracked 989 low-income, mostly African American children who attended preschool, compared with 552 peers who did not. The researcher found that those who attended preschool were "less likely to repeat a grade or to need special education" (Lord 2001, 48). We noticed during our year at Redbud that children who had attended preschool were more successful in academic and social endeavors.

EARLY VOICES OF OPPOSITION

By 1999, voices opposing high-stakes testing began to be heard, faintly at first and then ever louder. In "The Influence of Testing on the Curriculum," George Madaus (1999) issued a call to arms to his curriculum colleagues:

> To begin with, I feel that those concerned with curriculum and instruction need to lobby for a lowering of the stakes associated with test performance per se. Those concerned with curriculum, teaching, and learning must make the case that test information be *one* piece of information alongside other indicators. (105)

In the same year, the International Reading Association (IRA), a professional organization with 90,000 full and 250,000 affiliated members, mostly teachers, issued a position statement on high-stakes assessments. It said, in part, that the association "is opposed to high-stakes testing" (International Reading Association 1999). Problematic outcomes of high-stakes testing identified by IRA included narrowing the curriculum by inflating the importance of the test, losing instructional time, making bad decisions harmful to students, and centralizing decision making. The IRA's position paper stated that "narrowing of the curriculum is most likely to occur in high-poverty schools that tend to have the lowest test scores." The association recommended that decisions about graduation, grade promotion, and rewards utilize multiple indicators, including teacher informal assessments, portfolios, and teacher recommendations as well as standardized test scores.

One of the nation's two major teachers unions added its voice to the growing opposition to high-stakes testing during its annual convention in summer 2000. Bob Chase, president of the National Education Association (NEA), said, "In some states testing mania is quite literally devouring whole school systems like some education-eating bacteria" (Bradley 2000, 20).

Other organizations that expressed concern over holding students and schools accountable for performance on test scores were the Council of Chief State School Officers (CCSSO), whose members include state school superintendents and other state department officials, and the American Association of School Administrators (AASA), an organization of many of the nation's school district superintendents. Douglas Christianson, commissioner of education in Nebraska, stated, "We have rushed far too quickly in my opinion, to assessments with high-stakes testing, never giving a chance for standards to have meaning in the classroom" (Olson 2000a, 9). Paul Houston, executive director of the AASA, claimed, "Right now high-stakes testing is harming the educational process for many children" (Olson 2000a, 9).

At its 2000 annual convention, the members of the National Council of Teachers of English (NCTE) (2001) approved the following resolution:

> The efforts to improve the quality of education, especially in underachieving schools, are laudable, and the desire for accountability is understandable. However, high stakes tests often fail to assess accurately students' knowledge, understanding, and capability. Raising test scores does not improve education. Therefore, the use of any single test in making important decisions—such as graduation, promotion, funding of schools, or employment and compensation of administrators and teachers—is educationally unsound and unethical.
>
> High stakes testing often harms students' daily experience of learning, displaces more thoughtful and creative curriculum, diminishes the emotional well-being of educators and children, and unfairly damages the life-chances of members of vulnerable groups.
>
> We call on legislators and policymakers to repeal laws and policies that tie significant consequences to scores on single assessments. We further call on legislators and policymakers to join with professional organizations to develop better means of improving public education.
>
> BE IT FURTHER RESOLVED that NCTE invite other organizations to support, publicize, and promote a reconsideration of high stakes testing. (300)

The president of the National Council for the Social Studies, Susan Adler (2001), stated,

> Certainly, well-constructed tests can serve a real function, although important decisions should never be based on a single test. But we must not support testing programs that undermine the very foundations of social studies—the application of knowledge to thinking and decision making. We cannot support testing programs that hurt learners, and often hurt most those who are most at risk. As educators, we have, separately and together, expertise that can inform policy. (3)

Polls conducted in 2000 suggested a developing uneasiness about the growing emphasis on using standardized tests to make important education decisions about students. The AASA sponsored a bipartisan poll of eight hundred registered voters and found that "63 per cent of voters did not agree that a student's progress for one school year can be accurately summarized by a single standardized test" and "49 per cent opposed keeping students back a grade if they failed to achieve a passing score on a standardized statewide test" (Olson 2000b, 9). In Louisiana, a New Orleans–based parent group issued a legal challenge to using the LEAP test to decide whether students would be promoted to the next grade, but the challenge was rejected by a district judge. *USA Today* and the American Federation of Teachers conducted a poll of teachers and found that "91% believed that the focus on high-stakes test scores was forcing some schools to become nothing more than test-prep centers," and "94% agreed that politicians and school officials are placing unreasonable importance on the results of high-stakes tests" (Henry 2000, 10D).

A poll conducted by Public Agenda in October 2000 showed that while the public generally is supportive of the notion of accountability, "sixty-one percent said they 'strongly' agreed that 'it's wrong to use the results of just one test to decide whether a student gets promoted or graduates.' Another 17 percent said they 'somewhat' agreed with the statement" (Hoff 2000). The poll showed that nearly 80 percent of those surveyed were skeptical of using tests as the sole criterion for high-stakes assessment.

High-stakes testing spawned a number of books critical of the standards movement, including *One Size Fits Few: The Folly of Educational Standards* (1999) by Susan Ohanian, *The Schools Our Children Deserve: Moving beyond Traditional Classrooms and "Tougher Standards"* (1999) by Alfie Kohn, *The Case against Standardized Testing: Raising the Scores, Ruining the Schools* (2000a) also by Kohn, and *Will Standards Save Public Education?* (2000) by Deborah Meier. The central theme of all four books was articulated by Meier: "Standardized tests are too simple and too simple minded for high-stakes assessment of children and schools. Important decisions regarding kids and teachers should always be based on multiple sources of evidence that seem appropriate and credible to those most concerned" (17).

Leon Botstein (2000), in an article titled "A Tyranny of Standardized Tests," said, "The tyranny of testing has become so intense that teachers may find themselves spending more than half the year teaching specifically for tests; their jobs and the standing of their schools are on the line" (11). Testing pressures have begun to cause some students, teachers, and principals to cheat. Teachers in various states have been accused of using a variety of methods ranging from giving, filling in, or changing student answers to drilling their students on actual exam questions obtained in unknown ways. To some educators, the line is blurred between cheating and simply giving students extra help. Is drilling a class on sample or released test items cheating? This procedure is conducted routinely in Louisiana. Danny Bell, district test coordinator for the Lincoln Parish School System, said,

> We have a number of publications from the state which we distribute to our teachers on a regular basis. These give explicit examples of the types of questions which will be asked and how best to answer them. Some of these actually feature released test items from previous tests. Those are particularly helpful because they deal with the reality of what the students can expect. (Van Diest 2001, 1a)

The pressure to give as much help to their students as possible, even when it crosses that fuzzy line, is mounting. Scores have impact on school budgets, salaries, and whether administrators keep their jobs. Even parents have begun to feel similar pressures. In one northern Louisiana school district, a secured LEAP test was discovered missing the day before testing began; it was traced to an anxious parent who had access to the school building after hours.

Parents in Massachusetts have been organizing. "Much like revolutionaries of old, men and women are gathering in the halls of Harvard and the public spaces of Cambridge and Boston and well into the Berkshires to organize against the paper and pencil test" (Lindsay 2000, 34). The test they were organizing against is the Massachusetts Comprehensive Assessment System.

THE SILENCE OF NCATE

As of this writing, the voice that has not been heard opposing high-stakes testing is the voice of the nation's biggest organization that accredits teacher education programs in colleges and universities. The National Council for Accreditation of Teacher Education (NCATE) accredits more than five hundred of the nation's thirteen hundred teacher preparation programs. It is astonishing to us that although teacher organizations such as NEA and the American Federation of Teachers, administrator groups such as AASA and CCSSO, and professional associations of teachers exemplified by IRA and NCTE have taken a stand, the group that is most directly concerned with how teachers are prepared seems to have no problem with the way the standards movement is being played out in the schools and districts. Shame on NCATE for not using its Washington, D.C., and state capital connections and the other mechanisms of their great influence to try to turn the tide. Is it because NCATE is out of touch with the realities of classrooms today? Is it because NCATE is fearful of jeopardizing its standing with state legislators and other people of prominence who favor single-number indicators of student achievement?

QUESTIONS FOR OFFICIALS

We were warned by prepublication readers not to step on important toes. Nevertheless, we are convinced that we have a professional obligation to ask the following questions:

- How many federal or state lawmakers, state superintendents of education, or members of a state board of education or department of education ever have taught full time in one of the elementary schools under their jurisdiction?
- How many policymakers and lawmakers ever have taught in an underfunded school?
- How many policymakers and lawmakers have spent any significant amount of time in schools such as Redbud Elementary School to completely grasp the problems faced by the children, teachers, and administrators?
- How many executive directors and officers of associations such as NCATE ever have taught school full time? If they have taught, how many years ago? What were the conditions in the schools and the demographics of the pupils?

Perhaps some officials have been too concerned with reelection, reappointment, or the expansion and prominence of their organizations to feel they could be "spared" a year or two to get back to the classroom. But they make their rather comfortable livings forming, mandating, and monitoring the rules and regulations that affect the preparation of the nation's teachers. Wouldn't firsthand experience make sense for these people? It is high time these officials leave their well-appointed, air-conditioned offices and put their expense accounts and travel schedules on hold for a year to teach full time in public schools so they can acquaint themselves with life in schools today. It wouldn't hurt them to leave their usual salaries behind and try to budget on a teacher's salary, either. Then perhaps their voices of protest about some of the foolishness and harmfulness rampant in the schools would be heard in the same way the voices of many teachers, school administrators, and parents are being heard today.

It is in NCATE officials' own best interest to return to the public schools. Many new teachers don't stay long in the profession. Half the education graduates never enter the classroom, and of the rest, 20 percent leave the classroom by the third year (*Education Week* 2000, 9). They are overwhelmed by poor working conditions and the circumstances that are the theme of this book. Sooner or later, someone will be held *accountable* for the reasons these beginning teachers are so unprepared for the realities of contemporary classrooms. The buck eventually has to stop at the big shots' desks.

In "Standards for What?" Robert B. Reich (2001), former U.S. secretary of labor and professor at Brandeis University, pointed out,

> The latest rage in education is standardized tests. Tests have been around for a long time, of course, but have never been employed to the extent they are now. Young people are now being tested and then retested a year or two later, and then retested again and again. Our schools are morphing into test-taking factories. Politicians like tests because they don't cost much money and they reassure the public that children are at least learning something.
>
> Paradoxically, we're embracing standardized tests just when the new economy is eliminating standardized jobs. If there's one certainty about what today's schoolchildren will be doing a decade or two from now, it's that they won't all be doing the same things, and they certainly won't be drawing on the same body of knowledge. (64)

Reich's observations reiterate a warning sounded by former President Harry Truman in 1956:

> People must have freedom of mind for research that makes progress, otherwise there is no use in having an educational system. If everyone remained in the same groove and were taught exactly the same thing, we would end up with a nation of mediocrities. (Ayres 1998, 42)

We fear that the accountability movement sweeping American education and the high-stakes testing it has spawned are driving the nation in the direction Truman warned against.

SUMMARY OF OUR RECOMMENDATIONS

First, the use of high-stakes tests in some subjects is changing what goes on in classrooms to the detriment of the arts, problem solving, creativity, and the joy associated with learning and discovering. In recent years, schools such as Red-bud Elementary have become little more than test preparation centers whose teachers must spend disproportionate amounts of time teaching children how to take tests. Time is spent cramming the materials covered in the tests to the neglect of entire subjects such as science, social studies, art, drama, and music. Present policies place unwarranted stress on children and teachers because of the intense pressure to raise scores. State legislatures, boards of education, and school district authorities must back off from their commitment to raise test scores at the expense of providing children a well-rounded, well-grounded education across the curriculum. Passing a high-stakes test does not mean that students are well educated any more than passing a written or behind-the-wheel driver's test means that someone is a good driver. The continual drill-and-practice for the tests leaves the slower learners even farther behind. They become discouraged and give up on school at an early age. There are not enough adults available to help them catch up. "Work the teachers and the kids harder" is a simplistic, uninformed recommendation that we heard throughout our year at Redbud Elementary. States should redirect the money spent on testing into hiring an additional adult for each classroom in underfunded schools. This would be an example of real education reform.

Second, states and school districts must stop making important decisions about grade promotion or graduation based on a single test—even if given repeatedly. Listen to the experts in the classrooms and the professional organizations. Use multiple indicators such as test data, course grades, portfolios, and teacher judgments to determine who passes and who fails. Teachers know their students better than any single test can. They know the strengths and weaknesses and capabilities of the children with whom they work daily, week in and week out.

Third, states that give high-stakes tests should not only reexamine their testing policies but also examine the tests themselves. When fifty-four thousand fourth and eighth graders failed a test such as the LEAP in Louisiana in 2000 and forty thousand more failed in 2001, the problem is more likely with the tests themselves than with the students or their teachers. Who wrote the tests? What are their qualifications? What teaching experience have they had with students of the ages being tested? Who determines the pass–fail scores? On what basis? What are the content validity and the reliability of the tests? How developmentally appropriate are the content and format of the tests?

Fourth, schools in America are unequally funded. If every child in a state is expected to take the same test, every school should have the same proportionate quantity and quality of certified teachers; the same quantity and quality of instructional materials and resources; the same school environment in terms of building repair, cleanliness, and absence of vermin; the same playground and recreational equipment; and the same support personnel such as counselors and school nurses. Children of poverty have so many strikes against them in their homes, neighborhoods, and daily lives that they must, at the least, have the same in-school advantages as children of the middle classes and the affluent if they are to be held to the same standards as measured by the same standardized tests. This means that states must rethink their policies and procedures for funding local schools and must make a financial and moral commitment to equalize such funding.

Fifth, children of poverty must be provided with nursery school and pre-school education similar to what is typically available to more economically fortunate children. Many children in schools such as Redbud enter kindergarten and first grade seriously deficient in concept formation, vocabulary, and general language development. There is evidence that preschool programs help young children achieve a more equal footing. State legislation is needed, and the inherent financial commitment must follow, to provide preschool education for all.

Sixth, unequal funding of schools has been an indirect cause of some of the obvious resegregation of schools. The growth of private schools and academies, which often have mostly white students, is a result of parents' unwillingness to send their children to underfunded local schools whose student bodies have become mostly African American. If this type of resegregation is to be stopped, state and local (and perhaps federal) governments must see to it that public schools have adequate and equal funding. We also wonder if there isn't an unspoken and unwritten message to children who attend schools such as Redbud. The message is, "You're black and poor. A few of you are white and poor. These schools are good enough for you." The message is racist and smacks of social class elitism. State school officials must address this issue. Perhaps it is time for a federal review of these separate and unequal schools.

Seventh, decision making must again be entrusted to teachers rather than to state and district officials far removed from the classroom. Restore teacher dignity and autonomy by allowing teachers the freedom to teach—to plan and develop engaging and innovative instructional activities. State and district administrators must reduce and preferably eliminate the cumbersome burdens of redundant paperwork that currently engulf much of a teacher's time. They must stop the persistent and unnecessary monitoring of teacher activities and trust them to do their jobs.

Administrators must make life easier for teachers by providing them with time each day away from their children—even if it's just fifteen minutes to regroup or use the restroom. These minimal conditions are provided to factory workers and office workers. Give teachers a lunch period free from lunchroom duties and interacting with pupils. Districts need to provide private telephones that teachers can use to contact parents to discuss children's progress.

Eighth, it is time for a national commitment to raise teachers' salaries to a professional level so that the best teachers can afford to stay in the profession. No school should have to hire uncertified teachers who are there to mark time and collect a little money before they move on to their career of choice. Schools must have nurturing, sincere people behind the teacher's desk. Pay raises are especially needed for teachers willing to work in challenging rural and urban schools.

Ninth, underfunded schools need volunteers. It is one thing to talk about social injustice but quite another to do something about it. Parents and guardians who are among the working poor are too weary dealing with the grind of poverty to volunteer their time in schools the way some parents can. Teachers are too beaten down and worn out by the demands of accountability, benchmarks, codes, and other imposed minutiae to give more of themselves. There just isn't enough time or energy. Volunteers are needed to tutor children and read to them, to staff the lunchrooms so that teachers get a short break, and to paint and decorate classrooms and hallways. Volunteers are needed from among the expanding pool of retired persons who often live decades beyond their regular employment. Volunteers are needed from organizations and service clubs such as Junior League, Kiwanis, and Rotary. Volunteers are needed from colleges and universities whose professors in many disciplines could require service projects in poor schools. English and sociology classes could compile guides to food banks, dental clinics, and social service agencies. Business classes could organize and conduct fund-raising drives to support local schools. Journalism students could write articles that appeal for volunteers to work in the schools. Future teachers could work in instructional capacities to help busy teachers. Social injustice does not correct itself unless people do more than tsk-tsk it.

As a country, we need to realize what a mistake it is to not nourish, in every sense of the word, children of poverty. The year we spent at Redbud Elementary restored our hope for the future. The children came to us—and left us—with courage, ingenuity, eagerness to learn, trust, compassion for others, a warm sense of humor, and genuine kindness. Dwight D. Eisenhower, in a commencement address at Gettysburg College in 1946, captured the spirit we saw daily in the children of Redbud: "Fortunately for us and our world, youth is not easily discouraged. . . . The hopes of the world rest on the flexibility, vigor, capacity for new thought, the fresh outlook of the young" (Carruth and Ehrlich 1988, 633).

TWELVE

TODAY A NATION OF TESTING

POVERTY AND WEALTH AT HOME AND AT SCHOOL

Samantha Jones, one of our graduate students, is a high school teacher at an alternative school in New York City. The school has 220 students ranging in age from sixteen to twenty-one. New York is a high-stakes testing state. Third and fifth graders in New York City must pass a test to be promoted to the next grade, and high school students must pass a test to graduate. New York is one of the twenty-one states with such a graduation requirement. Samantha wrote the following description of her school:

> More than 85 percent of our students have not passed the English Language Assessment (ELA). Their English and reading skills are far below grade level. Trying to prepare the students for academic success is very difficult because they are having so many problems at home. We have students who have their own children. I am working with two students who are up for attempted murder. Their focus is far from schoolwork.
>
> My class size varies. One has 40 students, another 38. There are about 15 textbooks for the two classes combined. Many pages are ripped out, there is gum in or on them, and they are above the students' reading levels. The

other class I teach has 28 students. That class has no textbooks, so I am constantly making photocopies and handing out papers and folders.

The school has no nurse's office, no teachers' lounge, no library. The computer lab has 20 outdated, virus-embedded computers. That is our only technology. The computer room has one printer and students are not allowed to print out more than one page. I go to the public library and bring books into the school.

The security guards have to take away students' knives before they come into the building. Outbursts in classrooms and fighting are common. Yet, I am supposed to read a script on what and how to teach.

Every student gets a free breakfast and lunch and a Metro [subway] card. Teaching in a poor performing urban school is emotionally and physically draining. Most teachers here want the students to learn, but we have no support from the "powers that be." I have spent over $800 so far this year, and it is only November, on supplies and books for the classroom. Not only do we teach students but also critters such as the rat, mouse, and roach population. Some days they seem to pay more attention to me than the students.

The situation described by Samantha is in contrast with that of Elvira Berk, also one of our graduate students. Elvira is a teacher on Long Island. She wrote,

One of the great things that teachers enjoy in my district is the access to technology. There are several computers with high-speed Internet connections in every classroom. In the two middle schools, all sixth-graders are given a laptop that they use throughout the day.

Another great thing about my school district is that teachers don't need to spend their own money on things that they need. If we need supplies, all we have to do is fill out a supply request form, and then we are given whatever we need. If we want to go on a field trip, the district funds it without hesitation. We also never have to worry about our textbook supply because our students have a second copy of the texts for home use.

Students in both public schools and in all schools in New York State must take the same high-stakes tests.

The pattern of privilege and nonprivilege exists at home and at school in every state in our nation. There is ample documentation that poverty is negatively correlated to test scores; as the percentage of students who live in poverty increases, the test scores go down. Child poverty is an enormous problem in the United States, and in some states, one in four schoolchildren live in poverty (*Kids Count Data Book* 2004, 61). Louisiana, Mississippi, and New Mexico have the largest percentages of poor children with 24, 25, and 26 percent respectively (61). Superville (2004) reported that the number of people living in poverty grew by 1.3 million in 2003 to 35.8 million. Hunger affects 12.6 million families in the United States. She stated,

> In about one-third of the 12.6 million families, or 3.9 million, at least one person went hungry because there was not enough money to feed everyone. . . . More than 36 million people, including 13 million children, experienced hunger or worried about it last year. (A17)

These numbers are deplorable in a nation as wealthy as the United States. They become even more shameful when politicians and policymakers mandate that poor, hungry children compete on the same tests as their well-fed, well-cared-for peers in well-equipped schools.

Lynette Wilson (2004a), in an article that discussed poverty in Louisiana, stated, "The 2000 Census reported that 800,648 Louisianians live in poverty" (1). A Louisiana newspaper editorial noted that ten of the fifteen parishes (counties) in northeastern Louisiana had even higher percentage rates. The Mississippi delta parishes of East Carroll, Tensas, and Madison, with poverty rates of 39.9, 33.1, and 30.9, respectively, rank among the worst poverty areas in America ("Summit Can Help the Blight" 2004, 1). Sumrall (2004) reported that 26,327 housing units in Louisiana lack complete plumbing facilities and that 31,797 do not have complete kitchen facilities. He cited a resident of Alexandria, Louisiana, who said,

> The floors are dragging and shifting, the whole house really (is) in parts. The ceiling is twisting and turning, and it's hard to keep the tile up, it falls down, that sort of thing.
>
> With three kids in school and that sort of thing, it kind of left very little (money) for improvement, so that's where it kind of got the upper hand. (3)

Those three children must take the same high-stakes tests as children in affluent neighborhoods in the state.

Sumrall's (2004) article listed other prevailing housing problems, including bad electrical wiring, no indoor toilet, no indoor hot or cold water, no central air or heat, little insulation, walls that lean or sag, and doors that are loose or missing (3–4). In an article titled "The Third World Next Door," Jackson (2004) wrote, "While the stereotype of poverty might be one of dishonest, lazy creatures who abuse welfare and other charitable options, a truer face is one of minimum-wage earners, people working extra jobs and overtime to try to make ends meet" (1). Jackson cited a gas station attendant in Tensas Parish who said, "Poverty is being . . . hungry, and scared to burn your heat because you are scared you can't afford the utility bill" (2). Those Americans who have experienced a power failure or plumbing difficulties or lack of heat in cold weather know the inconvenience at first and then, if prolonged, the hardships such problems cause. Some people who live in poverty experience these hardships continuously, yet their children must take the same high-stakes tests as children of the middle classes and of affluence.

The importance of proper nutrition in maintaining a strong populace has been recognized for over half a century. According to the Food Research and Action Center (2003), the National School Lunch Program was established when a link was shown between soldiers rejected for the World War II draft and inadequate childhood nutrition. The program not only was a humanitarian endeavor but also was viewed as being in the best interest of national security.

Parents of children who attend some private schools are well aware of the importance of nutrition. For example, at The Calhoun School in New York City, a chef was hired from the French Culinary Institute to cook meals that are " 'all natural,' meaning from scratch with fresh ingredients and organic produce. . . . When paying $700 to $1,000 a year just for meals (compared with $315 a year in public school), as one parent put it, a certain level of quality is expected" (Hartocollis 2004, B4). The Calhoun School's (2005) lunch program website states,

> The chef frequently goes into classrooms, offering cooking demonstrations that focus on health, science-oriented lessons about herbs and chemistry, and social studies and linguistic lessons that expose children to diversity in cultures and foods. There are also a number of after-school cooking classes for students, at every age level, that reinforce the importance of high quality ingredients, recipe variety and well-seasoned food. (1)

A lunch menu from January 3–14, 2005, at The Calhoun School included, among other dishes, green beans with shallots; veggie goatcheese, sundried tomato, and arugula focaccia; hummus, cucumber, and tomato on wheat bread; fresh fruit; and couscous. In contrast, children in one underfunded Louisiana public school district had the following items, among others, on their weekly school lunch menus: pig 'n flapjackets with syrup, chili dogs, tater tots, cheeseburgers, sausages, Frito pie, mini honey buns, cinnamon rolls, French fries, and mini corn dogs (*Guardian-Journal* 2004a, 2004b, 2004c).

Steve Nelson (2005), head of The Calhoun School, pointed out,

> Food is not a utilitarian fuel, merely designed to provide some minimal level of glycogen for afternoon arithmetic. What our children eat is deeply important and the experiences they have in school will shape attitudes and be-

haviors for a lifetime. I've never understood how so many educators can examine each nuance of the science curriculum and, with no apparent awareness of irony, watch thousands of empty carbohydrates pass through young mouths each day. (1)

According to Wilson (2003), some poor public school children may not receive even the nutritionally suspect dishes listed above from the Louisiana public school menu. She noted that President George W. Bush had requested "more paperwork up front" for children who receive free school meals. Wilson stated, "The administration contends too many children are getting free meals because school districts don't check them out enough" (1). A child nutrition specialist in a Louisiana school district said that the proposal would be "devastating" to those children who receive the needed meals. We know from our experience in working with low-income pupils that some of their parents and guardians do not possess the literacy skills to complete even simple paperwork for free meals. Wouldn't it be better to allow some children who do not fully qualify for free meals to eat two meals a day than to risk having needy children miss the only meals they get all day because of paperwork?

In the spring of 2004, New York City Mayor Michael Bloomberg established a new policy that required grade retention for third graders who failed a citywide high-stakes test. The results of the test indicated that third-grade children from high-poverty areas dominated the retention ranks. Herszenhorn and Gootman (2004) reported that "children in impoverished, predominately black neighborhoods were likely to be most affected by the mayor's plan" (B4). Children from Harlem, Bedford-Stuyvesant, the Bronx, and other impoverished areas failed to achieve passing grades. As many as one out of three children in New York City's lowest-performing schools faced the prospect of repeating third grade.

The relationship between children's socioeconomic status and test performance is well established. Popham (1998) observed,

> If you want to predict how well a school's students will score on a standardized achievement test, simply find out what the average parental income is for that school. If parental income is high, students will usually score well; if parental income is low, anticipate lower scores. (7)

Watts (2003) conducted a study of sixty-six Louisiana school districts and found that students' socioeconomic status explained 60 percent of the variance in student achievement; the higher the rate of poverty as measured by eligibility for free and reduced lunch, the lower the student test scores. Borman and her colleagues (2004) conducted a study to explore the association between racial segregation in Florida and the percentage of students who passed high-stakes tests. The researchers found that as the percentage of poverty increased, the percentage of students who passed the Florida Comprehensive Assessment Test (FCAT) decreased. Johnson et al. (2005) examined the achievement test scores for ninety K–12 districts in Nassau and Suffolk counties on Long Island. They found that "in general, lower student achievement was associated with a higher percentage of students eligible for free lunch" (188). On all measures in their study, poverty was the significant variable, and the impact of poverty on test scores increased from fourth to eighth to twelfth grade. The longer a student stayed in school, the greater the effects of poverty on test scores.

The impressive connection between socioeconomic status and test performance is apparent when examining college entrance exams as well. On the 2004 SAT test, the average score for students whose family income was between $10,000 and $20,000 was 887, and the average score for test takers whose family income was more than $100,000 per year was 1,115 (FairTest, 2004b). On the ACT test, the average score for test takers whose family income was less than $18,000 was 18.0. For those with a family income of more than $100,000 per year, the average score was 23.5 (FairTest, 2004b). The issue is one of social justice, and it needs to be addressed aggressively by civil rights advocates across the country.

Winter (2004) reported on a widening gap in state funding for rich and poor schools. In twenty-five states, the wealthier districts received more local and state funding than did high-poverty school districts. Winter pointed out that in New York and Illinois, the gap in state funding was the largest in the nation with more than $2,000 less per child going to the low-income schools despite research evidence that it costs more to educate low-income children (A19). The picture may change in California. Madigan (2004) commented,

> If 16-year-old Eliezer Williams has his way, rats will no longer scurry through classrooms in California, and every student will have books, a place to sit and a clean bathroom to use.
>
> Eliezer is the lead plaintiff in a class-action lawsuit filed in 2000 by the American Civil Liberties Union on behalf of 1.5 million students, most from poor neighborhoods. The lawsuit accused the state of denying poor children adequate textbooks, trained teachers and safe classrooms. (A12)

California settled the case in the fall of 2004 by pledging to spend $1 billion to upgrade crumbling schools and provide educational supplies ("Calif. Public Schools to Post Notices on Adequate Conditions" 2005, 4).

California is not alone in its problems with dirty, rodent-infested schools. The *New York Times* reported that Chicago, for example, had shut down thirteen school cafeterias and ordered the cleaning of all six hundred public schools because of rat problems (Midwest: Illinois: Schools to Be Cleaned" 2004, A12). Gootman (2004) disclosed,

> At Abraham Lincoln High School in Brooklyn, the bathrooms are so bad that students have been known to use the toilets at Coney Island hospital, down the road. . . . Dirty bathrooms, broken toilets, faulty stall doors and a dearth of toilet paper are not new problems in New York City's 1,200 public schools but they persist, said Eva S. Moskowitz, chairwoman of the City Council Education Committee. (B3)

An Education Trust report listed Louisiana "as being among the worst 10 states for equitable funding between the richest and poorest school districts" (Gannett Capital Bureau 2004b, 1). A week later, the Gannett Capital Bureau pointed out, "More than one-third of Louisiana's school systems are in serious financial trouble" (Gannett Capital Bureau 2004a, 1). Nonetheless, Superintendent Picard, the Louisiana Department of Education, the state legislature, and the governor show no signs of easing up on the state's accountability and high-stakes testing mandates on which Louisiana spends tens of millions of dollars each year.

The differences in the funding of public schools across the country are disturbing. In Yonkers, New York, the financial picture was so bleak that the 2004–2005 school year began with 574 fewer teachers and support staff than the previous year. There were 27,000 students in the Yonkers public school system. The diminished budget meant that art, music, and foreign language classes in the elementary schools were eliminated, as were extracurricular programs such as instrumental music, drama, the yearbook, some varsity sports in the middle schools and high schools, and more. Security teams were reduced, most librarians were let go, and the social service staff (i.e., guidance counselors, psychologists, and social workers) was reduced (Semple 2004, B1).

The financial situation in Yonkers was sharply different from the Roslyn, Long Island, school district, in which there was such an abundance of money that the school superintendent and other school officials allegedly were able to embezzle approximately $8 million from the school budget before the shortage was discovered. Kolker (2004) reported that former Roslyn school superintendent Frank Tassone "allegedly had the district pay for two trips to London on the Concorde, one for $20,000 and another for $30,000, including $1,800-a-night suites, and a half-dozen jaunts to Las Vegas . . . where the district even staked some of Tassone's gambling money" (28). The district's website (www.roslynschools.org) notes that support staff include "math, reading, computer and library experts" and that pupils "begin the study of foreign language in kindergarten" (1). The site also points out that enrichment activities include marine biology and Great Books, among others, and that "Roslyn's vocal and instrumental music programs are exceptional and include performances, competitions and a joint concert annually with the New York Virtuosi" (2). The website states, "Roslyn students consistently score well above the county, state and national averages on standardized tests and the College Board exams" (1). The average home price in Roslyn is $750,000 (www.relocate-america.com). Students in Yonkers and those in Roslyn take the same New York–mandated high-stakes tests.

Roslyn is not the only affluent school district in New York that produces high test scores. Hevesi (2004) pointed out that families with children in the "highly regarded Public School 87 on the Upper West Side, or Public School 6 on the Upper East Side" of Manhattan must pay on average $1.1 million for a two-bedroom co-op and $1.6 million for a condo" (11.1). In these two schools, students test above the norm in reading and math. According to Ingrid Gould Ellen of the Furman Center for Real Estate and Urban Policy at New York University, property values and achievement as measured by tests "march in lock step" (11.9). Hevesi noted, "A statistical analysis by the Furman Center tracing both English language test scores for elementary and middle school students and median house prices in 26 New York City community school districts . . . drew ascending, virtually parallel lines" (11.9).

Susan Kramer (2004) of New York City felt compelled to write a letter to the editor of the *New York Times* about funding problems in the school district. The letter said, in part,

> My children attend P.S. 3, a top-rated New York City elementary school that has a relatively middle-class population. Every year we are asked to bring in soap, tissues, glue, paper towels and even pencils. Some bathroom sinks don't have running water. Our gym is a glorified hallway. Many of the classes are at the maximum of 33 children. The parents raise money so the children can have art, music and dance. I can only imagine what schools in less affluent areas are like. (12)

It is not difficult to understand why the turnover rate is so high for teachers in impoverished schools based on working conditions alone. Now there is an additional factor that further will deter people from wanting to teach in these schools. New York City Public Schools Chancellor Joel Klein is on record supporting teacher pay based on improvements in student performance (Herszenhorn 2004, B6), as are elected and appointed officials in other states. A year prior to Klein's pay-for-performance endorsement, Odden and Wallace

(2003) argued for compensating teachers based on gains in student achievement. Allan Odden is professor of educational leadership and policy analysis at the University of Wisconsin, and Marc J. Wallace Jr. is a founding partner of a compensation consulting firm in Illinois. The two conduct workshops on teacher pay-for-performance plans. Odden and Wallace do not seem concerned about the links between high test scores and parental affluence, children's background experiences, and school expenditures. We challenge Odden and Wallace, Chancellor Klein, and others who support the pay-for-performance notion to teach for one year in Samantha Jones's school, Redbud Elementary School in Louisiana, or a similar school that serves children of poverty and base the amount of their paychecks on their students' test scores.

THE GROWTH OF TESTING

In 2000, Louisiana became the first state in the nation to require elementary (fourth grade) and middle school (eighth grade) students to pass a standardized test for promotion to the next grade. Since 2000, seven additional states—Delaware, Florida, Georgia, Missouri, North Carolina, Texas, and Wisconsin—now have retention policies based on a single state test score (*Education Week* 2005, 90–91). By 2004–2005, twenty-one states based high school graduation on statewide exit or end-of-course exams, and three additional states were scheduled to do so beginning in 2006 and two more in 2008 (91). By 2004–2005, twenty-nine states sanctioned low-performing schools, and the sanctions included school closures, school reconstitution, permitting student transfers, and turning schools over to private management. Seventeen states provided rewards to high-performing or improved schools. Five states had policies to withhold funds from low-performing schools. The five states were Illinois, Louisiana, Maryland, Michigan, and Tennessee (90). When states withhold money from schools that need the funds the most, they are punishing children for being poor.

For the past thirty-six years, the Gallup polling organization and Phi Delta Kappa, a professional organization for educators, have conducted a survey of the public's attitudes toward the public schools. The thirty-sixth annual poll included telephone interviews with 1,003 adults between May 28 and June 18, 2004. Each interviewee was asked forty-two questions. One question was, "In your opinion, is it possible or not possible to accurately judge a student's proficiency in English and math on the basis of a single test?" Seventy-three percent of the respondents answered, "No, not possible." Another question asked, "In your opinion, will a single test provide a fair picture of whether or not a school needs improvement?" Sixty-seven percent of the respondents said, "No." A third question asked, "How much, if at all, are you concerned that relying on testing for English and math only to judge a school's performance will mean less emphasis on art, music, history, and other subjects?" Eighty-one percent said they were concerned "A great deal" or "A fair amount" (Rose and Gallup 2004, 46). If the respondents to the Gallup/Phi Delta Kappa poll accurately represent the national mood toward high-stakes testing, it should be apparent to lawmakers that taxpayers know it is wrong to base life-altering decisions on single test scores.

There have been a number of concerns raised about the use and misuse of test scores. Some people in Dallas, Texas, were not happy to learn that Juanita Nix, principal of Maple Lawn Elementary School, had displayed on bulletin boards class scores on the state's accountability test. Aimee Bolander, president of the Dallas affiliate of the American Federation of Teachers, said, "We think it is extremely unprofessional to do that. . . . It doesn't help to increase the learning of students by humiliating teachers publicly" (Galley 2003, 3). Across the country, newspapers routinely publish test performance scores for districts and individual schools. Realtors use these public listings to aid home sales in their territories. Some parents display school rankings and scores on bumper stickers. The executive directors of the National Association of Elementary School Principals, Vincent L. Ferrandino, and the National Association of Secondary School Principals, Gerald N. Tirozzi, decried the use of public shame as a mechanism to raise test scores. They stated,

> It is indeed discomforting, frustrating, and perplexing to have policymakers echoing a belief that the strongest weapon in the arsenal for improving public education is to shame the schools—in effect, principals, teachers, students, and parents. . . . Wouldn't shame be better focused on those policymakers who promote the use of testing as a punitive measure rather than as a diagnostic tool to improve instructional practices and student learning? (Ferrandino and Tirozzi 2003, 19)

High-stakes testing policies have spawned other questionable practices in some school districts. For example, a fourteen-year-old boy in Florida has been charged with a felony because he had a state test booklet in his possession. "He has been charged with burglary, petit theft, theft of intellectual property, which is a felony, and cheating on the FCAT which also carries a felony charge" ("Fla. Student Charged with Crime for Having Copy of State Test" 2004, 4). Not attending school can have a negative impact on district performance scores; therefore, some districts have established harsh attendance policies, and some dole out rewards for perfect attendance during test time. In Richland Parish, Louisiana, for example, students "who miss more than 20 days of school can be fined $250, jailed for 30 days or both" ("Skip School, Risk Trouble" 2004, 1). In Atlanta, Georgia, students who attended Brookwood High School each of the four days of the statewide tests were eligible to win an MP3 music player or a movie ticket (Robelen 2004, 1).

Some public elementary schools have eliminated recesses to allow more time for test preparation (Tyre 2003, 66). There are public schools in Alabama that have eliminated kindergarten nap time to free up time for test preparation ("Schools Drop Naptime for Testing Preparation" 2003, 1). High school students in ever-increasing numbers are dropping out or are being pushed out of school. According to Medina and Lewin (2003), New York City School Chancellor Joel Klein "acknowledged that significant numbers of students, most of them struggling academically, had been pushed out of city schools in recent years" (B6).

ERRORS IN TEST SCORING

Flaws in tests and test scoring have created additional problems for students. In New York, nearly two-thirds of tenth graders who took the statewide math Regents exam initially were failed in 2003. Then the state created a new scoring system that enabled most of those students to pass the test. The original test was judged to be unrealistically difficult for students after the state education department had been "bombarded" with complaints (Arenson 2003, B3). Henriques (2003) reported that Jennifer Mueller, a Massachusetts high school student, discovered a second correct answer for a question on the state exam, noting that "when statewide scores were adjusted to reflect Ms. Mueller's discovery, 95 dejected seniors who had failed the test by one point suddenly found they could graduate after all" (A1). Other testing and scoring errors have occurred in Nevada, where 736 students were incorrectly failed on the high school exit exam, and in Georgia, where statewide exams were cancelled for more than 600,000 fifth graders after a third testing error in three years was discovered (A1).

The National Board on Educational Testing and Public Policy at Boston College has published a report on systemic problems with standardized tests. The report documented more than one hundred reported errors and disputes (Henriques 2003, A20). Some of the largest testing corporations have been involved in testing errors. Scoring errors can have serious consequences. At the college and university level, students who want to become teachers must now pass a standardized test to attain state certification, and in some states a standardized test must be passed to receive a college or university diploma. The largest purveyor of such tests is the Educational Testing Service (ETS), which publishes the PRAXIS™ series of tests required in twenty-three states (Johnson et al. 2005, 232). Only five states—Idaho, Iowa, Kansas, South Dakota, and Wyoming—had no written test requirements for beginning teachers at the time of this writing.

Despite a lack of evidence that test scores relate to successful teaching, the National Council for Accreditation of Teacher Education (NCATE), the nation's largest teacher education accreditor, has endorsed the policy of testing future teachers. This endorsement flies in the face of the organizations, researchers, and educators who have opposed teacher testing because of its inability to determine who will succeed as a teacher. One opponent of teacher testing is the National Association for Multicultural Education. Its resolution, passed at their 2001 convention, stated,

> WHEREAS teacher admission and certification/licensure tests have been found to have questionable content, concurrent, construct, criterion-related, and predictive validity; and
>
> WHEREAS teacher admission and certification/licensure tests have been found to have psychometrically indefensible methods for establishing cutoff scores; and
>
> WHEREAS teacher admission and certification/licensure tests disproportionately eliminate Asian American, African American, Latina/Latino, Native American, Native Hawaiian, Pacific Islander, and other candidates of color, and individuals with disabilities; and
>
> WHEREAS teacher admission and certification/licensure tests are a chief obstacle to the national interest of recruiting a culturally, racially, and linguistically diversified national teacher force;
>
> BE IT THEREFORE RESOLVED that the National Association for Multicultural Education (NAME) calls for the elimination of teacher admission and certification/licensure testing until such time as testing instruments have been designed that can predict who will be academically successful in teacher education programs and who will be competent teachers in the school classroom. (1)

In response to the NAME resolution, Johnson et al. (2005) observed, "Common sense and experience tell us that there must be bias in these instruments because people of color, females, and the economically poor have the most trouble with them—even though these groups certainly are as bright as affluent White males" (245).

A test scoring mistake on the PRAXIS test, published by ETS, erroneously failed 4,100 prospective teachers nationwide, and the mistake cost many of the test takers a teaching license. The result was particularly grave for one student at Louisiana Tech University. According to the local newspaper ("Grading Errors Overturn Lives" 2004), the student was one of "the 486 prospective teachers in Louisiana whose plans were wrecked when [the] Education [Department] incorrectly notified them that they had flunked a test required for certification" (1). The student "failed" the test by one point; this meant no teaching license and no teaching job. At additional expense, he took the test two more times, and each time his score worsened. When the student was denied employment as a teacher, he joined the U.S. Army during the days of the Iraq War. ETS acknowledged that because of a grading error, the young man actually had passed the test the first time.

A study conducted by the University of Chicago has found that Chicago's much-touted retention policies for grades 3, 6, and 8 have not been helpful to students. The study reported by Trotter (2004) indicated that 78 percent of the students who were retained in grade 8 dropped out of school before graduation (8). Since 2000, the American Educational Research Association (AERA) has opposed grade retention based on failing a high-stakes test. In its position statement on high-stakes tests, AERA (2000) stated, "Decisions that affect individual students' life chances or educational opportunities should not be made on the basis of test scores alone" (2). In a *Boston Globe* editorial titled "The Grade Retention Fallacy," Edley and Wald (2002) observed, "For 40 years, study after study on grade retention has reached the same conclusion: Failing a student, particularly in the critical ninth grade year, is the single largest predictor of whether he or she drops out. . . . Research tells us that fear and humiliation are not the strongest motivators for struggling students" (1, 2).

We ask proponents of high-stakes tests how many times a failing student should repeat a grade. Some teachers say that there will be third graders too big for their desks if children continue to be repeatedly failed. In schools where a large number of children fail high-stakes tests, there are not enough support personnel to give them the individual help they need. In Chicago, the school board voted unanimously in 2004 to establish a new grade retention policy. *Education Week* ("Chicago Drops Math Scores as a Factor in Promotion" 2004) reported, "The new policy prohibits retaining students more than once in the same grade, and allows retention only once in kindergarten through 3rd grade, once in 4th through 6th grades, and once in grades 7 and 8" (4). Under Chicago's new policy, some middle school students will be old enough to drive to school.

State testing consequences have generated considerable citizen response in some states. In Michigan, parents, teachers, and administrators were in an uproar over tests mandated for the severely disabled. Winerip (2003) described the situation at Wing Lake Developmental Center in Bloomfield Hills:

> The 140 students, between the ages of 3 and 26, have IQs below 30. Ninety percent . . . wear diapers. Half are in wheelchairs. For the rest of their lives, they will need to be cared for by relatives or in supervised group homes. . . . So why the state tests? (D9)

Other parents, guardians, and students refuse to remain silent about testing. Lewin (2004) noted,

> Disabled children and their parents filed a federal class-action lawsuit yesterday against the Alaska Board of Education, the latest in a string of challenges to laws of various states requiring students to pass an exit exam to earn a high school diploma. The suit charges that Alaska's exit exam discriminates against students with disabilities, making a diploma hard—or impossible—for them to obtain. (A21)

Minority politicians in Florida have threatened boycotts of large state industries as a mechanism for forcing the state to suspend achievement tests failed by 13,000 high school seniors. Florida's black and Hispanic students failed the test "in disproportionate numbers" (Canedy 2003, A22).

Despite all of the evidence and some legal and threatened challenges against high-stakes testing, the practice continues unabated, and in some areas it is on the increase. For example, New York City Chancellor Joel Klein announced a plan to pay *The Princeton Review* (a test prep corporation) $8.2 million over three years to develop and administer three standardized tests in math and three in English to be given to grades "at strategic intervals next year, in addition to annual statewide and citywide exams" (Herszenhorn 2003, B5). The president of the teachers' union, Randi Weingarten, commented, "They are in danger of becoming the Department of Testing rather than the Department of Education" (B5). This is in a school district where classrooms do not have enough textbooks and school restrooms do not have necessary supplies. Alan Richard (2005) wrote, "Florida could become the first state to require students to pass a reading test to advance at every grade level, under a plan approved by the state school board last week" (22). The leading proponent of the plan is Florida Commissioner of Education John Winn, who urged school leaders not to "panic" over the proposed change (27).

NO CHILD LEFT BEHIND

Public Law 107-110, called the No Child Left Behind (NCLB) bill, was signed into law on January 8, 2002, as part of the reauthorization of the Elementary and Secondary Education Act. The publicly declared notion was that all children, regardless of socioeconomic status, race, physical or mental challenges, or other factors, should have equal access to a successful public education. No one could argue with that sentiment. The bill, however, expanded the federal government's role in education and increased its demand for testing of public school children. Richard Allington (2002), professor of education at the University of Tennessee, commented, "The accumulated weight of thirty years of scientific evidence on the effects of federal testing and accountability requirements indicates that this approach is largely devoid of any positive effects on student achievement. Is this new law another case of values trumping data? Of ideology trumping evidence?" (237).

NCLB mandated, among other things, the annual testing of every public school child in grades 3 through 8 and required that every child be "proficient" in reading and math by 2014. The bill established a new federal accountability system that linked standardized testing to heavy sanctions for schools that fail to make "adequate yearly progress" (AYP). This part of the bill has resulted in public listings of data on schools that fail to make AYP for each subgroup of students (e.g., minority, special needs, and low socioeconomic status groups) based on the annual test scores. In a 2003 listing of schools that did not make AYP, the range across the states varied from 4.6 percent in Alabama, 5.13 percent in Indiana, and 7.3 percent in Texas to 77.5 percent in Florida, 76.21 percent in South Carolina, and 66.4 percent in Idaho (Neill, Guisbond, and Schaeffer 2004, 30–31). States apparently interpreted the law in different ways, or the nature of their tests was highly dissimilar to produce such widely variant percentages of failing schools.

Newspapers in every state publish lists of schools that fail to meet AYP, and such listings place additional pressure and embarrassment on the students, teachers, and administrators in those schools. Hildebrand (2003) reported on the academic pressures on New York schools with the release of the list of 185 schools that failed to meet the ever-rising annual improvement targets (A7). A number of the schools such as Roosevelt High School, Wyandanch High School, and Park Avenue School in Amityville, all on Long Island, are communities with high rates of poverty. In the view of many critics of NCLB, the law equates raising test scores with a quality education, although there is no evidence that this is the case.

Those school subjects that are not tested usually get shortchanged, and the curriculum is pared down because teachers feel compelled to teach to the test—even if they disagree with the importance of specific test content and age appropriateness of the test questions. Theodore K. Rabb (2004), a history professor at Princeton University, pointed out, "No Child Left Behind is draining academic substance out of the classroom." He said that Americans "are being trained, not educated" (B24). It is only a matter of time before a cry goes out that students who graduate from the public schools do not know geography, history, or other content not measured by high-stakes standardized tests. Will those who supported the NCLB law take responsibility for these shortcomings, or will the schools again be blamed?

Another requirement of NCLB is a demand for "highly qualified" teachers in every classroom. This has been challenged by many states with large rural populations because they must have teachers who can teach classes across several disciplines. Other aspects of the law require schools to provide tutoring for children who fall behind and permit the transfer of students out of schools that do not make AYP. Each of these provisions is fraught with problems. The tutoring provision has led to the proliferation of private, for-profit enterprises, but tutoring is effective only if the tutors are skilled teachers. The transfer policy has resulted in serious overcrowding of some schools. In recent years, Norman Thomas High School in Manhattan, for example, has had an enrollment surge from 1,800 to 2,981 students because of transfers. Such growth clearly strains resources at the school. Norman Thomas has seen its students' performance on the English Regents test fall, its attendance rate drop, its classes bulge, and its students without books, chairs, or desks (Freedman 2004, A27).

In New York City, 8,000 students of the 300,000 students eligible to transfer switched schools in 2003, causing overcrowding and staff shortages (Neill et al. 2004, 88). In some cities, such as Chicago, the transfer problem is dire. There "the odds of a Chicago student finding a transfer spot were worse than ever, with 190,000 elementary students eligible to vie for 500 seats" (91). That means there is one seat available for every 380 eligible students.

With the passage of NCLB, the federal government has added to the testing pressures that states and school districts already have placed on children—particularly children from low-income families. At the same time that public school students are being overtested, private school students, many of whom come affluent families, are free to learn without draconian accountability consequences. We fear that a nation with an educated elite and a test-weary, lock-step-thinking underclass is just around the corner unless there is a grassroots effort to bring common sense to education policies for America's public school children. Some organizations are beginning this effort. On October 21, 2004, thirty-one education, civil rights, children's, disability, and citizens' organizations issued a joint statement that expressed their concerns with NCLB. The statement said,

> Among these concerns are: over-emphasizing standardized testing, narrowing curriculum and instruction to focus on test preparation rather than richer academic learning; over-identifying schools in need of improvement; using sanctions that do not help improve schools; inappropriately excluding low-scoring children in order to boost test results; and inadequate funding. (FairTest 2004a, 1)

Among the organizations that signed the statement were the American Association of School Administrators, the Children's Defense Fund, the National Association for the Advancement of Colored People, the American Association of University Women, and the National School Boards Association.

It is disheartening that NCATE was not among the thirty-one organizations that went on public record calling for changes in NCLB. This organizations exists for the preparation and accreditation of teachers, but it seems to be content with NCLB. It has voiced no concerns since the first edition of this book was published in 2002.

Former Secretary of Education Rod Paige's view of NCLB was quite different from the thirty-one organizational signatories. Paige stated,

> Four years ago, this is what we saw when we arrived in Washington: we saw a de facto system of educational apartheid. This is no exaggeration of the facts. Millions of children were being left behind . . .
>
> We know that *No Child Left Behind* is starting to generate some amazing results, transforming the educational landscape. We already see considerable evidence that the law is working. ("Secretary Paige Lauds NCLB" 2004, 1)

We have not seen these "amazing results," and it still is not difficult to find examples of "educational apartheid" such as Samantha Jones's school in New York City and elsewhere.

President Bush said, "If you teach a child how to read, [he or she] will pass a reading test. I've heard every excuse in the book why not to measure. But if you can't measure, how do you know?" ("Secretary Paige Lauds NCLB" 2004, 3). Reading, however, is a complex, integrated process. It is more than word identification, that is, mouthing the words. Our former elementary pupils, who have had difficulty comprehending passages, have told us that they can "sound out" the words, but they don't know what they mean and therefore can't "read" the passage. More than twenty-five years of literacy research has established the essential role that prior knowledge plays in reading comprehension and vocabulary development. Reading is an interaction between what is in the reader's mind (i.e., background experiences) and what is on the page. Hayes-Roth and Thorndyke (1979) demonstrated that good readers bring prior knowledge to what they read, and it is this prior knowledge that enables them to comprehend text. The research of van Dijk and Kintsch (1983) showed that readers' abilities to make inferences beyond the information given in text is heavily dependent on their prior knowledge.

It does not take a literacy researcher to understand the essential role of prior knowledge in reading a passage. When readers casually pick up printed material on unfamiliar topics, the material looks strange and perhaps incomprehensible. The text contains words they do not know. Authors assume that their readers have at least a basic understanding of what they have written. When readers lack such understanding, they often put down the printed matter because of comprehension difficulties. Even a proficient, mature reader, for example, might have a problem comprehending passages about eukaryotes, baryons, and heaving-line bends unless the reader has prior knowledge of cell structure and function, nuclear and particle physics, and nautical knots. The reader probably would not want any life-altering decisions made that were based on a test of these topics—even if the reader had some test prep sessions.

It does not take an education researcher to know that we are more interested in things and places if we have had firsthand experiences with these things and places. A reader who has visited the Washington, D.C., monuments, the Grand Canyon, Old Faithful, Mount Rushmore, New Orleans, San Francisco, and Boston probably will have an interest in passages about these things and places, and this interest and prior knowledge will aid reading comprehension in passages about these topics. Large numbers of American students who have difficulty with high-stakes tests are children of poverty—children whose parents or guardians have not been able to provide the resources at home or elsewhere that contribute to the kind of prior knowledge required by high-stakes test passages.

TESTING AND CORPORATE PROFITS

Whether NCLB has been good for children is a matter of political, ideological, and experiential debate. What is not debatable is that NCLB has been very good for the corporate world.

The combination of state-mandated testing and federal mandates related to NCLB have led to a bonanza for corporations in the testing, publishing, and tutoring industries. In *Education Week*, Olson (2004) reported that the federal Government Accountability Office has estimated that testing requirements will cause states to spend between $1.9 billion and $5.3 billion in the next six years (1). Olson noted that nine companies have garnered about 87 percent of the business for state tests. The largest of these companies in terms of state contracts for tests are CTB/McGraw-Hill, Harcourt Assessment, Pearson Assessment, and Riverside Publishing. Smaller firms, including nonprofit players such as Measured Progress and ETS, also have respectable chunks of the testing business (18).

ETS, for example, is a newcomer to the state testing market. For years it has published the Graduate Record Exam and the PRAXIS series of tests used by many states for entry into the teaching profession. The nonprofit ETS estimates $90 million in revenues from state contracts in 2004–2005. Measured Progress, which developed Louisiana's LEAP tests, has moved from $26 million in revenue in fiscal 2000 to about $62 million in 2004–2005. Data Recognition Corporation, which administers Louisiana's state tests, generates approximately $100 million in revenues per year—primarily from K–12 testing (Olson 2004, 19). Corporate executives predict a rapidly expanding market as more states add more grades and more subjects to their state testing mandates.

Another growth industry spurred on by NCLB and state accountability mandates is the private sector that engages in tutoring. Reid (2004) stated, "For-profit education companies are ramping up their businesses to tap into millions of federal dollars set aside to provide tutoring for students attending struggling schools" (1). In addition, children whose parents can afford it get private tutoring help in preparation for high-stakes tests. An estimated $2 billion has been earmarked for tutoring nationwide; there are more than 1,500 tutoring providers already approved by the states. It is imperative to remember that this tutoring is geared toward passing tests—not toward creating a broadly educated citizenry. There are twenty-three major for-profit tutoring corporations. Among the largest are Plato Learning Inc., Kaplan K-12 Learning Services, Huntington Learning Centers Inc., and The Princeton Review Inc. Nonprofit organizations that are providers of government-financed tutoring include the Boys and Girls Club and the YMCA (Reid 2004, 19).

Reid (2004) also reported that there is concern about inadequate monitoring and evaluation of the tutoring services, although "most for-profit companies require training for their tutors, and some mandate ongoing professional development" (19). Liz Wolff, national research director for the Association of Community Organizations for Reform Now (ACORN), an advocacy group for low-income families, pointed out that private companies haven't been required to demonstrate progress on state tests—in other words, they have not been held accountable like children, teachers, and schools have been. According to Reid, Ayeola Fortune of the Council of Chief State School Officers explained that "many state education agencies lack the capacity and money to develop a monitoring process for tutoring. The council will request funding from the U.S. Department of Education to produce a common evaluation system that states could adapt" (19). Billions are being spent on tests and tutoring, but no one clearly knows if any of this is worthwhile. Reid noted that Seppy Basili, vice president of Kaplan Educational Services, "acknowledged that it would be difficult to isolate the academic effects of tutoring programs" (19). Public school teachers, however, are held accountable for the academic effects of their teaching even though variables such as pupils' home life, school funding, and neighborhood conditions confound the issues of teacher effectiveness. Why are the testing and tutoring companies not being held accountable?

The publishers of schoolbooks, supplementary materials, computer software programs, and other test preparation materials make up a third segment of the corporate world that reaps huge profits from America's current testing obsession. Nearly every school that faces high-stakes tests feels compelled to purchase test preparation materials. The exhibit halls at teacher conferences and professional meetings are filled with test prep items available for purchase. Struggling schools that serve children of poverty are most likely to buy these wares in large numbers because they face sanctions and even school closure if test scores do not climb. Test prep purchases reduce funds that might be available for library materials, field trips, and real prior-knowledge-building enrichment resources. Estimates of the billions of dollars spent on test prep materials are difficult to locate. Although it is easy to find the scores of "failing" schools, it is not easy to track down the precise amount of money that each district spends for materials to prepare their students to get higher test scores.

ACCOUNTABILITY AND STANDARDS

An underlying problem with the accountability movement involves the standards to which schools must conform. Yale University professor Robert Sternberg (2004) commented on the ambiguities of state standards:

> There is no clear standard of accountability for the standards of accountability. The standards in the law, despite all the hoopla, are largely arbitrary and even punitive. So schools are being held accountable to standards that themselves meet no standard of accountability. (56)

Where do standards originate? Who sets the standards? What are the standards setters' qualifications? What special interest groups or pressure groups are at work in developing standards? What research evidence exists that the standards are worthwhile, realistic, age appropriate, and attainable? Standards usually are drawn up by committees or task forces that have been given that charge by some organization or government body. Committee members engage in give-and-take discussions about what should be included in the standards. The end result often means that a set of standards is a compromise document that accommodates various points of view. Those who write standards must have blocks of time available for the undertaking. This requirement leaves out most classroom teachers who work closely with children throughout a school year because they cannot get time off from their jobs. Yet teachers have the knowledge and experience that should be a requirement for setting standards for schools.

Standards can be politically motivated and therefore fickle, depending on who holds political power at the time of their establishment. For example, former Minnesota Education Commissioner Cheri Pierson Yecke issued a new set of social studies standards in 2003 that caused concern among school district officials and social studies teachers. Stolle (2003) cited Craig Sheets, an instructional facilitator for the Rochester, Minnesota, school district, who claimed that fifty years of curriculum development were eliminated in a few days when a state committee, appointed by Commissioner Yecke, rewrote the social studies standards. Sheets pointed out, "This is exactly what happens when people put the blinders on and you charge into something and don't take the time and ask the input (of stakeholders)" (1E). Rochester school officials estimated that the cost of rewriting their social studies curriculum and buying new materials for that curriculum would cost the district at least $1.8 million—with no money provided by the commissioner. An editorial in the *St. Paul Pioneer Press* titled "Minnesota Academic Standards" (2003) revealed that

> the curriculum for fourth-grade world history students is especially burdensome—the kids are expected to know pre-history through 1500 A.D., including archeological types and ancient civilizations of the Chinese, Egyptians, Indians, Greeks, Romans, the Byzantine Empire, Medieval Europe, Japan, Africa and the Middle East. For good measure, they're also to know about world religions, including Judaism, Hinduism, Buddhism, Christianity, Islam, and indigenous traditions. They are to understand regional trade patterns in Europe, East Asia and the Middle East and analyze contributions of the Aztec and Incan civilizations. In addition, the 9-year-olds must know the significance of the Renaissance; it's suggested that they consider contributions from Michelangelo, Leonardo da Vinci and Johann Gutenberg.
>
> Recall that the above is one portion of the social studies requirement, followed by geography, economics and government/citizenship. Add to the above the usual fourth-grade math, science, reading and writing classes. (14A)

One wonders if the writers of the social studies standards in Minnesota ever have taught fourth graders. Most of the topics covered are not developmentally appropriate for pupils of that age. How many college graduates could meet these standards?

Many adults think that there should be standards for schools, teachers, and students. But what kinds of standards? Is the purpose of standards to serve as instructional targets, or guidelines, or mandates? How specific should standards be? How quantifiable? Should standards be uniform nationwide, ignoring geographic and demographic needs? The standards adopted in each state for each subject area become the basis, presumably, for the high-stakes testing, the tutoring, the publication of test results, the labeling of schools, and the retention of children. Some of our graduate students who teach in New York City have told us that for every lesson they teach, they must write the New York State standards addressed in their lesson on the chalkboard. Similarly, teachers in Louisiana must key and code their daily lesson plans to the state standards. Teachers in Louisiana, however, are not even allowed to see the items on the standardized high-stakes tests that ostensibly measure children's attainment of these standards. Similar practices prevail in most states.

Colleges and universities are by no means exempt from the requirement to meet a multitude of standards and all the time-wasting notations that go with standards. This especially is true in the nation's schools of education that have accreditation from NCATE. Johnson and colleagues (2005) found that a teacher education program in New York, for example, that wants to prepare future reading and language arts teachers for elementary and middle schools must address the following: six standards and thirty elements established by NCATE, ten principles and 126 elements established by the Interstate New Teacher Assessment and Support Consortium, four standards and thirty-seven performance indicators to meet New York State English language arts requirements, five standards and nineteen elements for the International Reading Association, and five standards and twenty elements for the Association for Childhood Education International. These standards with their coding systems must appear on each course syllabus for every topic taught. If a professor's objective is to prepare students to teach idiomatic expressions, for example, the entry on the syllabus for that objective would be similar to the following: Objective 7.b (Candidates will demonstrate effective teaching of idiomatic language recognition and comprehension), NCATE 1a, INTASC 6.1, New York 2.3, IRA 1.4, and ACEI 2b. All of this to teach idiomatic expressions such as *out in left field* and *asleep at the switch*. In addition, schools of education must meet state standards for all the other disciplines as well as the standards established by each professional organization of the disciplines for which the institution prepares teachers. Yet there is no evidence that teaching to all these standards ensures competent educators.

ADDITIONAL TESTING

The fixation on accountability and testing now has spread from elementary and secondary schools to preschool and Head Start programs. In 2003, President Bush called for a major overhaul of Head Start, the federally funded preschool program for economically disadvantaged children. His goal was to transform Head Start's emphasis on health, nutrition, and social skills to academics. According to Bumiller (2003), Bush said that Head Start programs were "working O.K.," but "we want better than O.K. in America. We want excellence" (A1). Bush's bill proposed to modify Head Start so that the employees would focus on teaching early reading, writing, and math skills. He stated, "We want Head Start to set higher ambitions for the million children it serves" (A18). In discussing Bush's plan, Sarah Greene, president and chief executive officer of the National Head Start Association, said, "We think it would absolutely destroy Head Start" (A1). Senator Ted Kennedy, in opposition to the Bush plan, commented, "It makes no sense to start down a totally new path with a program that's been proven effective by three full decades of research" (A18).

The new Head Start direction as seen by President Bush seems to reflect an accountability trend in preschool education. Jacobson (2004) reported that researchers at Columbia University had learned that

> thirty-six states now have standards for what children should know and be able to do before they enter kindergarten, particularly in literacy and other academic areas. But many of those documents don't give the same level of attention to other aspects of development, such as social and emotional skills and physical growth. (13)

The researchers found a great variety in the number of preschool standards that states had developed, ranging from fifty standards to 370 standards. Those of us who have worked with young children know that some come to preschool not knowing how to hold a pencil or scissors, and some are not even reliably toilet trained. Sharon Lynn Kagan, professor of early childhood policy at Teachers College, Columbia University, stated that the early childhood educators who wrote such standards governing reading, writing, and math in the preschool ran the risk of "misunderstanding nearly a century of research" on how young children learn (Jacobson 2004, 13). When states have established fifty to 370 standards for preschoolers, the tests to measure those standards are sure to follow.

The influence of corporate America—and the Business Roundtable in particular—on public school accountability and the use of high-stakes tests has been well documented elsewhere. Readers are referred to works such as *Why*

Is Corporate America Bashing Our Public Schools? (Emery and Ohanian 2004), *The War against America's Public Schools: Privatizing Schools, Commercializing Education* (Bracey 2002), and *America's "Failing" Schools: How Parents and Teachers Can Cope with No Child Left Behind* (Popham 2004). The business agenda behind accountability and its "blame the schools, blame the students" attitude has led to the charter school movement; scripted, "teacher-proof" curricula; and school vouchers. The movement began with the publication of a small report, *A Nation at Risk*, in 1983. The report spoke of the need to make American education more rigorous and demanding, and it decried education policies that permitted the social promotion of undereducated youth. It put the blame for graduates who lacked academic skills on the shoulders of teachers and implied that if teachers and students were made to work harder, the problems identified in the report would be solved. Critics of *A Nation at Risk* have referred to it as a "propaganda-laden document" sponsored by the Reagan administration and its secretary of education, William Bennett (Bracey 2002, 7).

Those who cheer the finger-pointing of *A Nation at Risk*, as well as the business community, fail to acknowledge that America did not become the leader in technology, medicine, and nearly every other field by sending all its children to private schools. Nor did the United States become an intellectual leader in the world by inundating public school students and their teachers with ever-increasing testing demands.

Despite the lack of evidence that the more than twenty-year accountability movement has produced commendable results, the shaming of students and their teachers continues. In an *Education Week* commentary, Louis V. Gerstner Jr. (2005), former chairman and chief executive of the IBM Corporation, called for "revolutionizing teaching, which years of neglect has turned into a second-rate profession" (60). Gerstner said, "It's time to hold every teacher to the higher bar we are starting to set for new teachers" (34). He decried the low standards and undemanding training programs of the teaching profession. When will corporate America learn that schools are not factories or businesses and cannot be dealt with in the same business-model way? We ask Mr. Gerstner how many of his IBM employees would have stayed on the job—or even applied for a position—if his buildings were as roach and rat infested as Samantha Jones's public school in New York City. How many would have stayed on the job without even basic tools required of their work—not to mention to low pay? The Business Roundtable does not have the firsthand experiences working with children in public schools, rich and poor, to make pronouncements about how to improve public education.

Peter McAllister (2003), a graduate student majoring in teacher education at Dowling College on Long Island, pointed out some of the differences between corporate life and life in schools:

With 25 years of experience as an executive with Citigroup and, prior to that, having earned a Ph.D. from Columbia University, I don't consider myself a stranger either to hard work or to stress. . . . This semester I embarked upon my Student Teaching Practicum in The Mathematics Department at Commack High School. Although I had no expectations regarding the assignment, several professors at Dowling warned me that teaching is tougher than many people think it is. This may very well be the greatest understatement of the new millennium. In all of my previous experiences, I was judged by how knowledgeable I was or, at least, by how knowledgeable I appeared to be. As a teacher, subject matter expertise is taken for granted. The dominant criterion here is how knowledgeable my students become.

Communicating even the most fundamental concepts to a group of students with different backgrounds and aptitudes requires an enormous amount of preparation. Moreover, a dry, factual presentation simply won't cut it. In all of the classes at CHS I've observed, the lessons were fast-paced, interesting, and clear. When I got up to teach my first lesson, I realized how daunting it is to teach in such a manner. I've always taken pride in my ability to make presentations to all levels of management in an organization. Now I'm finding that when the other teachers in the department teach it's like listening to a concert. When I'm up there, it's like walking outside and listening to street noise. I simply had no idea of how much hard work and training goes into teaching even the most basic high school lesson.

Since I've started teaching, I've had to disabuse myself of the notion that any skills I may have acquired as a manager are directly transferable to the classroom.

How much control do I have over any of my students? I can't fire them or deny them a bonus or hold up any promotion they might have earned.

I am finding classroom management and, by extension, student relationship management to be two of the hardest tasks I have ever faced.

They constitute a completely different ball game from traditional managerial situations and they are tremendously more challenging. How do I motivate a disaffected child to master the fundamentals of mathematics? What techniques can I use to bring a fractious group of adolescents to order so that learning can occur? The tools and incentives at my disposal are meager when compared to my previous work. To make matters worse, the teachers at CHS have deceived me. Their skills in this area have made the job seem effortless. I can assure you it is not. (1–2)

Epilogue

REDBUD ELEMENTARY SCHOOL

Since our school year ended at Redbud Elementary in June 2001, Super-intendent Miller has left the district for another superintendency in Louisiana. Pam Porter, the principal of Redbud Elementary, accepted a principalship in Arkansas. Ms. Dawson, the assistant principal, has left the school, and several teachers with whom we worked have moved to other schools or have retired. Only three of the ten third- and fourth-grade teach-ers still are teaching at Redbud Elementary. Ms. Tremain, the former third-grade student teacher, is now a fourth-grade teacher at the school. The principal of Redbud High School left for a job in Wisconsin, and there is a new principal of Redbud Junior High. The average teacher salary at Red-bud remains among the lowest in the state—fiftieth of the sixty-six school districts (Herring 2004e, 5). Teachers in Redbud Elementary School now must use a "scripted program" instead of "balanced reading" to teach chil-dren to read. The district employs "coordinators" to monitor this "teacher-proof" instruction. Deerborne Parish schools currently receive checks from the Louisiana Department of Education when they have reached their "growth targets." Those schools, however, that show "growth" but do not reach the targeted number of points set by the department receive nothing but bad publicity.

The town looks as it did when we taught there. We occasionally see some of our former pupils' names on the junior high school honor roll—but not enough of them. Most of our pupils were so bright and eager, but poverty and the continuing pressures of high-stakes testing exact a toll on young minds and bodies. We also see reports in the local newspaper that give us further pause: the death of a sibling of one of our former pupils, the jailing of a former pupil's mother, and other crushing events.

Three years after the year we taught in Redbud, results of the Iowa Test of Basic Skills scores still are below the national median of the fiftieth percentile. The LEAP scores continue to be below most other districts in the state. What good did all the pressures on the children and all the money spent on accountability do?

In 2002, voters in the Deerborne Parish district approved a bond issue to "consolidate the [Redbud] schools on one campus, construct new wings on the elementary and high schools, move the fifth grade to the elementary school, construct a track, expand the cafeteria, and renovate the existing high school and elementary school" (Herring 2004c, 1). The district, however, ran short of money to complete the project. Nonetheless, some Redbud Elementary School pupils and teachers moved into two new wings at the end of April 2004. There were community members who blamed low architect estimates for the shortfall of funds; some blamed former Superintendent Miller. Renovation of the junior high, rather than rebuilding it, was entertained, but the principal pointed out the "serious termite problem" at the current site (Herring 2004d, 13).

Complaints about Deerborne Parish Schools were filed with the U.S. Justice Department. The complaints were about "expulsion, suspension, and unfair treatment" (Herring 2004f, 1). The U.S. Justice Department Office of Civil Rights has requested information such as "the names, races, and addresses of students in each classroom, on each bus route, and in each school activity" and has questions about "the race ratios" at some schools and "what efforts were being made to desegregate those schools" (Herring 2004b, 1, 5). One elementary school in Deerborne Parish has 182 African American children enrolled in the school and no white children. Another school has 191 African American students and 39 white students. A third school has 218 white pupils and 101 African American pupils. The district has hired a New Orleans attorney, for $125 per hour, "to represent the school district regarding potential litigation involving the U.S. Justice Department" (Herring 2004f, 1). In referring to the Justice Department requests, the Redbud superintendent stated,

This is difficult for a school system to go through. When we are really putting an emphasis on improved test scores, when we are having to meet the
No Child Left Behind obligations, not only for students but for teachers,
when we have to meet high stakes testing standards . . . we are doing our
very best to educate children and this makes it very difficult. . . . This is difficult for me but it is equally difficult for principals who have to take the
time to answer the bulk of these questions. (Herring 2004c, 9)

MISPLACED PRIORITIES: NEWS FROM ACROSS LOUISIANA

It appears to be business as usual within the powerful Board of Elementary and
Secondary Education (BESE). The newly elected governor, Kathleen Blanco,
reappointed eight-year board member Leslie Jacobs, "the architect of accountability." Blanco also reappointed Cecil Picard as state superintendent of education. Polly Broussard was newly elected to the BESE. An article in the Baton
Rouge newspaper, *The Advocate*, noted that

> Broussard strongly backs the accountability program, which requires stu-
> dents to pass tests to earn promotion in certain grades . . . and threatens pun-
> ishment against schools that don't improve. Broussard wants to consider
> vouchers, which would allow students in bad schools to attend private and
> even religious schools at state expense. The Louisiana Association of Busi-
> ness and Industry financed much of Broussard's campaign. ("Broussard Wins
> Seat in BESE 6" 2003, 1)

The status quo, therefore, and the state accountability system continue despite
a new governor.

Louisiana is facing a severe budget shortfall. Estimates range from $300
million to $686.5 million (Hasten 2005, 1). Some school districts are facing
teacher layoffs (La Plante 2004, 1–2). According to Macolm Duplantis, president of the Louisiana Association of School Superintendents, "About half of
the districts are going to have to do some type of reduction in teaching force
to balance their budgets" (Brown 2004, 1–2). Teachers at Franklin Parish High
School held a sick-out because of taxpayers' lack of support for education.
Comer (2005) reported, "The parish has not passed a tax to support education
in 33 years" (1). Many districts lack basic supplies such as Band-Aids, staples,
and tape. Teachers are expected to pay for these supplies out of their own
pockets. One district reported that teachers have not received their $80 supply
stipend for the past two years ("Teachers Prepare Out of Their Pockets" 2004,
1). Conditions in some schools are dire. One teacher said, "We have weapons

in the school and an infestation of rodents. . . . Everyone wants to cover up the problem, but we need the truth to be told." An eleven-year-old boy told newspaper reporters that some students were afraid to attend school (Cannon and Faulkner 2003, 2).

According to an article in the Monroe, Louisiana, *News-Star*, "The State of Louisiana will cut a check using borrowed money to keep the Saints in New Orleans. The Legislature agreed Monday to borrow $7.1 million from a Louisiana Economic Development Commission fund to complete the state's $15 million obligation made three years ago by former Gov. Mike Foster" (Hasten 2004b, 1). There does not seem to be a lack of big money for a professional football team, but the public schools are doing without even basic supplies. Do the New Orleans Saints bring in so much revenue that children's educations can be mortgaged? What are the priorities in Louisiana? Where is the tally—so far—of how many millions have been shoveled into the accountability system? Why isn't this figure public knowledge? School scores on high-stakes and district performance scores are readily available to taxpayers. Why are the total dollar amounts spent on accountability not publicized within the state?

Despite the lack of classroom supplies, teacher layoffs, rodent-infested school buildings, and the highest poverty rate in the United States, there has been no suggestion from lawmakers or policymakers to eliminate the high-stakes testing policies and the spending (such as employing district accountability coordinators) that are related to the tests. Louisiana has a number of alarming problems that should be the lawmakers' and policymakers' highest priorities. The state ranks near the bottom on every indicator of child well-being as reported in the *Kids Count Data Book* (2004). Louisiana ranked as follows:

- Forty-third in the percentage of teens who are high school dropouts (58)
- Forty-fifth in teen birthrate (57)
- Forty-sixth in rate of teen deaths by accident, homicide, and suicide (56)
- Forty-seventh in child death rate, ages one to fourteen (55)
- Forty-eighth in percent of children living in poverty (61)
- Forty-eighth in percent of teens not attending school and not working (59)
- Forty-eighth in percent of children living in families where no parent has full-time, year-round employment (60)
- Forty-eighth in infant mortality rate (54)
- Forty-ninth in percent of low-birth-weight babies (53)
- Forty-ninth in percent of families with children headed by a single parent (62)
- Forty-ninth in overall rank on child well-being (52).

The state ranks poorly on other factors as well. The *New York Times* reported that "Minnesota is the nation's healthiest state, while Louisiana is the least healthy, a ranking it has held for 14 of the last 15 years of a national survey," according to the United States Health Foundation ("Minnesota Leads in Health Survey" 2004, A16). The ranking is based on many of the factors cited in the *Kids Count Data Book* but also considers such other factors as health insurance coverage, public health spending, prevalence of smoking, and violent crime. These are the problems on which Louisiana should be spending its money. Dealing with child poverty, health care, nutrition, and dropouts and repairing public schools and purchasing basic school supplies should precede expenditures to raise test scores at all costs—or expenditures to support a professional football team.

MISPLACED REWARDS

We participated in one of the first pep rallies for tests in the nation during our year at Redbud Elementary in 2000–2001. The test prep rallies now have become extravaganzas in some school districts. A reporter for the New Orleans *Times-Picayune*, described a multiple-district rally:

> [The rally] will emphasize test-taking tips using costumed characters and skits, will bring together 800 bands members, 400 cheerleaders, local elected leaders and television news personalities to help psych students. Navy pilots are also scheduled to fly over the field. Students will receive pencils, cups emblazoned with test tips and stickers that read, "I Can. I Will. . . ." Coca-Cola signed on as a corporate sponsor. (Nelson 2003, 2)

At a more modest test pep rally in a central Louisiana school district, fourth graders shouted cheers and were given "I'm a LEAP All-Star" T-shirts (Peters 2004, 1). Pizzas and sodas were distributed at a school pep rally in northeastern Louisiana, but other rewards were more enticing. Domingue (2004) wrote,

> The names of one student in each third- and fourth-grade class . . . who attend the testing days, are quiet and read their books without being told after testing, will be put into a hat and the winners will get a limousine ride to C.C.'s Pizza. Ten winners will be selected. . . . The students who score the highest on the Iowa and LEAP 21 will receive a watch. (3)

The principal of the school added that "each student scoring basic and mastery in language arts and math will receive a $25 gift certificate to Barnes & Noble," and "those students who score advanced will get a $50 gift certificate to Barnes & Noble" (3). If the scores at this elementary school reflect the scores at nearly all other elementary schools in Louisiana and across the country, it will be the more affluent children who score the highest on the test. The children of poverty, who do not have books at home, will not be the ones receiving the Barnes & Noble certificates. Even young children have a sense of fairness, and they know it is unjust when free books are given to children who most likely have books at home but are not given to children who are less fortunate.

There seems to be abundant money available to tout the state's accountability system. A Louisiana Department of Education (2004a) press release issued on April 15, 2004, stated, in part, "Gov. Kathleen Blanco, along with State Superintendent of Education Cecil J. Picard and the Board of Elementary and Secondary Education, honored 333 schools that met or exceeded their accountability goals during a reception at the Governor's Mansion Thursday afternoon" (1). The reception was attended by district superintendents and school board presidents of the honored schools. These special guests were given flags to be presented to their schools that achieved Recognized Academic Growth or Exemplary Academic Growth. The release noted that

> Schools of Recognized Academic Growth met or exceeded their growth targets by five points or less while Schools of Exemplary Academic Growth exceeded their growth targets by more than five points. In addition to flags, schools were given financial rewards totaling nearly $4.4 million based on their academic growth. (1)

Nearly 1,000 Louisiana schools did not fly these flags or find ways to put financial rewards to good use despite the pressures they endured to raise test scores. One wonders how much stress is being placed on children in these un-rewarded schools to score higher on tests so that their schools can, in the words of the governor, "fly their growth reward flag high" (1).

What effects does all the hoopla to pass a high-stakes test have on children? We saw firsthand the effects in our year at Redbud, and in our current work with New York teachers, we hear about them as well. For example, a veteran fourth-grade teacher said, "High-stakes testing is putting an unprecedented form of pressure on districts, teachers, and students. When we have to hire extra janitorial staff on high-stakes testing days to clean up the vomit, we know that things are getting ridiculous" (personal communication, November 2003). Domingue (2004) reported, "Sometimes students feel so much pressure and responsibility to show up on test day that they'll come to school sick." She quoted an elementary school principal as saying,

> We had one that came to school with a 102 (degree) temperature. . . . We sent him home, of course, but they are so ingrained with the fact that they have to take the test he came with a fever of 102. (2)

Some young children work on stress-control techniques during testing time (Peters 2004, 2), and others worry about how their school will be represented in the media. A fourth grader in central Louisiana whose school had low scores on the high-stakes test the previous year said, "I'm scared about our school being back in the newspaper with a big 'X' on it" (1). At a school in Shreveport, Louisiana, the teachers "wear inspirational T-shirts during testing that read, 'We believe in you'" (Brumble 2004, 3). Most elementary school children do not want to let their teachers down. If the teacher "believes" in the children and the children do poorly on the test despite their best efforts, how does this make these "failing" children feel?

The effects of high-stakes testing are troublesome enough for children without special needs, but they are even more disturbing for special education students. Nelson (2004) wrote about a nine-year-old Louisiana child who was a victim of a car accident caused by a speeding teenager trying to evade police. The crash killed her brother and sister. The fourth grader received "head injuries that led to mental disabilities and have forced her to re-learn basic math and how to hold a pencil." Nelson noted, "This week, another challenge awaits the youngster . . . taking the state-mandated Louisiana Educational Assessment Program test." The child's teacher, who was attempting to prepare her special needs children for the test, said, "I would like to say I'm optimistic, but it's unrealistic to say this is a fair test for them." The child's father pointed out, "She's not even ready for a first-grade test. . . . She had to start all over with everything." Her mother said, "I don't want her to be ashamed" (A1, A8).

But the tests continue. Herring (2004a) quoted a northern Louisiana citizen as saying, "I've been in homes where floors were dirt and there was no running water." Herring added, "Children in these homes do not have a lamp, a pencil or a table, yet they are expected to have homework or reports from the library ready for school the next day" (5). Louisiana had a $500 million state budget shortfall in 2004, but the tests continue ("Blanco Sees No Pay Raise for Teachers" 2004, 4). The new governor of the state, Kathleen Blanco, who, according to a teachers' union representative, promised to raise teacher salaries to the Southern Regional Average, said budget problems preclude teacher raises, but the tests continue. Some support workers in Louisiana schools must apply for food stamps (3), but the tests continue.

Amidst the accountability scramble, the state has devised a catchy new visual way of displaying school rankings. Thevenot (2003b) observed,

> The state also released a new ranking system, mimicking movie ratings, that gives schools from one to five stars, five being the best, based on test performance. The rankings give a snapshot of performance, regardless of recent improvement. Only 20 percent of schools earned at least three stars, which roughly correlates to average score of "basic" on the LEAP test, meaning a student meets grade-level standards. Just 3 percent of schools earned four or five stars. Of the remaining schools, 62 percent scored one or more stars. Eighteen percent received no stars, scoring either "academically unacceptable" or "academic warning." (3)

Perhaps the Achilles' heel in Louisiana's testing obsession will be its effects on schools that serve more affluent pupils. Brumble (2004) wrote,

> Schools like Stockwell Place Elementary and Elm Grove Middle School that have scored at or above the federal goal—100 percent proficiency by 2013—since 2001 are still expected to show a significant yearly improvement. . . . Stockwell Place scored 127.3 . . . in 2001 [making it a School of Academic Achievement], and even though the school's score improved by an additional seven points by 2003, the school was not eligible for rewards. The same was true for Elm Grove Middle School. Although Elm Grove scored above the 100 point mark and improved by almost three additional points, it was shy of the five point improvement mark needed to make it eligible for rewards. But both Stockwell Place and Elm Grove are initiating similar methods to improve their students' scores through mind, body and soul. (2)

If these "mind, body, and soul" techniques do not produce the "desired results," perhaps some influential parents will start questioning high-stakes test consequences for children; after all, their children will be attending schools that are not flying reward flags.

LOUISIANA ACCOUNTABILITY AWARDS

Power brokers' takes on ratings and rankings reveal curious individual interpretations of the facts. For example, under the headline "Journal Ranks Louisiana's

Testing Seventh," Hasten (2002) wrote, "*The Princeton Review*, a leading education journal, has rated Louisiana's testing program as one of the top procedures in the country" (3A). Hasten added that Superintendent of Education Cecil Picard referred to the announcement as "'another prestigious organization commending us for all of the hard work done by Louisiana teachers, department staff and others since we started this in 1996. This report shows we're on the right path'" (3A). Leslie Jacobs, Louisiana's "architect of accountability," said the report was "yet another unbiased, third-party affirmation that the testing and accountability policies we've put into place are among the best in the nation" (5A).

In 2003, the state moved up a notch in the eyes of *The Princeton Review*, and the Louisiana Department of Education (2003a) issued a press release with the headline "Louisiana's Testing Program Ranked 6th in Nation." The body of the release stated, in part,

> The Princeton Review collected information from each state and the District of Columbia for Testing the Testers 2003: An Annual Ranking of State Accountability Systems. The magazine rated them on four key areas. . . . Accountability is working in Louisiana because we have the right plan in place," State Superintendent Cecil J. Picard said. "I'm proud that Louisiana is finally at the top of education lists. We are truly leading the way. . . ." "This confirms, once again, that Louisiana is on the right path with its testing and accountability policies," Board of Elementary and Secondary Education President Paul Pastorek said. "We definitely put Louisiana's children first." (1)

The Princeton Review is not a "leading education journal," nor is it a "magazine." It is a corporation that sells test-related goods and services. The company does not hide its mission. In a full-page ad in the April 12, 2004, issue of *U.S. News & World Report*, for example, *The Princeton Review* (2004) states, "Raise Your Score with Proven Test-Taking Strategies" (53). The company lists its website and its 800 number in the ad and notes, "The Princeton Review is not affiliated with Princeton University or ETS." According to Reid (2004), *The Princeton Review* has tutoring contracts in thirty states (19). FairTest (2003), an organization that opposes high-stakes tests, issued a press release on May 4, 2003, that pointed out, "Princeton Review sells multiple titles of test coaching books for seven of the top ten state programs in its rankings [of state accountability systems]. It does not market similar products for any of the ten bottom-ranked programs" (1). In light of this information, why do Louisiana education officials refer to the ranking as "unbiased" and by "another prestigious organization"? Do they know what *The Princeton Review* is?

Education Week's *Quality Counts 2004* ranked Louisiana number one in the nation in standards and accountability. The *News-Star* reported, "State education officials are pleased with a ranking from Education Week that shows Louisiana has the best and most effective education system ("La. Education Earns Good Grades" 2004, 1). Cecil Picard said, "It's great news. . . . We were in the top five last year and now we are No. 1." (1).

In 2005, Louisiana's standards and accountability program was given a grade of A by *Education Week* in its annual listing titled *Quality Counts 2005*. With a score of 98, Louisiana dropped to second highest in the nation behind New York, which received a score of 100. The grades were based on a combination of factors: having state standards in core subjects, using statewide assessments, and having in place five components of accountability (i.e., report cards, ratings, assistance, sanctions, and rewards) (104). The tougher the state standards and accountability mechanisms, the higher the state grade as determined by *Education Week*. Santell (2004) noted, "The magazine [*Education Week*] heaped praise on how the state measures student performance" and cited Cecil Picard, state superintendent of education, as saying, "We have become the national model and this is just another indication that we are doing it the right way" (1).

Louisiana also was awarded an A by *Education Week* for its efforts to improve teacher quality (*Education Week* 2005, 92). The grade was based on such factors as financing and regulating alternative routes to teacher certification, written tests for teacher licensing, required performance assessments of teaching, and a requirement that teacher evaluations be tied to student achievement (104–5). In other words, Louisiana scored near the top of all states in factors that are based on regulation, testing, monitoring, and mandating.

In contrast to the grade of A awarded by *Education Week* for its efforts to improve teacher quality, according to Keller (2004), the National Council on Teacher Quality gave Louisiana a grade of D on teacher quality. Keller's report noted that the state grades were based on "the quality of the standards they have set to assess whether teachers now in the classroom have adequate knowledge of the subjects they teach" (21). Keller pointed out that the Washington-based National Council is a proponent of alternative routes to certification. The Council wants veteran teachers to be held "to the same content-knowledge standards as new teachers" (21). In the area of teacher quality, therefore, Louisiana has received contrasting grades of A and D.

On other measures in *Education Week's Quality Counts 2005* report, Louisiana did not fare as well as it did on standards and accountability. It received a grade of D+ on school climate (82), which is based on such factors as school facilities, school safety, state funding dedicated to capital outlay or construction, state tracking of school facilities, parent involvement, and more. With a score of 67, Louisiana tied with Maryland for last place in the nation for school climate. "Louisiana is one of only nine states that neither provide money for school construction nor monitor the condition of school facilities" (119). The state earned grades of F from *Education Week's Quality Counts 2005* for these two factors (104). Furthermore, Louisiana ranked forty-sixth in the nation on the percent of total taxable state resources spent on education (102), and it also ranked forty-sixth on total money spent on categorical programs such as special education (101). Louisiana ranked forty-fifth in the nation in average teacher salaries with an average annual salary of $37,116 (95). In other words, Louisiana does not spend much money on public education compared to other states. Much of what it does spend is directed toward its public school accountability system.

Also in contrast to *Education Week's* grade of A for Louisiana's standards and accountability was an analysis conducted by Morgan Quitno Press (2005), a research/publishing company that prepares annual state and city rankings for education, health, and safety. The press "is not a subsidiary of any other company nor is it subsidized by any outside interest groups" (1). One of its publications, *Education State Rankings*, awards its "Smartest State" rankings based on twenty-one factors, including high school graduation and dropout rates; average class size; percentages of public school expenditures used for instruction; percentages of fourth and eighth graders proficient in reading, writing, and mathematics; pupil-to-teacher ratio; and more. In its 2004–2005 rankings, Morgan Quitno Press (2004) ranked Louisiana forty-sixth in the nation.

Some might think that standards and accountability equate to quality of the education experience and to how well students are learning, but there are numerous indicators that this is not the case. Learning must transfer to other situations. If individuals could not transfer what they had learned to other situations, every task that deviated in some aspect—no matter how small—from the original situation would require "from scratch" teaching and learning. For example, a young person can learn to drive a specific vehicle for a driver's test. It is assumed that there is some transfer of learning when that driver gets behind the wheel of a similar but different vehicle. A child learns to read and comprehend a grade-appropriate and prior-knowledge-appropriate passage in a text. It is assumed that the child will be able to read and comprehend a similar grade- and prior-knowledge-appropriate passage. Transfer of learning, according to teaching and learning experts, undergirds the whole concept of schooling. Over two decades ago, Bigge (1982) stated,

> The effectiveness of a school depends, in a large measure, upon the amount and quality of transfer potential of the materials that students learn. Thus, transfer of learning is the cornerstone upon which education should ultimately rest. Unless students learn in school those matters that help them in

meeting situations more effectively further along the academic sequence and later in life as well as in the present, they are wasting much of their time. (253)

The lack of transfer of learning, most likely due to the persistent drilling for high-stakes test items, becomes evident when Louisiana students are scored on time-tested national measures.

The National Assessment of Educational Progress (NAEP) was authorized by Congress more than thirty-five years ago to conduct ongoing, comparable, representative assessments of the achievement of American students. These periodic assessments in reading, writing, mathematics, science, and other subjects have been conducted since 1971. The most recent NAEP assessments of reading and mathematics were conducted in 2003. Scores were reported at four levels of achievement: below basic, at or above basic, at or above proficient, and at advanced. The 2003 assessment indicated that 30 percent of all students tested nationally scored at or above proficient in reading in grades 4 and 8. In math, 31 percent in grade 4 and 27 percent in grade 8 scored at that level. The range among the states scoring at or above proficient was 18 to 43 in fourth-grade reading, 20 to 43 in eighth-grade reading, 17 to 43 in fourth-grade math, and 12 to 44 in eighth-grade math.

On each of the four 2003 NAEP tests, Louisiana ranked forty-seventh in the nation. In fourth-grade reading, Louisiana and Nevada tied for forty-seventh place with 20 percent of the children scoring at or above proficient (*Education Week* 2005, 84–85). What the NAEP data reveal is that Louisiana's A grade in standards and accountability is not reflected in scores on the nationally respected thirty-five-year-old NAEP tests. Seven states, however, that received low grades of C+ to F from *Education Week's Quality Counts 2005* for standards and accountability were among the top ten states in fourth-grade reading on the 2003 NAEP test. They were Connecticut, New Hampshire, Minnesota, Vermont, Maine, Montana, and Iowa (84).

Furthermore, the NAEP designation of proficient is apparently much more rigorous than the Louisiana designation of proficient. Only 20 percent of Louisiana's fourth graders scored at or above proficient on the 2003 NAEP reading test, but 61 percent of the fourth graders scored at the proficient level on Louisiana's 2004 LEAP test in reading (*Education Week* 2005, 84). This wide gap in proficiency percentages was brought about by Louisiana's changed labeling of test performance in recent years. Louisiana's original five levels of test performance were unsatisfactory, approaching basic, basic, proficient, and advanced. In 2003, the label "proficient" was changed by Louisiana's Board of Elementary and Secondary Education to "mastery." Then, to satisfy requirements of Adequate Yearly Progress for the federal No Child Left Behind Act,

Louisiana defined proficient to include everyone who scored at the basic, mastery, and advanced levels on the LEAP test or the secondary Graduate Exit Examination (GEE) (Louisiana Department of Education 2003b, 8). On the spring 2004 LEAP test, only 3 percent scored advanced and 18 percent mastery (the former proficient) in fourth-grade reading. With the new definition of including "basic" within "proficient," however, another 39 percent of the students were labeled "proficient" for No Child Left Behind—therefore the discrepancy between NAEP proficiency and Louisiana proficiency in reading.

Amrein and Berliner (2002) analyzed testing data from eighteen states that have severe consequences attached to their high-stakes tests. The researchers wanted to determine if the high-stakes testing programs had a positive effect on student learning, which is purportedly the intended outcome of such testing. They examined results of four separate standardized tests in common use, the NAEP, the American College Testing Program (ACT), the Scholastic Aptitude Test (SAT), and the Advanced Placement (AP) to determine if there was any transfer from the state tests to these established measures. Based on their analyses, the researchers concluded,

> Evidence from this study of 18 states [including Louisiana] with high-stakes tests is that in all but one analysis, student learning is indeterminate, remains at the same level it was before the policy was implemented, or actually goes down when high-stakes testing policies are instituted. Because clear evidence for increased student learning is not found, and because there are numerous reports of unintended consequences associated with high-stakes testing policies (increased drop-out rates, teachers' and schools' cheating on exams, teachers' defection from the profession . . .), it is concluded that there is a need for debate and transformation of current high-stakes testing policies. (2)

Who is going to be held accountable for the lack of transfer of learning and the failure of high-stakes testing? After untold millions of dollars have been wasted on accountability mandates, the taxpayers and especially the test takers deserve some answers.

The 2003 NAEP tests also revealed serious gaps in achievement levels by race and ethnicity and by family socioeconomic status as determined by eligibility for free or reduced school lunch. In Louisiana, 30 percent of white fourth graders scored below basic and 70 percent at or above basic in reading. For African American children, the reverse was true: 70 percent of African American fourth graders scored below basic in reading and only 30 percent scored at or above basic. At the at or above proficient level, the difference was large: 34 percent of white children scored at that level, but only 8 percent of African

American children did. On the socioeconomic factor, 62 percent of Louisiana fourth graders eligible for free or reduced lunch scored below basic—twice as many as the 30 percent of fourth graders not eligible for free or reduced lunch who scored below basic. The same pattern held in every state and in the nation as a whole (National Center for Education Statistics 2003).

Test score differences by race and by family income level have been apparent on numerous standardized tests. For example, on the 2004 SAT test used for college entrance, the average total score for African American test takers was 857, and the average score for white test takers was 1,059, a more than 200-point disparity (FairTest 2004b). The reasons for these major differences in test scores by race and income level reflect the bias of test content as well as the lack of the type of prior knowledge required on standardized tests. Gene R. Carter (2005), the executive director of the Association for Supervision and Curriculum Development, observed,

> According to [former UCLA professor and testing expert] James Popham, 40–80 percent of test questions are linked to socio-economic status (SES), meaning that they are more likely to be answered correctly by students from higher SES families, regardless of academic instruction. As one example, Popham cites a 6th grade science question that asks children to select the tool they would use to discover whether a distant planet had mountains or rivers on it. The correct answer—a telescope—favors children whose families have taken them to museums or who have telescopes in the home, making it a great measure of SES but not of instruction. (13)

OTHER TESTING DEVELOPMENTS

Louisiana has not been exempt from the type of accountability and testing errors discussed in chapter 12. Brian Thevenot (2003a) of the New Orleans *Times-Picayune* reported that the Louisiana Education Department misprinted some of the more than 700,000 school report cards delivered to parents of every public school student in the state. The mistake was caused by a computer programming error according to the state accountability director, Robin Jarvis. Parents and guardians were misinformed about whether various subgroups, including children of different income levels and different races, had met state requirements. Jarvis indicated that her staff would complete "a hand-check of every single report card of every single school in the state . . . after which the state will reprint the cards and reissue them" (2). According to Thevenot, state officials were unable to tell how much money this error would cost the taxpayers.

Late reporting of test scores by the Louisiana Department of Education still is a problem. Wilson noted that the department released retake test scores on the Friday in August just before some schools opened on Monday. Wilson (2004c) quoted an accountability coordinator as saying, "So many of these students are waiting on scores to know if they are promoted. . . . High school counselors are waiting to schedule ninth-graders . . . principals are waiting" (1).

Jefferson Parish, near New Orleans, embarked on a new procedure in spring 2004. Waller (2004) wrote that the parish had instituted a program of basing part of the fourth-quarter report card grades in middle school on achievement levels on the LEAP test and the Iowa test. Letter grades of A to F were assigned to performance at the five LEAP test achievement levels from advanced to unsatisfactory. On the Iowa tests given in grades 6 and 7, percentile rankings "were divided into five categories, with a 75–99 earning an A, and a 1–15 earning an F. The rule grew out of concerns from middle school principals that students were not taking the Iowa test seriously because it carried no consequences" (2). Both tests contribute to a school's performance score. BESE member Leslie Jacobs criticized the plan because its intent seemed to be more toward raising school performance scores than toward helping students. According to Waller, Jacobs said, "I think we put enough pressure on the students, making LEAP high-stakes" (3). As the "architect of accountability," Leslie Jacobs ought to be well aware of the pressures these tests put on children, their parents, their teachers, and their schools.

Swerczek (2004) reported that the St. Charles Parish School Board had toughened its testing policy after it was discovered that some teachers had helped students with test questions. The new policy reads, "A breach of test security by any employee, as determined by the superintendent, will constitute willful neglect of duty with grounds for dismissal" (2). After students had reported to a monitor that a teacher had given them some answers or some hints, the school district recommended termination, and the teacher resigned her position (2). Another teacher in a northeastern Louisiana school district wrote,

> I was called into the principal's office around 1:30. A man, who did not bother to introduce himself, said, "I was monitoring the halls during the Iowa test and I saw you give answers to two students." I was floored. I replied, "You saw me tell two boys that they didn't erase their answers very well and it looked like they had two answers on one line." He said, "Well, what you say and what it looked like are two different things." I said, "Why don't we call the boys in here and ask them?" But he refused. This man was

from the state department and he, of course, doesn't know me. (personal communication, March 21, 2003)

The teacher, who had received national recognition for her contributions to education, finished the remaining months of the school year and then left Louisiana for a position in another state.

Three child advocates have mounted a strong opposition to Louisiana's high-stakes testing policies. Sandra Hester, host and producer of *The Hester Report*, a popular New Orleans television talk show, is founder and executive director of the Parent Empowerment Center, an organization dedicated to teaching parents to become effective advocates for their own children. C. C. Campbell-Rock and Raymond Rock, human rights and education activists and cohosts of *Speak Now or Forever Hold Your Peace*, a weekly New Orleans television show, are cofounders of Parents for Educational Justice. These activists have been instrumental in keeping unjust high-stakes testing in the forefront of the public's mind. They work tirelessly for no pay and no tangible rewards to make things better for children, especially the poor and those not well served by accountability mandates.

When Tony Amato was hired as superintendent of the New Orleans schools in 2003, he promised the community that the New Orleans public schools would "make the biggest leap on the LEAP in spring, 2004" (Rasheed 2004, 1). At his first meeting with state education officials, Amato had boasted, "Write it down and hold me to it" (2). Results of state testing announced in May 2004 indicated that his predictions fell far short. "Thirty-five percent of the district's 6,600 fourth-graders failed English and 43 percent failed math" (2). Yolanda Williams, the district accountability officer, confirmed that New Orleans failed to do better than any other Louisiana school district in any category (3). On April 12, 2005, Superintendent Amato announced his resignation (Thevenot 2005, 1).

One Louisiana truant officer has expressed concern that the state's high-stakes testing policies have led to higher dropout rates, according to a report by Wilson (2004b, 1). Truant officer James Smith of Rayville was quoted as saying, "The children that can't get past the LEAP21 are sometimes 15, 16 and 17 years old by the time they get to high school" (1). He developed a vocational construction program at the school to provide an option for students unlikely to earn a high school diploma.

Smith's program, however, may not succeed. In July 2004, Hasten (2004a) reported that Governor Kathleen Blanco "vetoed legislation . . . that would have allowed high schools to issue certificates to students who complete graduation requirements but fail the Graduation Exit Exam . . . because I share Superintendent Picard's concerns that the bill could have the effect of reducing the importance of the state's accountability program" (1). Representative Wayne Waddell (R-Shreveport), who authored the bill, stated, "How tragic that our young people will continue to leave the public education system with nothing to account for the 12-plus years spent in the classroom. Because they could not pass a part of one test, they join the ranks of high school dropouts" (1).

Louisiana State Senator Cleo Fields (D-Baton Rouge) also has become a voice of opposition to the state's high-stakes testing policies. Senator Fields introduced a bill to stop the state from using the LEAP and the GEE tests for promotion and graduation decisions ("Tests Provide a Good Tool" 2004, 1). Senator Fields had stressed the need for uniform school quality as a prerequisite to mandatory state testing. In other words, Senator Fields wanted the state high-stakes testing program put on hold until all schools were brought to the same level of building repair with the same quantity and quality of instructional materials and technology and with the same percentage of certified teachers. The Senate Education Committee, however, prevented the bill from going forward.

WHAT DOES IT ALL MEAN?

Louisiana embarked on its "award winning" public school accountability system in 1999 and began retaining fourth and eighth graders who failed the LEAP test in 2000. Since that time, Louisiana has spent many millions of dollars each year (in 2000–2001, Louisiana spent $56 million, but we have been unable to locate data on subsequent years) on tests, test preparation, test remediation, and promotion of the accountability system. Tens of thousands of students have had to repeat either fourth or eighth grade, thousands of high school students have dropped out, and numerous teachers have left the state or the profession because of stress and frustration. Have the results been worth it?

The Louisiana Department of Education regularly publishes high-stakes test results, school scores, and district scores on its website and in its publications. Its multiyear results summary (2004b, 1) provided the following tabulation of the percentages of Louisiana students scoring at each achievement level in fourth-grade English and math in the annual spring testing from 1999 to 2004. They are representative of the other subjects and other grades:

Percentage of Fourth Graders at Each Achievement Level in English and Math

			English		
	Advanced	Mastery	Basic	Approaching Basic	Unsatisfactory
1999	1	15	39	24	21
2000	2	14	39	25	20
2001	1	14	44	24	16
2002	3	16	38	29	14
2003	1	13	45	26	15
2004	3	18	39	22	19

			Math		
	Advanced	Mastery	Basic	Approaching Basic	Unsatisfactory
1999	2	8	32	24	35
2000	2	10	37	23	28
2001	2	11	41	23	23
2002	2	10	38	25	25
2003	3	13	42	23	19
2004	2	13	38	23	24

This table shows there has been little change in the percentages at each of the five achievement levels during this six-year period. In any given year, only a tiny percentage of children scored at the advanced level, and fewer than 20 percent achieved mastery. At the unsatisfactory level in fourth-grade English, the percentage range was 14 to 21. In math, only about 12 percent scored at the mastery level, but more than 20 percent scored unsatisfactory except in 2003. The years 2001 and 2003 showed more students scoring basic on both tests than in other years. The eighth-grade LEAP and the high school GEE results were similar to those in fourth grade. One must ask if the anguish, humiliation, and expense have been worth it. Any change in test scores has not been impressive, and differences might be attributable to students' prior knowledge or other factors in a given year. In addition, as discussed earlier, the high-stakes "learning" has not transferred to other tasks and measures.

Louisiana is a microcosm of what is happening to education in each of the fifty states. We urge lawmakers and policymakers to heed the advice of author Philip K. Howard (2004), who stated,

> Once the idea of rule-based management takes root, the bureaucracy grows like kudzu. . . . Is legal micromanagement the way to run schools? Maybe teachers and principals should be allowed to think for themselves. That's how successful schools have always worked. . . . Schools depend on the en-

ergy, skill, judgment, humor and sympathy of teachers and principals. Liberate them to draw on all their human traits. (A29)

Louisiana policies mirror those of other states in their reluctance to tackle the real issues that account for low test scores. Barry S. Levy (2005), past president of the American Public Health Association, said, "As funds for essential public health systems are cut, we, as a society, are ignoring the true enemies that threaten our country: poverty, disease, malnutrition and the social injustices that underlie these problems" (A18). Each year, billions of dollars are spent trying to force test scores a few points higher. It is in our citizens' best interests to redirect these monies toward solving societal problems, such as poverty, racism, and underfunded schools, that are reflected in performances on high-stakes tests.

References

Adler, S. 2001. High-stakes testing: We should not sit quietly by. *Social Studies Professional* 162 (March–April):3.

Aitchison, J. 1994. *Words in the mind: An introduction to the mental lexicon.* 2nd ed. Oxford: Blackwell.

Allington, R. L. 2002. *Big Brother and the National Reading Curriculum: How ideology trumped evidence.* Portsmouth, N.H.: Heinemann.

American Educational Research Association. 2000. AERA position statement concerning high-stakes testing in prek-12 education. November 27. Retrieved March 30, 2004, from www.ncme.org/news/newsdetail.ace.

Amrein, A. L., and D. C. Berliner. 2002. High-stakes testing, uncertainty, and student learning. *Education Policy Analysis Archives* 10, no. 18:1–69.

Arenson, K. W. 2003. Scores on math Regents exam to be raised for thousands. *New York Times*, August 30, B3.

Ayres, A., ed. 1998. *The wit and wisdom of Harry S. Truman.* New York: Meridian.

Banks, J. A., B. K. Beyer, G. Contreras, J. Craven, G. Ladson-Billings, M. A. McFarland, and W. C. Parker. 1998. *Louisiana: Adventures in time and place.* New York: McGraw-Hill School Division.

Barham, D. 2000. BESE wants more options, not lesser ones. *The News-Star* (Monroe, La.), November 30, 3.

Bigge, M. L. 1982. *Learning theories for teachers.* 4th ed. New York: Harper and Row.

Blair, J. 2001. Iowa approves performance pay for its teachers. *Education Week*, May 16, 1, 24–25.

Blanco sees no pay raise for teachers. 2004. *The News-Star* (Monroe, La.), March 26. Retrieved March 26, 2004, from www.thenewsstar.com/localnews/html.

Borman, K. M., T. M. Eitle, D. Michael, D. J. Eitle, R. Lee, L. Johnson, D. Cobb-Roberts, S. Dorn, and B. Shircliffe. 2004. Accountability in a postdesegregation era: The continuing significance of racial segregation in Florida's schools. *American Educational Research Journal* 41, no. 3:605–31.

Botstein, L. 2000. A tyranny of standardized tests. *New York Times*, May 28, 11.

Bracey, G. W. 2002. *The war against America's public schools: Privatizing schools, commercializing education*. Boston: Allyn and Bacon.

Bradley, A. 2000. Union heads issue standards warnings. *Education Week*, July 12, 1, 3.

Brooks, R. 2001. Blizzard of grievances joins a sack of woes at U.S. Postal Service. *Wall Street Journal*, June 22, A1, A4.

Broussard wins seat in BESE 6. 2003. *The Advocate* (Baton Rouge, La.), November 16. Retrieved November 16, 2003, from www.2theadvocate.com/stories.

Brown, M. 2004. BESE offers little to bail out schools. *Times-Picayune* (New Orleans, La.), March 13. Retrieved March 13, 2004, from www.nola.com./archives.

Brumble, M. 2004. Students get psyched for higher stakes testing. *The Times* (Shreveport, La.), March 13. Retrieved March 13, 2004, from www.shreveporttimes.com/news/html.

Bumiller, E. 2003. Bush, to criticism, seeks change in Head Start. *New York Times*, July 8, A1, A18.

Calhoun School. 2005. Lunch program. Retrieved January 8, 2005, from www.calhoun.org/lunch_program.htm.

Calif. public schools to post notices on adequate conditions. 2005. *Education Week*, January 12, 2005, 4.

Canedy, D. 2003. Critics of graduation exam threaten boycott in Florida. *New York Times*, May 13, A22.

Cannon, C., and L. Faulkner. 2003. Lake Providence teachers walk off job in protest. *The News-Star* (Monroe, La.), November 13. Retrieved November 13, 2003, from www.thenewsstar.com/localnews/html.

Carruth, G., and E. Ehrlich. 1988. *American quotations*. New York: Wings.

Carter, G. R. 2005. When assessment defies best practice. *Education Week*, January 12, 13.

Chicago drops math scores as factor in promotion. 2004. *Education Week*, March 31, 4.

Clark, E. 1993. *The lexicon in acquisition*. Cambridge: Cambridge University Press.

Comer, C. 2005. Franklin Parish teachers stage sick-out, turn high school into ghost town. *The News-Star* (Monroe, La.), April 30. Retrieved April 30, 2005, from www.thenewsstar.com/apps.

Domingue, S. 2004. LEAP of excellence. *The Advertiser* (Lafayette, La.), March 9. Retrieved March 16, 2004, from www.theadvertiser.com/news/html.

Eakin, S., and M. Culbertson. 1992. *Louisiana: The land and its people*. 3rd ed. Gretna, La.: Pelican.

Edley, C., Jr., and J. Wald. 2002. The grade retention fallacy. *Boston Globe*, December 16. Retrieved March 30, 2004, from www.civilrightsproject.harvard.edu/research/articles/retention_edley.php.

Education officials get raises: Teachers wait. 2000. *The Times* (Shreveport, La.), October 27, 5B.

Education Week. 1999. *Quality counts 1999: Rewarding results, punishing failure.* Bethesda, Md.: Education Week.

———. 2000. *Quality counts 2000: Who should teach?* Bethesda, Md.: Education Week.

———. 2001. *Quality counts 2001: A better balance: Standards, tests, and the tools to succeed.* Bethesda, Md.: Education Week.

———. 2004. *Quality counts 2004: Count me in: Special education in an era of standards.* Bethesda, Md.: Education Week.

———. 2005. *Quality counts 2005: No small change: Targeting money toward student performance.* Bethesda, Md.: Education Week.

Elias, M. 2000. Parents battle schools over discipline for kids: Confrontation, litigation are becoming commonplace. *USA Today*, December 11, 1D, 2D.

Emery, K., and S. Ohanian. 2004. *Why is corporate America bashing our public schools?* Portsmouth, N.H.: Heinemann.

Evans, B. N. 2000. Eighth-graders could have another option. *The Times* (Shreveport, La.), November 30, 1A, 3A.

FairTest. 2003. Princeton Review state test rankings equivalent to Arthur Anderson audit of Enron: Financial self-interest leads to misleading reports. May 4. Retrieved May 14, 2003, from www.fairtest.org/pr/princtonenronrelsease.html.

———. 2004a. Joint organizational statement on No Child Left Behind (NCLB) act. October 21. Retrieved December 4, 2004, from www.fairtest.org/joint%20statement%20civil%20rights%20grps%2010-21-04.html.

———. 2004b. 2004 college bound seniors test scores: SAT, ACT. Retrieved December 4, 2004, from www.fairtest.org/nattest.

Ferrandino, V. L., and G. N. Tirozzi. 2003. For shame. *Education Week*, June 4, 19.

Fla. student charged with crime for having copy of state test. 2004. *Education Week*, March 17, 4.

Food Research and Action Center. 2003. Federal food programs: National school lunch program. Retrieved January 22, 2004, from www.frac.org/html/federal_food_programs/programs/nslp.html.

Foster, M. 2001. Accountability is key to continued education improvements. *The Times* (Shreveport, La.), May 19, 7A.

Freedman, S. G. 2004. An overcrowded school boils over. *New York Times*, December 22, A27.

Galley, M. 2003. Texas principal posts test scores of classes. *Education Week*, September 17, 3.

Gannett Capital Bureau. 2004a. Many schools run on empty. *The News-Star* (Monroe, La.), October 21. Retrieved October 21, 2004, from www.thenewsstar.com/localnews/html.

————. 2004b. School funding gap closing slowly. *The News-Star* (Monroe, La.), October 11. Retrieved October 11, 2004, from www.thenewsstar.com/localnews/html.

Gerstner, L. V., Jr. 2005. An education reform agenda for the next four years—and beyond. *Education Week*, January 5, 60, 34.

Gootman, E. 2004. Dirty and broken bathrooms make for a long school day. *New York Times*, January 29, B3.

Grading errors overturn lives. 2004. *The News-Star* (Monroe, La.), August 8. Retrieved August 8, 2004, from www.thenewsstar.com/localnews/html.

Guardian Journal. 2004a. Parish public school breakfast and lunch menu. December 16, 7.

————. 2004b. Parish school lunch and breakfast menus. December 2, 7.

————. 2004c. Public school breakfast and lunch menus. October 14, 8.

Harrington, M. 1962. *The other America: Poverty in the United States.* New York: Touchstone.

Harris, P. 2000. "Grassroots" testing response. *Council Chronicle*, November, 1, 5.

Hartocollis, A. 2004. At private schools, healthier food wins favorable reviews (mostly). *New York Times*, November 26, B4.

Hasten, M. 2002. Journal ranks Louisiana's testing seventh. *The News-Star* (Monroe, La.), June 19, 3A, 5A.

————. 2004a. Governor vetoes certificates for those who fail high school exit exam. *The Times* (Shreveport, La.), July 10. Retrieved July 10, 2004, from www.shreveport times.com/news/html.

————. 2004b. Lawmakers do cash shuffle so Saints will stay in N.O. *The News-Star* (Monroe, La.), June 22. Retrieved June 22, 2004, from www.thenewsstar.com/local news/html.

————. 2005. Louisiana's budget picture is hazy. *The Times* (Shreveport, La.), January 22. Retrieved January 22, 2005, from www.shreveporttimes.com/apps/pbcs.d11/article.

Hasten, M., and M. Brumble. 2001. Area scores improve. *The Times* (Shreveport, La.), May 12, 1A, 6A.

Hayes-Roth, B., and P. W. Thorndyke. 1979. Integration of knowledge from text. *Journal of Verbal Learning and Verbal Behavior* 18:91–108.

Henriques, D. B. 2003. Rising demands for testing push limits of its accuracy. *New York Times*, September 2, A1, A20.

Henry, T. 2000. Test pressure blamed for cheating. *USA Today*, July 13, 10D.

Herring, S. T. 2000a. Every classroom in parish will be connected to Internet. *Guardian-Journal* (Redbud, La.), December 14, 1.

————. 2000b. Failure of LEAP test prompts suicide attempt by fifteen year old student. *Guardian-Journal* (Redbud, La.), September 7, 1.

————. 2000c. Governor's resource team impressed by Redbud's beauty. *Guardian-Journal* (Redbud, La.), October 19, 1, 5.

————. 2000d. Stachybotrys fungus found at Redbud Memorial Hospital has been removed. *Guardian-Journal* (Redbud, La.), December 7, 1.

————. 2001a. Panel fields questions on drug problem in Redbud. *Guardian-Journal* (Redbud, La.), March 8, 1, 8.

References   243

———. 2001b. Picture caption. *Guardian-Journal* (Redbud, La.), February 22, 7.

———. 2004a. Community seeks solutions for poverty. *Guardian-Journal* (Redbud, La.), November 25, 1, 5.

———. 2004b. Justice Dept. requests information from school board. *Guardian-Journal* (Redbud, La.), May 13, 1, 5.

———. 2004c. [Redbud] school project oversight committee sets meeting. *Guardian-Journal* (Redbud, La.), August 26, 1, 9.

———. 2004d. [Redbud] school project short needed funding. *Guardian-Journal* (Redbud, La.), June 17, 1, 13.

———. 2004e. School board gets report on [Redbud] schools. *Guardian-Journal* (Redbud, La.), July 15, 1, 5.

———. 2004f. School board hires attorney for Justice Dept. *Guardian-Journal* (Redbud, La.), December 16, 1, 5.

Herszenhorn, D. M. 2003. City plans to add 6 standardized tests in math and English. *New York Times*, July 17, B5.

———. 2004. Chancellor urges broad changes in way teachers are paid. *New York Times*, January 28, B6.

Herszenhorn, D. M., and E. Gootman. 2004. 3rd graders in poor areas bear the brunt of promotion rules. *New York Times*, June 18, B4.

Hevesi, D. 2004. Finding a neighborhood and a school. *New York Times*, December 12, 11.1.

Hildebrand, J. 2003. Pressure to perform. *Newsday*, September 6, A7, A21.

Hoff, D. J. 2000. Polls dispute a backlash to standards: But public fears giving tests too much weight. *Education Week*, October 11, 1, 16–17.

Hoffman, J. V., L. C. Assaf, and S. G. Paris. 2001. High-stakes testing in reading: Today in Texas, tomorrow? *Reading Teacher* 54, no. 5:482–92.

hooks, bell. 2000. *Where we stand: CLASS MATTERS.* New York: Routledge.

Howard, P. K. 2004. You can't buy your way out of a bureaucracy. *New York Times*, December 3, A29.

Ingram, J. 1992. *Talk talk talk: An investigation into the mystery of speech.* Toronto: Penguin.

International Reading Association. 1999. *High-stakes assessment in reading.* Newark, Del.: International Reading Association.

Jackson, T. P. 2004. The third world next door. *The News-Star* (Monroe, La.), December 5. Retrieved December 5, 2004, from www.thenewsstar.com/localnews/html.

Jacobson, L. 2004. Pre-K standards said to slight social, emotional skills. *Education Week*, July 14, 13.

Johnson, D. D., B. Johnson, S. J. Farenga, and D. Ness. 2005. *Trivializing teacher education: The accreditation squeeze.* Lanham, Md.: Rowman & Littlefield.

Katz, M. B. 1971. *Class, bureaucracy, and schools: The illusion of educational change in America.* New York: Praeger.

Keizer, G. 2000. What we really think of teachers. *Yankee*, September, 78–83, 130.

Keller, B. 2004. States receive poor marks for teacher-quality standards. *Education Week*, April 21, 21.

Kids count data book: State profiles of child well-being. 2004. Baltimore: Annie E. Casey Foundation.

Kohn, A. 1999. *The schools our children deserve: Moving beyond traditional classrooms and "tougher standards."* Boston: Houghton Mifflin.

———. 2000a. *The case against standardized testing: Raising the scores, ruining the schools.* Portsmouth, N.H.: Heinemann.

———. 2000b. Standardized testing and its victims. *Education Week*, September 27, 60, 46, 47.

Kolker, R. 2004. The bad superintendent. *New York*, September 27, 27–31, 85, 89.

Kozol, J. 1991. *Savage inequalities: Children in America's school.* New York: Crown.

Kramer, S. 2004. Shame of the schools. *New York Times*, November 21, 12.

La. education earns good grades. 2004. *The News-Star* (Monroe, La.), January 8. Retrieved January 8, 2004, from www.thenewsstar.com/localnews/html.

La Plante, J. 2004. Schools fear layoffs from budget shortfall. *The Advocate* (Baton Rouge, La.), June 11. Retrieved June 11, 2004, from www.2theadvocate.com/stories/061104.

Levy, B. S. 2005. Why are infants at risk in America? Letter to the editor. *New York Times*, January 14, A18.

Lewin, T. 2004. Disabled Alaska students sue over exam. *New York Times*, March 17, A21.

Lindsay, D. 2000. Contest. *Education Week*, April 5, 30–36.

Longaberger, D. 2001. *Longaberger: An American success story.* New York: HarperBusiness.

Lord, M. 2001. Getting a jump on kindergarten. *U.S. News & World Report*, May 21, 48.

Louisiana Department of Education. 2000. *LEAP for the 21st century: High stakes testing policy, revised May, 2000.* Baton Rouge: Louisiana Department of Education.

———. 2001a. *LEAP for the 21st century: Grade 4: English language arts, mathematics, science, and social studies: Test administration manual.* Baton Rouge: Louisiana Department of Education.

———. 2001b. *Louisiana statewide norm-referenced testing program: 2001 test administration manual grade 3: Iowa Tests of Basic Skills Form M.* Itasca, Ill.: Riverside.

———. 2001c. *Reaching for results: A message from the superintendent.* Baton Rouge: Louisiana Department of Education.

———. 2003a. Louisiana's testing program ranked 6th in nation. May 5. Retrieved May 15, 2003, from www.doe.state.la.us.

———. 2003b. *2002–2003 school accountability subgroup component report.* Baton Rouge: Louisiana Department of Education.

———. 2004a. Gov. Blanco honors schools receiving growth awards. April 15. Retrieved January 20, 2005, from www.doe.state.la.us.

———. 2004b. LEAP 21, GEE 21, and the Iowa tests: Multi-year state/district test results summary. Retrieved December 21, 2004, from www.doe.state.la.us.

———. 2005. School Analysis Model (SAM). Retrieved May 19, 2005, from www.doe.state.la.us/lde/ssaa/1591.html.

Madaus, G. F. 1999. The influence of testing on the curriculum. In M. J. Early and K. J. Rehage, eds., *Issues in curriculum: Selected chapters for NSSE yearbooks*, 73–111. Chicago: National Society for the Study of Education.

Madigan, N. 2004. California will spend more to help its poorest schools. *New York Times*, August 13, A12.

McAllister, P. 2003. Dowling student teachers: Making a difference as they learn. Retrieved January 29, 2005, from www.dowling.edu/news/year2003/st01.shtm.

Medina, J., and T. Lewin. 2003. High school under scrutiny for giving up on its students. *New York Times*, August 1, B6.

Meier, D. 2000. *Will standards save public education?* Boston: Beacon.

Midwest: Illinois: Schools to be cleaned. 2004. *New York Times,* January 24, A12.

Miller, D. W. 2001. Scholars say high-stakes tests deserve a failing grade. *Chronicle of Higher Education*, March 2, 14–16.

Minnesota academic standards. 2003. *St. Paul Pioneer Press*, December 23, 14A.

Minnesota leads in health survey. 2004. *New York Times*, November 9, A16.

Morgan Quinto Press. 2004. Results of the 2004 smartest state award. Retrieved January 21, 2005, from www.morganquinto.com/edfact04.htm.

———. 2005. About us. Retrieved January 21, 2005, from www.morganquinto.com/aboutus.htm.

National Association for Multicultural Education. 2001. Resolution on teacher testing. November 11. Retrieved January 15, 2004, from www.nameorg.org/resolutions/teachertesting.html.

National Center for Education Statistics. 2003. Reading: The nation's report card. Retrieved December 31, 2004, from http://nces.ed.gov/nationsreportcard/reading/results2003/stateachieve-g4-compare.asp.

National Commission on Excellence on Education. 1983. *A nation at risk: The imperative for educational reform*. Washington, D.C.: U.S. Government Printing Office.

National Council of Teachers of English. 2000. Standardized minds: Summing up the damage. *Council Chronicle*, September, 24.

———. 2001. NCTE members pass resolutions on high stakes testing and on the rights of test takers. *Language Arts* 78, no. 3:300.

Neill, M., L. Guisbond, and B. Schaeffer. 2004. *Failing our children: How "No Child Left Behind" undermines quality and equity in education*. Cambridge, Mass.: FairTest.

Nelson, R. (2003). Rally to psych LEAP students. *Times-Picayune* (New Orleans, La.), February 28. Retrieved February 28, 2003, from www.nola.com/archives.

———. (2004). Testing the limits. *Times-Picayune* (New Orleans, La.), March 17, A1, A8.

Nelson, S. 2005. The Calhoun School. Retrieved January 8, 2005, from www.calhoun.org/eat_right_now2.pdf.

O'Brien, E. 2001. Teachers get locked down, but paid up: Educators bust out of schools for better pay. *The News-Star* (Monroe, La.), January 29, 1.

Odden, A., and M. J. Wallace Jr. 2003. Leveraging teacher pay. *Education Week*, August 6, 64.

Officials: Hold-back numbers show LEAP works. 2001. *Ruston Daily Leader* (Ruston, La.), March 23, 1, 5.

Ohanian, S. 1999. *One size fits few: The folly of educational standards*. Portsmouth, N.H.: Heinemann.

Olson, L. 2000a. Officials worry about pressures placed on assessments. *Education Week*, July 12, 9.

———. 2000b. Poll shows public concern over emphasis on standardized tests. *Education Week*, July 12, 9.

———. 2004. NCLB law bestows bounty on test industry. *Education Week*, December 1, 1, 18, 19.

Orleans plan would dismiss uncertified teachers. 2001. *The Times* (Shreveport, La.), April 1, 6B.

Payne, R. K. 1998. *A framework for understanding poverty*. Highlands, Tex.: R. F. T. Publishing.

Peters, E. 2004. Fourth-graders prep for LEAP. *The Town Talk* (Alexandria, La.), March 13. Retrieved March 16, 2004, from www.thetowntalk.com/html.

Picard, C. J. 2001. *Reaching for results: LEAP 21, Grade 4*. Baton Rouge: Louisiana Department of Education.

Pinker, S. 1994. *The language instinct: How the mind creates language*. New York: Harper-Perennial.

Popham, W. J. 1998. A message to parents: Don't judge your child's school by its standardized test scores. Paper presented at the annual meeting of the American Educational Research Association, April 13–17, San Diego.

———. 2004. *America's "failing" schools: How parents and teachers can cope with No Child Left Behind*. New York: Falmer.

Princeton Review. 2004. Raise your score with proven test-taking strategies. *U.S. News & World Report*, April 12, 53.

Publisher recalls state's Iowa results. 2001. *The News-Star* (Monroe, La.), May 20, 1A, 4A.

Rabb, T. K. 2004. What has happened to historical literacy? *The Chronicle Review*, June 4, B24.

Rasheed, A. 2004. LEAP results fall short of vow. *Times-Picayune* (New Orleans, La.), May 12. Retrieved May 15, 2004, from www.nola.com/news.

Raspberry, W. 2001. Let states equalize education. *The News-Star* (Monroe, La.), April 8, 3B.

Reich, R. B. 2001. Standards for what? *Education Week*, June 20, 64.

Reid, K. S. 2004. Federal law spurs private companies to market tutoring. *Education Week*, December 8, 1, 18–19.

Richard, A. 2005. Fla. board seeks social-promotion ban in all grades. *Education Week*, January 26, 22, 27.

Robelen, E. W. 2001. Bush promises swift action on education. *Education Week*, January 10, 42.

———. 2004. Schools seek participation on test days. *Education Week*, March 31, 1, 14.

Rose, L. C., and A. M. Gallup. 2004. The 36th annual Phi Delta Kappa/Gallup poll of the public's attitudes toward the public schools. *Phi Delta Kappan* 86, no. 1:41, 52.

Roza, M. 2001. The challenge for Title I: Teacher shortages feed the downward spiral for poor schools. *Education Week*, April 4, 56.

Sacks, P. 2000. *Standardized minds: The high price of America's testing culture and what we can do to change it.* New York: Perseus Books.

Santell, W. 2004. Magazine praises La. on school accountability. *The Advocate* (Baton Rouge, La.), January 8. Retrieved January 8, 2004, from www.2theadvocate.com/stories.

Schools drop naptime for testing preparation. 2003. *Atlanta Journal-Constitution,* October 3. Retrieved October 29, 2003, from www.ajc.com/news/content/news/1003/03naptime.html.

Secretary Paige lauds NCLB: "The law is working." 2004. *The Achiever,* September 1, 1, 3.

Semple, K. 2004. After cutbacks, Yonkers awaits a school year with few extras. *New York Times,* September 7, B1.

Skip school, risk trouble. 2004. *The News-Star* (Monroe, La.), August 1. Retrieved August 1, 2004, from www.thenewsstar.com/editorial/html.

State school reform gets praise of U. S. education secretary. 2000. *The Times* (Shreveport, La.), December 3, 2B.

Sternberg, R. J. 2004. Good intentions, bad results: A dozen reasons why the No Child Left Behind Act is failing our schools. *Education Week,* October 27, 56, 42.

Stolle, M. 2003. Schools are in quandary: Standards could change again next year. *The Post-Bulletin* (Rochester, Minn.), December 20–21, 1E.

Stricherz, M. 2001. Greater expectations. *Education Week,* May 2, 32–37.

Summit can help the blight. 2004. *The News-Star* (Monroe, La.), December 4. Retrieved December 4, 2004, from www.thenewsstar.com/editorial/html.

Sumrall, B. 2004. Pineville housing program to provide "fresh start." *The Town Talk* (Alexandria, La.), December 10. Retrieved December 10, 2004, from www.thetowntalk.com/html.

Superville, D. 2004. Hunger hit 12 million families in '03. *Boston Globe,* November 20, A17.

Swerczek, M. 2004. Schools toughen testing policy: Teachers can be fired for giving answers. *Times-Picayune* (New Orleans, La.), May 6. Retrieved May 16, 2004, from www.nola.com/education.

Teachers prepare out of their pockets. 2004. *The Town Talk* (Alexandria, La.), July 14. Retrieved July 14, 2004, from www.thetowntalk.com/html.

Tests provide a good tool. 2004. *The News-Star* (Monroe, La.), April 23. Retrieved April 23, 2004, from www.thenewsstar.com/editorial/html.

Thevenot, B. 2003a. Report cards on schools sent with misprints. *Times-Picayune* (New Orleans, La.), November 22. Retrieved November 22, 2003, from www.nola.com/news.

———. 2003b. Schools gain, but many miss targets. *Times-Picayune* (New Orleans, La.), November 21. Retrieved November 22, 2003, from www.nola.com/education.

———. 2005. Besieged Amato calls it quits. *Times-Picayune* (New Orleans, La.), April 13. Retrieved April 14, 2005, from www.nola.com/search.

Thomas, M. D., and W. L. Bainbridge. 2000. The truth about "all children can learn." *Education Week,* December 6, 34.

Torrans, A. 2001. Poor language skills often behind failure. *The Times* (Shreveport, La.), March 15, 9A.

Trotter, A. 2004. Studies fault results of retention in Chicago. *Education Week*, April 14, 8.

Turner, D. 2001. Statewide riverboat tax increase passes. *The Times* (Shreveport, La.), March 23, 1A, 2A.

Tyre, P. 2003. Reading, writing, recess. *Newsweek*, November 3, 66.

Van Diest, M. M. 2001. Local schools prepare for March LEAP testing. *Ruston Daily Leader* (Ruston, La.), February 23, 1A.

van Dijk, T. A., and W. Kintsch. 1983. *Strategies of discourse comprehension*. New York: Academic.

Wagner, T., and T. Vander Ark. 2001. A critical fork in the road. *Education Week*, April 11, 56, 40.

Waller, M. 2004. More at stake during testing. *Times-Picayune* (New Orleans, La.), March 13. Retrieved March 13, 2004, from www.nola.com/education.

Walsh, M. 2001. Pearson hopes to "widen the definition of education." *Education Week*, February 21, 8.

Watts, R. S. 2003. The education production function: An analysis of the relationship between fiscal resource variables and student achievement across Louisiana school districts. Unpublished doctoral dissertation, University of Louisiana at Monroe.

Williams, T. H. 1969. *Huey Long*. New York: Vintage.

Wilson, L. 2003. Bush makes move to streamline free lunch programs. *The News-Star* (Monroe, La.), February 4. Retrieved February 4, 2003, from www.thenewsstar .com/html.

———. 2004a. "I want to get out." *The News-Star* (Monroe, La.), November 14. Retrieved November 14, 2004, from www.thenewsstar.com/localnews/html.

———. 2004b. Program targets test-weary students. *The News-Star* (Monroe, La.), March 15. Retrieved March 15, 2004, from www.thenewsstar.com/localnews/html.

———. 2004c. Students do better on LEAP. *The News-Star* (Monroe, La.), August 14. Retrieved August 14, 2004, from www.thenewsstar.com/localnews/html.

Winerip, M. 2003. Testing fad is farce for the disabled. *New York Times*, April 16, D9.

Winter, G. 2004. Financial gap is widening for rich and poor schools. *New York Times*, October 6, A19.

Yardley, J. 2001. Well-off but still pressed, doctor could use tax cut. *New York Times*, April 7, A1, A8.

INDEX

AASA. *See* American Association of School Administrators
accountability movement: for-profit enterprises and, xviii, 37, 44, 125, 146, 215–16; high-stakes testing and, x, xi; learning and, 32; origins of, x, xvi; politicians and, x, 125–26, 172–73, 181; poverty and, 180–81; state standards and, 212–13. *See also* high-stakes testing; Louisiana; No Child Left Behind; teachers
American Association of School Administrators (AASA), 184, 185, 186, 209
American Federation of Teachers, 34, 186

Bainbridge, William L., 86
Bigge, M. L., 229–30
Blanco, Kathleen, 221, 225–26, 234–35
Bossier Parish, 104–5, 162

Bridges, Kim (Redbud reading specialist), 43, 70, 74, 96, 114
Brumble, M., 166, 225, 226
Bush, George W.: administration policy on high-stakes testing, 176–77, 209; Head Start reform, 215; school nutrition and, 197. *See also* No Child Left Behind

Calhoun School, 196–97
Carter, Gene R., 232
CCSSO. *See* Council of Chief State School Officers
Chicago, 198–99, 205, 208
computers: disrepair of, 24, 126; inappropriate websites, 68; Internet access, 24, 95–96, 126, 146, 150, 155, 163; learning on, 50, 71, 103; student assessment software, 44, 47, 50–51, 64–65, 71, 103
consultants, 48, 51, 63, 64, 70

Council of Chief State School Officers
    (CCSSO), 184, 186, 212
crime: crack cocaine, 9, 31, 105, 113;
    gangs, 13, 14; guns at school, 155;
    murder, 105–6, 107, 113; robbery, 49;
    theft, 38–39; vandalism, 81, 83, 87. *See
    also* Louisiana

Dawson, Greta (Redbud assistant
    principal), 26–27, 45, 56, 60, 62–63,
    68, 70, 74, 75, 87, 89, 96, 109, 112,
    114, 155, 219. *See also* school
    discipline
Deerborne Parish (La.): household
    income, 3, 13; poverty rate, 3, 48;
    racial resegregation, 220; school
    funding, 219–20; teacher shortage,
    160–61; test performance, 176
Department of Education, United States.
    See U.S. Department of Education
developmental reading assessment
    (DRA), 28, 39, 159, 169, 171

Educational Testing Service (ETS), 204,
    211
Education Week, 44, 102, 125, 164, 172,
    211, 228, 229

Green, Mr. (Deerborne Parish secondary
    supervisor), 16, 20, 26, 119

Harrington, Michael, 180
Harris, Peggy, 77
Hasten, M., 166
Head Start, 215
Hevesi, D., 200
high-stakes testing: administration of,
    128–29, 132–33, 136; compared to
    multiple performance indicators, 189;
    criticism of, ix, xvi–xvii, 77, 152,
    183–86, 202, 205–6, 208, 224–25,
    234; errors in, 203–4, 205; failure and
    grade repetition, xv, 115, 197, 205;

Florida Comprehensive Assessment
    Test (FCAT), 198, 202, 206; for-profit
    enterprises and, x–xi, 28, 123, 135,
    177, 211, 227; Graduate Exit
    Examination (GEE), 161, 231, 235,
    235; Iowa Test of Basic Skills, 4, 12,
    28, 30, 39, 41, 71, 85, 97, 103, 104,
    113–14, 120, 123, 128–29, 132–33,
    134, 135, 137, 138, 160, 171, 176,
    220, 233; instructional time and, 102,
    104, 115, 140, 168, 208; learning-
    disabled children and, 17, 86, 206,
    225; Massachusetts Comprehensive
    Assessment System, 186; pep rallies
    for, 113–14, 120; poverty and, 78,
    85–86, 152, 177, 190, 194, 198, 210,
    237; practice tests, 104, 130; public
    opinion of, 185, 201–2; Scholastic
    Aptitude Test (SAT), 231, 232;
    security measures for, 128–29, 133,
    134, 137, 138, 186, 233–34;
    socioeconomic status and, 197, 200;
    student stress and, 115, 116, 224–25;
    teacher pay and, 172, 200–201;
    "teaching to the test," xvii, 152, 161,
    177, 185, 189, 208; test scores, xvi,
    160, 202; Texas Assessment of
    Academic Skills (TAAS), 36, 115,
    117; tutoring for, 71, 211, 227;
    United States, 201. *See also*
    accountability movement; LEAP tests
hooks, bell, 147
Howard, Philip K., 236–37

instruction: art, 7, 13, 47, 104, 136,
    138–39, 146, 148, 175–76; culturally
    appropriate, 100; drug awareness, 61,
    67–68; history, 48–49, 96, 108, 146,
    208; language arts, 13, 74–75, 149;
    mathematics, 27, 63; reading, 20, 37,
    38, 41, 48, 59–60, 70, 73, 157,
    209–10, 219; science, 34–35, 45, 70,
    146; social studies, 6, 37, 43, 46, 59,

101, 131, 136, 143–44, 151, 158; writing, 49, 96–97, 98, 114, 136. *See also* Bridges, Kim (Redbud reading specialist); developmental reading assessment (DRA); Project Read
International Reading Association (IRA), 77, 183, 186, 214
Iowa Test of Basic Skills. *See* high-stakes testing
IRA. *See* International Reading Association

Jacobs, Leslie, 82, 112, 164, 166, 221, 227, 233
Jacobson, L., 215

Katz, Michael B.: *Class, Bureaucracy, and Schools*, 16
Keizer, Garrett, 17
King, Martin Luther, Jr., 99
Klein, Joel, 200, 203, 206
Kohn, Alfie, 44

LEAP tests, 4, 12, 28, 36, 39, 86, 97, 133, 145–46, 150, 235; administration of, 128, 146–47; dropout rates and, 234; failure and grade retention, 4, 17, 36–37, 52, 116, 126, 127, 131, 140, 165, 185; instructional time and, 131; learning-disabled children and, 112, 165, 167, 225; legal challenges to, 185; Louisiana content standards and, 30, 117; pep rallies for, 114, 120–21, 126, 223–24; practice tests, 101, 112; private school exemption from, 10, 113, 162, 167; security measures for, 135; student performance on, 133, 220, 226, 230–31, 233, *236*; student stress from, 31, 85, 126, 131–32, 167; summer school and, 78, 165, 167, 176; teacher absenteeism and, 16; "teaching to the test," 4–5, 50; test

preparation, 42, 59, 116, 117; tutoring for, 103, 116, 117. *See also* high-stakes testing; Louisiana
Longaberger, Dave, 64
Louisiana: accountability movement and, 85, 164, 173, 224, 226, 227, 232, 235; African Americans in, 179; Board of Elementary and Secondary Education, 32, 82, 112, 128, 164, 172, 221, 224; children's well being in, 222; content standards, 12–13, 15, 29–30, 43, 55, 63, 74, 214; crime in, 19–20; Department of Education, 16, 17, 103, 129, 137, 141, 143, 146, 153, 154, 219–20, 232, 233, 235; educational rankings, 227–30; health of population, 223; history of, 1–2, 179; poverty rate, xviii, 48, 194–95; school funding, 221–22; statewide achievement test results, 78, 165, 166, 189, 230–31, 232, 235–*36*; tax referenda, 71, 78; teacher salaries, 225–26. *See also* Blanco, Kathleen; Jacobs, Leslie; LEAP tests; Picard, Cecil
Louisiana Educational Assessment Program for the 21st Century. *See* LEAP tests

Madigan, N., 198
Marshall, Thurgood, 48, 49
Miller, D. W., 125
Miller, Mark (Deerborne Parish superintendent), 13, 50, 82, 119, 137, 173, 219, 220
Minnesota, 213–14

National Assessment of Educational Progress (NAEP), 230, 231–32
National Association for Multicultural Education (NAME), 204
National Board on Educational Testing and Public Policy, 203–4

National Commission on Excellence in Education: *A Nation at Risk*, ix–x, xvi, 216

National Council for Accreditation of Teacher Education (NCATE), 186–87, 188, 204, 209, 214

National Council for the Social Studies, 184

National Council of Teachers of English (NCTE), 32, 77, 184, 186

National Education Association (NEA), 183

NCATE. *See* National Council for Accreditation of Teacher Education

NCLB. *See* No Child Left Behind

NCTE. *See* National Council of Teachers of English

New Orleans, 234

New Orleans Saints (football team), 57–58, 94, 222, 223

New York City, 193–94, 197, 200, 203, 206, 208

New York State, 193, 194, 198, 200, 207, 214

No Child Left Behind (NCLB), 207–11 passim, 221; accountability movement and, 207; adequate yearly progress (AYP), 207, 208, 230–31; for-profit entities and, 208, 210–11

Orleans Parish (La.), 140, 144–45

Paige, Rod, 209

paraprofessionals, 41, 50, 70, 182, 189

parents: child neglect by, 28–29, 74, 112; incarcerated, 29, 68, 71, 95, 97, 126, 163, 174, 220; involvement of, 4, 43, 156; middle-class, 200; occupations of, 33, 53; religious views of, 38, 89; teachers, conferences with, 51–52, 57; teachers, relations with, 39, 52, 89; test preparation and, 42, 43

Parent-Teacher Organization (PTO), 36, 63, 64, 89, 97, 105

Pearson Education, 125

Picard, Cecil, 39, 65, 140, 141, 166, 172, 199, 221, 224, 227, 228, 235

Porter, Pam (Redbud principal), 3, 25, 36, 41, 43–44, 46, 54, 55, 64, 70, 74, 78, 87, 89, 94, 113, 137, 138, 174, 176, 219

Princeton Review, 206, 211, 227

private schools, 10, 78, 100, 110, 140, 164, 190, 208, 216. *See also* Calhoun School; LEAP tests

Project Read, 36, 44

race relations, 99, 179, 190, 198, 220

Redbud (La.): drug problems, 61, 130; history of, 2; housing in, 2, 9; population, 3; poverty of, x, 4, 8–9, 61; white population, 9–10. *See also* crime; Deerborne Parish (La.)

Redbud Elementary School: balanced literacy program, 18, 19, 48, 72–73, 99, 219; bathrooms, 8, 22, 23; book fair, 69–70; building, xv, 3; charitable contributions to, 25, 40, 53, 57–58, 124–25, 138–39, 148; classrooms, 5–6; cleanliness, state of, 100; contests, writing, 158–59; dress code, 97, 148; heating and air conditioning, xvi, 5, 8, 29, 87–89, 90, 92, 94, 132; library, lack of, xvi, 8, 44, 47, 136, 146; medical facilities, lack of, 8, 81, 150; as microcosm, xvii–xviii, xix; mold problem, 88; playground, xvi, 8, 11, 22–23, 57–58, 146, 157; reference resources, 6, 44, 50, 53, 131; school closings, weather-related, 90, 93; school supplies, 6–7, 55–56, 107; staff, xvi; student population, xv, 4, 78, 162; student sales campaigns, 118; test performance, 4, 41, 74, 78, 165–67, 173, 220; vermin problem, 5, 6, 7, 29,

47, 79, 126. *See also* computers; crime; instruction; Porter, Pam (Redbud principal); school attendance; school discipline; students; teachers

Reich, Robert B., 188

Reid, K. S., 211–12

Roslyn (N.Y.), 199–200

Roza, M., 180–81

school attendance, 78, 98, 162, 202–3, 234; truancy, 79, 100, 118–19, 137, 165

school discipline, 26–27, 62–63, 75, 87, 148, 155; corporal punishment, 11, 13, 71, 75; suspension, in-school, 45, 70, 158. *See also* Dawson, Greta (Redbud assistant principal)

school funding, xvii, 32, 105, 181, 189–90, 198–99, 221–22

school vouchers, 109–10, 221

standardized tests. *See* high-stakes testing

Sternberg, Robert, 212

students (by name): Andrenna, 166, 175, 177; Antinesha, 43, 48, 62, 70, 72, 73, 75, 99, 101, 122, 123, 135, 157, 160, 175; Antron, 24, 45, 116, 143, 177; Ashley, 70, 125, 152, 175, 178; Carlonna, 25, 49, 58, 126, 175; Chalese, 24, 45, 72, 167, 177; Cherise, 22, 41, 62, 72, 77, 79, 137, 160, 169, 175; Chikae, 24, 49, 56, 72, 96, 123, 153, 175; Damien, 22, 124, 175, 177; Danielle, 166, 175, 177; Dario, 22, 69, 88, 112, 126, 131, 166–67, 177; Dawnyetta, 25, 53, 108, 127, 177; De'Lewis, 22, 24, 45, 49, 52, 79, 136, 166, 177; Demetrius, 24–25, 41, 81, 116, 177; Derek, 22, 124, 143, 158, 166, 175, 177; Dwayne, 21, 41, 52, 57, 69, 76, 80–81, 136, 149, 165, 175, 177; Earvin, 108, 112, 123, 124, 149, 177; Emerald, 22, 57, 68, 86, 97, 108, 123, 158, 177; Garrison, 102, 174, 177; Gerard, 38, 80, 83, 91, 94, 101, 123, 130, 133, 152, 155, 159–60, 164, 174, 178; Graham, 49, 175, 177; Haden, 23, 46, 62, 99, 101, 122, 134, 175; Jaheesa, 24, 33, 35, 46, 72, 91, 101, 105, 107, 130, 158, 178; Jamal, 45, 69, 167, 173, 177; Jaron, 22, 33, 43, 49, 70, 77, 99, 123, 151, 167, 169, 175; Jatoyia, 121, 132, 175, 177; Jaylene, 22, 45, 50, 79, 116, 151, 167; Jelani, 22, 27, 68, 73, 95, 97, 122–23, 138, 150, 168–69; Jesse, 35, 56; Jimmy, 56, 59–60, 75–76, 81, 101, 137, 149, 161; Joshua, 21, 35, 45, 57, 69, 79, 133, 143; Kanesha, 76, 108, 123, 175; Kanzah, 22, 24, 35, 38, 65, 68, 71, 73, 76, 79, 89, 130, 161, 169; Keaziah, 22, 77, 158, 168; Kelvin, 62, 69, 96, 99, 121, 130, 133, 152, 174; LaDelle, 22, 57, 61, 116, 133, 136, 139, 143, 150, 167, 175, 178; Leon, 22, 24, 35, 48, 73, 75, 123, 137, 146, 148, 152, 153, 156, 161; Letrinette, 22, 52, 57, 127, 138, 139, 145, 178; Lynette, 108, 177; Malcolm, 22, 68, 100, 102, 158, 177; Manuel, 22, 34, 43, 49, 61, 69, 73, 76, 96, 99, 127–28, 152, 157, 159, 174, 175; Melissa, 116, 178; Milo, 23, 57, 97, 133, 149, 159, 161, 177; Nicole, 153, 175; Nikeya, 23, 52, 79, 91, 116, 121, 136, 150, 175, 178; Nikos, 45, 177; Perry, 45, 116, 143, 155; Rachael, 108, 124, 172, 174, 177; Randall, 62, 76, 111–12, 137–38, 150, 175; Rashand, 116, 126, 175, 177; Rhonda, 80–81, 95, 97, 98, 122, 177; Roland, 97–98, 99, 157, 158–59; Sam, 45, 62, 130, 134, 152, 174; Shantel, 22, 41, 61, 72, 73, 75, 77, 99, 114, 146, 157, 175; Shonora, 25, 122, 153, 163, 165, 175, 177; Tony, 24, 29, 45, 107, 126, 177; Travis, 45, 177; Tyler,

99, 166, 177; Verlin, 57, 76, 98, 99,
100, 102, 149, 151, 177; Victavius, 22,
28–29, 31, 45, 69, 158, 175, 177;
Wendice, 24, 34, 35, 37, 68, 73–74,
77, 89, 95, 105, 108, 113, 123, 136,
153, 163–64; Yolande, 24, 79, 100,
118–19, 137, 165, 177
students: African American, xv, 4, 45,
78, 162, 174, 179, 183, 190;
bedtimes, 77, 111, 148; bullies and,
46; clothing of, 35, 88, 166, 173;
dental problems, 8, 26, 35, 38, 65, 79,
89, 166, 169; drugs and, 61, 67–68,
113; evaluations of, 27–28; family
problems, xv, 24–25, 49, 68, 101,
107, 111–12, 135, 146, 156, 163,
166; field trips, 65, 72, 101, 121, 139;
gifts to, 69, 76, 92, 145, 152–53, 178;
grades for, 42–43, 170; holidays and,
69, 91, 92, 116, 143; house fires
affecting, 86, 108, 112, 122–23, 149;
housing of, xv, 109, 169; language
skills, 24, 33, 42, 59, 72–73, 97, 131,
182; letters and notes by, 52, 57–58,
91, 94, 96, 108, 109, 113, 121–22,
124–25, 127, 139, 152–53; medical
problems, 8, 26, 29, 34, 37, 76–77,
79, 80–81, 91, 97, 101, 109, 166,
168–69; nutrition, 4, 23, 34, 70, 109,
196–97; pen pals, 107–8, 149–50;
poverty of, xv, 7, 88, 98, 101, 109,
166; preschool and, 182–83, 190;
progress reports, 62; report cards,
100, 232; school funding and, 61–62;
school pictures, 48, 88; shoes of, 73,
137–38, 151, 166; special education,
xvii, 21, 45, 101, 112, 134, 156, 160,
162, 165, 167, 178; theme days, 72;
travel by, 99–100; uniforms, 3, 21;
violence, exposure to, 33, 49, 68,
105–6, 152; white, 22–23, 70, 95;
writings by, 98, 99, 158–59, 174–75.
See also high-stakes testing;

instruction; parents; Redbud
Elementary School
student teachers (by name): Avalon, Mrs.,
139, 143, 167, 171–72, 178;
Hammond, Ms., 81, 100, 102,
121–22, 178; Schwartz, Melody, 81,
91, 101, 107, 111, 122, 178, 219;
Tomah, Mrs., 150, 158, 159
Sumrall, B., 195

teachers (by name): Belinda, 7, 32;
Glenda, 18–19, 33, 90; Henderson,
Mrs., 37, 45, 87, 89, 177; Larson,
Mrs., 28, 33–34, 87, 109, 128, 132,
136, 138, 176; Marlow, Mrs., 79, 94,
129, 134; Nikki, 7, 31, 90; Quigley,
Mrs., 109, 130, 163, 173; Tina, 8, 9,
31; Waverly, Ruth, 6, 7, 79, 87, 88, 94,
109, 128, 133, 134, 141
teachers: absenteeism, 12, 16;
accountability movement and, xviii,
15, 16–17, 30, 54–55, 80, 100, 129;
awards for, 34; break-times, 22, 151,
182, 190–91; corporate views of,
216–17; gifts to, 87, 91, 92; high-stakes
testing, views of, 168, 185; leave policy,
16; lesson planning, 14–15, 16, 26, 96,
106, 134, 214; liability insurance, 34;
monitoring of, 39–40, 44, 54–55, 63,
87, 128, 129, 134, 136, 144, 153–55,
160; paperwork, 14–16, 25, 29–30, 33,
37, 39, 40, 42, 53–55, 63, 86–87, 153,
160, 169–71, 181–82, 190, 214;
professionalism, 16–17, 19, 80, 119–20,
134, 151, 190; rules governing, 11–14;
salaries, 4, 6, 14, 18–19, 46, 65, 71, 78,
106, 107, 140, 191; school supplies,
purchase of, 6–7, 18, 38, 221; self-
esteem, 56–57; shortage of, 160–61;
technology training, 58–59; testing of,
14, 203–4, 205, 211; time demands, 39,
60, 64, 74, 80, 119–20; turnover, 52,
85, 180–81, 188, 219; uncertified, 14,

35, 145, 146; whole-faculty study groups, 63, 64, 87; workshops and meetings, 17–19, 27, 29–30, 36, 42, 47, 51, 63, 64, 70, 74. *See also* instruction; teachers (by name)
testing. *See* high-stakes testing
Thevenot, B., 226, 232
Thomas, M. Donald, 86
Truman, Harry S., 188

U.S. Department of Education, 85, 177

Vander Ark, T., 152
violence, 31, 41, 57, 85. *See also* crime; students
vocational programs, 82
volunteers, 191

Wagner, T., 152
Warton Correctional Institution, 8, 9, 10, 97

Yonkers (N.Y.), 199

ABOUT THE AUTHORS

DALE D. JOHNSON earned his Ph.D. from the University of Wisconsin–Madison, and is professor of literacy education at Dowling College, Long Island, New York. His most recent books are *Trivializing Teacher Education: The Accreditation Squeeze*, coauthored with Bonnie Johnson, Stephen J. Farenga, and Daniel Ness, and *Vocabulary in the Elementary and Middle School*. Dr. Johnson is a past president of the International Reading Association. He worked as a teacher of English as a second language in Nigeria with the Ford Foundation and has taught in elementary and middle schools as well as colleges and universities in several states.

BONNIE JOHNSON earned her Ph.D. at the University of Wisconsin–Madison. She is currently professor of human development and learning at Dowling College, Long Island, New York. Her most recent books are *Wordworks: Exploring Language Play* and *Trivializing Teacher Education: The Accreditation Squeeze* (coauthored with Dale D. Johnson, Stephen J. Farenga, and Daniel Ness). Dr. Johnson has taught at all levels from prekindergarten through graduate school. She received a Distinguished Teacher of Teachers Award from the University of Wisconsin.